50 HIKES
IN NEW JERSEY

OTHER BOOKS IN THE 50 HIKES SERIES

50 HIKES
IN NEW JERSEY

FIFTH EDITION

Daniel Chazin

NEW YORK–NEW JERSEY
TRAIL CONFERENCE

THE COUNTRYMAN PRESS

A division of W. W. Norton & Company

Independent Publishers Since 1923

AN INVITATION TO THE READER

Over time trails can be rerouted and signs and landmarks altered. If you find that changes have occurred on the routes described in this book, please let us know so that corrections may be made in future editions. The author and publisher also welcome other comments and suggestions.

Address all correspondence to:
Editor, 50 Hikes Series
The Countryman Press
500 Fifth Avenue
New York, NY 10110

Manufacturing by Versa Press
Series book design by Chris Welch

The Countryman Press
www.countrymanpress.com

A division of W. W. Norton & Company, Inc.
500 Fifth Avenue, New York, NY 10110
www.wwnorton.com

978-1-68268-444-3 (pbk.)

10 9 8 7 6 5 4 3 2 1

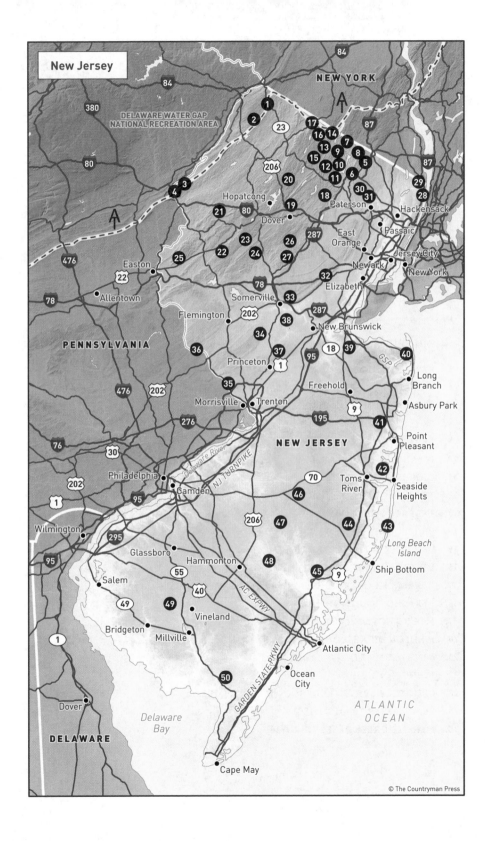

New Jersey

Contents

III. PIEDMONT | 161

IV. COASTAL PLAIN | 213

Hikes at a Glance

HIKE	COUNTY	DISTANCE (miles)	DIFFICULTY	RISE (feet)	TIME (hrs)
1. South of High Point	Sussex	6.3	M/S	500	4
2. Blue Mountain Loop Trail	Sussex	8.5	M	950	5
3. Rattlesnake Swamp—Appalachian Trail Loop	Warren	5.2	M	500	3
4. Mount Tammany	Warren	3.5	M/S	1,200	3
5. Ramapo Valley County Reservation	Bergen	3.8	M	650	2.5
6. Ramapo Lake and the Van Slyke Castle	Passaic/Bergen	5.5	M	700	3.5
7. Ringwood Manor Circular	Passaic	3	E	250	2
8. Skylands Manor	Passaic	8.5	M	1,200	5
9. Lake Sonoma and Overlook Rock	Passaic	4.5	M	700	3
10. Wyanokie Circular	Passaic	7.1	M/S	1,500	5.5
11. Carris Hill	Passaic	4	M/S	800	4
12. Torne Mountain—Osio Rock	Passaic	2.7	E/M	750	3
13. Terrace Pond	Passaic	4.5	M	350	3.5
14. Bearfort Ridge	Passaic	7	M/S	1,200	5.5
15. Pequannock Watershed	Passaic	8 or 9.5	M/S	400	6
16. Wawayanda State Park	Sussex/Passaic	7.5	E/M	530	4
17. Appalachian Trail—Stairway to Heaven	Sussex	2.8	M/S	1,000	2.5
18. Pyramid Mountain	Morris	3	E/M	500	2.5
19. Mount Hope Historical Park	Morris	2.7	E	350	2
20. Mahlon Dickerson Reservation	Morris	4.9	E/M	400	3
21. Jenny Jump State Forest	Warren	5	M	950	3.5
22. Point Mountain	Hunterdon	2.8	M	535	2.5
23. Schooley's Mountain County Park	Morris	2.3	E/M	500	2
24. Black River Trails	Morris	6.6	M/S	800	4
25. Merrill Creek Reservoir	Warren	6.7	E	400	4
26. Dismal Harmony Natural Area	Morris	2.6	E/M	380	2

VIEWS	KIDS	CAMP	X-C SKI	FALLS	SHUTTLE	Comments
✓		✓				Hike on Appalachian Trail; open ridges with views
✓						Cascading brook; west-facing views from rock ledge
✓		✓				Rugged and remote trail; excellent east-facing views
✓			✓			Steep climb and descent, views, heavily used
✓				✓		Great views, scenic lake, waterfall
✓						Views, lake, stone ruins of mansion
✓	✓		✓			Historic manor house and cemetery, scenic pond
✓						Manor house, gardens, views
✓	✓		✓			Scenic lake and panoramic views
✓			✓			Two iron mines, spectacular views from Wyanokie High Point
✓			✓			Steep, rocky sections, good views
✓						Panoramic views from two peaks
✓						Rock scrambling, beautiful glacial lake
✓						Puddingstone rock ledges, pristine wilderness lake
✓				✓	✓	Historic features, views, deep woods
✓			✓			Rhododendron stands, lakes, historic furnace
✓						Steep climb to viewpoint; excellent views
✓	✓					Unusual boulders, views
✓						Historic mines
✓	✓	✓	✓			Unusual pine swamp, views, cross-country skiing
✓						Glacial boulders, good views, lake
✓			✓			Cascading stream, open fields, views from rock ledge
✓				✓		River gorge, waterfalls, views
				✓	✓	Grist mill, wild river gorge, meadows
✓	✓		✓			Walk around scenic reservoir, historic ruins
	✓			✓		Cascading brook, unusual boulder

HIKE	COUNTY	DISTANCE (miles)	DIFFICULTY	RISE (feet)	TIME (hrs)
27. Jockey Hollow	Morris	5.3	E/M	670	3
28. Scherman Hoffman Wildlife Sanctuary	Morris	1.5	E	300	1
29. Palisades	Bergen	5.50	M	600	4
30. Rockleigh Woods Sanctuary and Lamont Reserve	Bergen	2.2	E/M	400	1.5
31. High Mountain	Passaic	4	M	400	2.5
32. South Mountain Reservation	Essex	9.3	M	750	6
33. Watchung Reservation	Union	6.5	M	500	4
34. Sourland Mountain Preserve	Somerset	4.7	E/M	500	3
35. D & R Canal—Washington Crossing to Scudder's Falls	Mercer	6.3	E	100	3
36. D & R Canal—Bull's Island to Stockton	Hunterdon	7.2	E/M	M	3.5
37. D & R Canal—Kingston to Rocky Hill	Somerset	4	E/M	M	2
38. D & R Canal—Weston to East Millstone	Somerset	4.3	E	M	2
39. Cheesequake State Park	Middlesex	3.3	E/M	200	2.5
40. Hartshorne Woods Park	Monmouth	2.7	E/M	300	1.5
41. Allaire State Park	Monmouth	3.7	E	120	2.5
42. Cattus Island	Ocean	3.7	E	M	2.5
43. Island Beach State Park	Ocean	3.7	E	M	2.5
44. Wells Mills County Park	Ocean	4.5	E/M	500	3
45. Bass River State Forest	Burlington/ Ocean	4.3	E	M	2.5
46. Brendan T. Byrne (Lebanon) State Forest	Burlington	8.1	M/S	M	5
47. Carranza Memorial to Apple Pie Hill	Burlington	8.2 or 5.2	M/S	166	4–5
48. Mullica River Wilderness	Burlington	12	M/S	M	6
49. Parvin State Park	Salem	4.0	E	M	2.5
50. Belleplain State Forest—East Creek Trail	Cape May	7	E/M	M	4.5

VIEWS	KIDS	CAMP	X-C SKI	FALLS	SHUTTLE	Comments
✓			✓			Revolutionary War historic site
						Interesting trees and boulders; scenic river walk
✓	✓			✓		Scenic walk along Hudson River, historic Kearney House
✓	✓					Pleasant hike on western slope of Palisades
✓	✓					Panoramic view of New York City skyline
✓			✓	✓		Views, waterfall, historic features, unusual rocks
✓						Suburban park, historic village and cemetery
	✓					Many unusual boulder formations
	✓		✓	✓		Historic buildings, canal towpath
	✓		✓			Historic bridges over Delaware River, historic gristmill
	✓		✓			Historic features, water, easy walking
	✓		✓			Tranquil, peaceful section of D & R Canal
✓	✓					Freshwater and cedar swamps, varied woods
						Holly and oak forests, mountain laurel thickets
	✓	✓				Historic Allaire Village
✓	✓					Views of marsh and bay
✓	✓					Ocean and bay views
						Hills in the Pinelands
	✓		✓			Sand roads, cedar bog
✓		✓				Explores cedar swamps and cranberry bogs
✓		✓			✓	Classic Pinelands hike, views from fire tower
						Parallel streams in the Pinelands
	✓	*				Pinelands vegetation, scenic lake
✓	✓	✓				Pinelands vegetation, scenic lake

Acknowledgments

Continuing to build on the foundation set by Stella Green, Bruce Scofield, and H. Neil Zimmerman, the authors of the first two editions of the book, this fifth edition incorporates many changes and enhancements. For this edition, I have added three completely new hikes to the book: Hike #2 (Blue Mountain Loop Trail); Hike #5 (Ramapo Valley County Reservation), and Hike #26 (Dismal Harmony Natural Area). In addition, many other hikes have been significantly revised and updated, and many new photos have been included.

My friends Ryan Chombok, Akiva Grimaldi, Devin McDermitt, Reuben O'Neill, Benny Oppenheim, Shimon Oppenheim, Ariel Schwartz, Eitan Schwartz, and Matt Wikfors accompanied me on trips to check out some of the hikes in this book, for which I am grateful. For this edition, all of the photos used (except for the cover image) are my own.

—Daniel Chazin

Introduction

New Jersey boasts an abundance of fine hiking trails. The famous Appalachian Trail crosses the northern part of the state, as does most of the 150-mile Highlands Trail; the 60-mile Delaware & Raritan Canal State Park extends from New Brunswick to Raven Rock, north of Trenton; the 50-mile Batona Trail traverses the New Jersey Pinelands; and the Long Path commences its journey northward on the Palisades at the George Washington Bridge. Some trails are located on old roads and footpaths that existed prior to the acquisition of the land for public use, and some date back to the Depression and the days of the federally funded Civilian Conservation Corps, whose members built park and recreation facilities still used today. Many trails, including the Appalachian Trail, are maintained by volunteers, whose dedication is evidenced by the fresh paint marks, water bars, and trails cleared of blowdowns and other hazards.

Hiking in the Garden State is varied, from the flat sandy trails in the southern part of the state to the hilly and rocky highlands in the northern part. There are swamps, beach areas, woods, and grasslands. Nine-tenths of New Jersey borders water; of its 480 miles of boundary, all but 48 are along either the seacoast or a riverbed. Except for the northwest section, the typical New Jersey landscape is a low, flat plain filled with meandering streams; four-fifths of the state is no more than 400 feet above

LAKE RUTHERFORD

sea level, and most of it is less than 100. The highest point, in the northwest corner, is 1,803 feet above sea level.

THE GEOLOGY AND TOPOGRAPHY OF NEW JERSEY

Geologists divide New Jersey into four primary provinces. In the northwest, running roughly southwest to northeast, is the Appalachian Ridge and Valley Province, containing the highest elevations in the state. Here, in what was once a major mountain range (since leveled by erosion), is a series of parallel valleys and ridges composed of faulted and folded Paleozoic (Cambrian to mid-Devonian) sandstones and conglomerates between 375 and 540 million years old. The mountains we see today are former marine basins of sandstone, shale, and limestone, tipped by the compression of moving continental plates, which have eroded at varying rates, creating a series of parallel ridges and shallow valleys. Hawk sightings along the main ridges are frequent during the fall migration. The Delaware Water Gap National Recreation Area, Worthington and Stokes State Forests, and High Point State Park together preserve nearly all the mountainous portions of this province. The Appalachian Trail follows the crest of the main ridge, the Kittatinny Mountains, for more than 40 miles on its way from Georgia to Maine. The hiking in this province can be challenging because of steep inclines and extremely rocky footing.

Southeast of the Ridge and Valley Province and paralleling it lies the New Jersey Highlands Province. This mountainous area is composed primarily of Precambrian gneisses, granites, and schists, which formed between 750 million and 1.3 billion years ago. These rocks were formed from high pressures and temperatures deep within the Earth. From a distance, the Highlands appear to be a mass of elevated land at a constant elevation. But the Highlands have a very rugged topography, with erratic and disconnected ridges and deep valleys between them. The elevations of the flat-topped summits typical of this province lie only a few hundred feet lower than those of the Kittatinny Mountains. The range extends north into New York State as the Hudson Highlands and south into Pennsylvania as the Reading Prong. Hikers will find not only more trails in this province than in any other in the state but also numerous lakes and reservoirs. The province includes Ramapo Mountain State Forest, Ramapo Valley County Reservation, Norvin Green State Forest, Ringwood State Park, Wawayanda State Park, and the vast holdings of the city of Newark, which supply drinking water to New Jersey's largest city. A number of other state and county parks and forests preserve segments of the natural features of the area.

Comprising most of northeastern and central New Jersey, the Piedmont Lowlands Province is a low-lying plain composed mainly of Mesozoic (Triassic and Jurassic) sandstones and shales that are 190 to 240 million years old. It is separated from the Highlands by a fault line that runs from Mahwah, in the north, to Milford, on the Delaware River. The Ramapo Fault in the northern part of the state shows this distinction dramatically, the boundary being apparent to the discerning eye on both road and contour maps. The more erosion-resistant Highlands rise above the Piedmont by as much as 800 feet in this region. Within the Piedmont

ALONG THE DELAWARE CANAL

Province, evidence of former rifting is found in a series of old lava flows that have withstood erosion better than the shales and sandstones and now stand as mountain ridges. Following the deposition of shales and sandstones, rifting of the North American plate occurred in several places. Rifts are where a series of openings form between the earth's surface and the hot mantle miles below the surface. Basalt and related rocks are formed from such mantle extrusions. One such rift, to the east of present-day New Jersey, continued to expand and became the Atlantic Ocean. The rift that is now in New Jersey failed to open, leaving behind a number of igneous flows and intrusions. Just across the Hudson River from New York stand the Palisades, the eastern edges of a sill of igneous rock that, in places, rises more than 500 feet above the river. Farther west are the Watchung Hills, roughly parallel ridges made up of the resistant edges of westward-sloping, basaltic lava flows, which rise about 250 feet above the surrounding plans. Cushetunk Mountain and others near it are

somewhat similar features called dikes. Composed of diabase, related to basalt, they are found in the southwestern portion of the province, where it extends into central New Jersey.

Extensive development has marred much of the natural beauty of the Piedmont Lowlands Province, though a few parks offer an opportunity to explore what was once the forest frontier of the New York region. The Palisades Interstate Park preserves much of the northern portion of the rock ramparts overlooking the Hudson. Several reservations along the crest of the first Watchung Ridge and the Round Valley Recreation Area on Cushetunk Mountain preserve some of the remaining high woodlands. In this province are also found several tracts of land that, though low and flat, offer some interesting hiking possibilities. The federally owned Great Swamp Wildlife Refuge and neighboring county parks have miles of trails, some on boardwalk, that penetrate the wetlands of a former glacial lake of immense proportions. From Raven Rock on the Delaware River to New

Brunswick on the Raritan, the towpath of the old Delaware & Raritan Canal (now a state park) offers the hiker 66 miles of wooded walkway along a quiet but very alive body of water. During its heyday, the canal was the scene of intense activity. In fact, for a while, the Delaware & Raritan Canal did more business than the much better-known Erie Canal in New York State.

Encompassing nearly all of New Jersey south of an imaginary line drawn between New Brunswick and Trenton is the Coastal Plain, the largest geomorphic province in the state. This entire area is composed of ocean and stream deposits of sands, silts, and clays laid down during the late Mesozoic to the early Cenozoic (late Cretaceous to Miocene) eras, 50 to 80 million years ago. The lowest elevations in the state are here, ranging from only a few hundred feet above sea level inland to water level on the seashore. From the gently rolling topography of the Pinelands to the sandy beaches along New Jersey's 127-mile coast, this province offers the hiker an environment very different from that found in the rest of the state. The Pinelands (also known as the Pine Barrens), a sparse pine and scrub oak forest of about 1 million acres, has been saved in large measure from the pressures of development. The heart of the Pinelands is preserved in several state forests, the largest of which is Wharton, headquartered at the old bog iron-mining town of Batsto. The Batona Trail (named for the BAck TO NAture Club of Philadelphia) penetrates the forest for some 50 miles from Lake Absegami to Ong's Hat. This marked footpath passes deep cedar swamps, parallels rivers of cedar water, and climbs Apple Pie Hill, at 205 feet the highest summit in the Pinelands. Throughout the Pinelands are sand roads—some more than 200 years old—that make for excellent walking through this wilderness of pines.

Several areas along the Jersey coast have been preserved in their original state, by contrast with the overdevelopment that has occurred elsewhere. Here, dunes, marshes, and moving sands pushed by the ocean currents present interesting walking opportunities. The New Jersey coast lies along the Atlantic Flyway, the route taken by migrating birds as they wing their way toward warmer climates. To avoid crowds, we recommend that the coast be hiked during the off-season.

LONG-DISTANCE TRAILS

Three long-distance trails pass through New Jersey. The Appalachian Trail (AT), a National Scenic Trail, enters from Pennsylvania at the Delaware Water Gap on its 2,185-mile journey from Georgia to Maine. From the Delaware Water Gap, it heads northeast along the ridge of the Kittatinny Mountains for 45 miles, then turns east and parallels the New Jersey–New York state boundary for another 25 miles until it turns north and heads into New York State. Blazed with white rectangles, the AT is administered by the Appalachian Trail Conservancy, headquartered in Harpers Ferry, West Virginia. Responsibility for the section of the AT in New Jersey has been delegated to the New York–New Jersey Trail Conference, and it is maintained by volunteers.

The Long Path (LP), blazed in parakeet aqua, begins its northward journey at the George Washington Bridge. For years, its northern terminus was at the town of Windham in the Catskills, but it has now been extended north to the Mohawk Valley. It is maintained by volunteers of the New York–New Jersey Trail Conference, and there is a plan to extend the trail into the Adirondacks. The first 10 miles of the LP are in New Jersey. The Shawangunk Ridge Trail (SRT) was established as a trail alternative to the LP road walk through Orange County. Only 3.1 miles are located in New Jersey—the remaining miles are in New York.

The 150-mile Highlands Trail (HT) links the Delaware and Hudson Rivers, traversing many county, state, and federal parks. It is the result of cooperation among the New York–New Jersey Trail Conference, the New Jersey Conservation Foundation, and the National Park Service. There is a plan to extend the HT across the Hudson River and into Connecticut.

THE NATURE OF HIKING

Being out in the woods entails a certain element of risk. All hikers should be prepared with emergency gear and be able to look after themselves. Taking precautions will ensure that your trip is pleasant. Enjoy your hobby.

The times assigned for the hikes in this book are based on an average pace, allowing for breaks and exploration of interesting features along the way. Some hikers will be able to complete the hikes faster than the assigned time; some will take longer. Every hiker develops a pace at which he or she feels most comfortable. The slow amble with frequent stops that many beginning hikers adopt soon gives way to a more rhythmic stride. Begin with short walks on a regular basis and, as your skills and muscle power build, move on to more challenging hikes. In addition to the physical elation of exercising in the outdoors, hobbies such as birdwatching, tree and flower identification, wildlife observation, photography, and local history can be made a part of almost any hike.

To enjoy the outdoors requires a certain amount of planning. Study the route and allow sufficient time to complete the

BOARDWALK THROUGH THE CEDAR SWAMP, CHEESEQUAKE STATE PARK

trip before darkness falls. Some prefer hiking alone, but it is safer and generally more enjoyable to hike with a small group. A group of four people is recommended; if someone is injured, two of the hikers can go for help while one stays with the injured party. Large groups tend to destroy the feeling of isolation that one experiences in the wilderness and can spoil the hike for others who encounter large groups along the way. If you decide to hike alone, tell someone dependable where you are hiking and when you expect to return, and do not deviate from the established plan.

As a hiker, your body is your resource. It needs enough food to keep energy levels high; above all, it needs water, and it should not be pushed to the point of exhaustion. Hiking is pleasurable if adequate preparations are taken. Keep your body at a comfortable temperature—neither so warm that excessive perspiration occurs, nor so cold or wet that hypothermia becomes a problem. Getting wet, either from rain or sweat, should be avoided. Hypothermia can creep up unawares. The outdoor temperature does not have to be very low. You can become hypothermic in 50-degree weather if there is rain or wind and you are unprepared. Watch your companions for signs of poor reflex actions: excessive stumbling, the need for frequent rest stops, or a careless attitude toward clothing and equipment. Once uncontrollable shivering has started, it may only be a matter of minutes before the body temperature has cooled beyond the point of recovery. Immediate warmth for the afflicted person is the only solution.

Suitable clothing and equipment are essential as safeguards against emergencies. It is assumed—and highly recommended—that new hikers will start their hiking careers during the warmer months, so the pieces of equipment discussed here are only the basics. Winter hiking is superb, with fewer people in the woods, no bugs, and a completely different feeling from summertime hiking, but remember: rocks may be icy, wet leaves and lichen make rocks slippery, and clothing and equipment must be adjusted to fit the conditions.

CLOTHING

While clothing is largely a matter of personal choice, there are some important rules that should be followed. Cotton clothing should be avoided, especially in cold weather. When cotton becomes wet, it is heavy, dries slowly, and does not retain warmth. Instead, wear nylon or polypropylene, especially next to your body. Wearing layers of clothing is recommended; this way, one can remove a layer or two if one gets too warm and then put them back on at rest stops to avoid getting chilled. For emergency use, we recommend you carry a wool shirt or sweater, wool or polypropylene hat and gloves, a small flashlight, a simple first-aid kit, a pocketknife, toilet paper, and (in summer) bug repellent. In winter, it is a good idea to bring Stabilicers, MicroSpikes, or similar lightweight devices that provide traction on icy portions of the trail. If you would be helpless without your eyeglasses, carry an extra pair.

Boots: It is essential that one wear well-fitting, rubber-soled footwear on all hikes. Some hikers prefer lightweight sneakers, and these are minimally adequate for most hikes described in this book. However, lightweight hiking boots provide ankle support—something that sneakers do not provide. Many hikers choose to wear hiking boots on all but the easiest hikes, and they are strongly recommended for backpacking and for the more rugged hikes. If you need new boots, to ensure a good fit, take with you to the store the socks you plan to wear on the trail (see below). There should be ample room in the boots so your toes are not cramped, and there should not be much forward movement of your feet in them. Most good outfitters employ salespeople experienced enough to advise on boot choice. If possible, walk around in your home or office for several days before determining whether the pair you purchased will be suitable for hiking. Your first hike in new boots should be a short one and should a "hot spot" form on your foot, stop immediately and apply moleskin or molefoam to reduce the likelihood of a blister.

Socks: To help prevent blisters, wear two pairs of socks with hiking boots: an inner pair of lightweight polypropylene or wool and an outer of thicker wool.

Rain/Wind Protection: Ideally, your rain jacket should have a hood. The hood will prevent cold wind from penetrating between your collar and neck. Remember, though, that hiking will generate perspiration, and some rain jackets will retain wetness inside the garment even if it is not raining. A waterproof, breathable fabric such as Gore-Tex is highly recommended.

PACK

A lightweight day pack is indispensable for carrying those pieces of equipment that you will need to take with you on the trail. Most day packs are basically small backpacks that ride high on the back. Some of the newer fanny packs, as well as a hybrid called a lumbar pack, will hold nearly as much as a small backpack and may be more comfortable.

You will want to take these items with you:

Water: The time has long since passed when you could be refreshed at that beautiful stream by drinking the pure, cold water. Giardia lamblia and other intestinal parasites and bacteria have destroyed that pleasure. Always carry water with you. The amount you need to take will vary depending on the length of the hike, the temperature and humidity, and your personal needs. Some people require more water than others. One quart may suffice for a moderate hike in cool temperatures, but you might need two or three quarts if you take the same hike on a hot summer day. Monitor your urine, and if it is dark, increase your water intake, particularly in colder weather, when thirst is not as apparent as it is in the heat.

Lunch: Even if lunch is not planned on the trail, take an emergency ration—fruit, trail mix, a chocolate bar, or "gorp" (good old raisins and peanuts—with M&Ms, if you wish).

MAPS

The maps in this guide, along with the text, are all you really need for these hikes. As you become experienced, though, you may want to explore areas in more depth. Each hike refers you to other maps, as keyed at the end of this introduction. For hiking in New Jersey, it is not usually necessary to carry a compass, particularly if you are on a described hike; however, if you stray from the trail, having a map and compass—and knowing how to use them—can return you to the path or to civilization. Today, the Global Positioning System (GPS) is an additional navigational tool. When used in conjunction with mapping software, a GPS unit can produce a map of the hike just walked.

You will need a good New Jersey road map to find your way to the trailheads. Each hike tells you how to reach the trailhead itself, but getting to the nearby town from where the directions begin is often up to you. New Jersey, like most states, publishes an official highway map, and it is free. Write to the New Jersey Division of Travel and Tourism, P.O. Box 820, Trenton, NJ 08625; call 609-292-2470 or 1-800-VISITNJ (1-800-847-4865) or go to www.state.nj.us/travel. Even if you have a GPS receiver in your car, it is a good idea to bring along a map, as GPS receivers sometimes fail to work properly.

GEOCACHING

This is a high-tech treasure hunt. In 2000, a new dimension was added to the adventure of being outdoors. A game called geocaching, which uses Global Positioning System (GPS) technology, was designed and developed in the Seattle area and now delights more than 6 million participants. Caches are mostly hidden containers, sometimes plastic, sometimes metal, that contain a logbook and trinkets, with its coordinates posted on a log page accessed on the Web at www.geocaching.com. Players choose code names for themselves, enter a zip code, and find the names and coordinates for caches in their vicinity. Then it's up to the skill of the player to use a portable GPS unit to find the treasure. The pleasure is in the hunt, though. When the cache is found, the cacher signs the log using his nom de plume, replaces what he removes from

the cache with an item of equal value, and then logs his find on the cache page, which keeps track of the number of "finds." It is estimated that caches exist in every state and in more than 200 countries, and there are many variations on the main theme.

Letterboxing is a similar pastime (www.letterboxing.com), but instead of a GPS using satellites to obtain coordinates, this game uses instructions and puzzles to help hikers locate the treasure, and you need a rubber stamp and pad to validate the find. Other sites such as www.navicache.com are also available.

FACTS FOR HIKERS

TRAIL MARKERS

The trails in the Garden State are mostly color-coded with paint blazes on trees. Sometimes metal or plastic tags affixed to trees with nails are used instead. Three blazes in a triangle indicate the beginning or the end of a trail, and major turns are indicated by two blazes, with the turn direction indicated by the upper blaze.

Ideally, trail blazes are spaced so that you can easily see the next as you move along the trail. At times, blazes become obscured by new growth or blowdowns, or, if a trail is not maintained properly, they may become faded. The hikes described in this book are mostly on marked trails, but we cannot vouch for the quality of the marking, which varies from trail to trail.

TICKS AND CHIGGERS

During the hot summer, in grassy areas with damp soils, hikers may come into contact with chiggers. Chiggers are a species of mite and are parasitic on humans only in the juvenile stage of their life cycle. They are extremely small and are identifiable by only the itchy red spots that appear after the mite has attached itself to the skin. Welts may appear for several days after exposure as the mites move around the body. Immersion of the affected areas with alcohol is recommended as a treatment.

Ticks are a problem in New Jersey and other nearby states. Lyme disease is not to be trifled with. The deer tick (Ixodes scapularis) that carries Lyme disease is very small (the size of a period in this text). Do not confuse it with the common wood tick, which is the size of a match head, or—when engorged with blood—the size of a pea. Deer ticks are more abundant in shore areas where deer are common. A bite from an infected deer tick will often result in a rash (sometimes, but not always, in the shape of a bull's-eye), which should be immediately treated by a doctor. Learn to look for and remove ticks after hiking in an infested area. Long-sleeved shirts and pants with the legs tucked into socks are a must in these areas. Spray your feet and legs with a tick repellent containing DEET. A flyer on Lyme disease is available from the New Jersey State Department of Health, P.O. Box 360, Trenton, NJ 08625; call 609-292-7837. Or check the Web site of the New York–New Jersey Trail Conference at www.nynjtc.org.

WILDLIFE

The black bear is the largest animal in New Jersey and is native to the Garden State. In recent years, the bear population has increased, particularly in areas close to Pennsylvania, and near areas in New Jersey where new homes have invaded the territory that was once exclusively the domain of these animals.

Food smells attract bears, and in many cases they learn that where there are campsites, there will be food. When camping, it is advisable to use a commercial bear-proof box (available from outfitters) to store all foods, as well as such items as soap, deodorant, and toothpaste. Never store anything edible in the tent or shelter, and prepare meals at least 100 feet away from your tent. Do not take the clothing worn while cooking into the tent, because food odors and food spatters cling to fabric.

The next best protection from bears is to hang food from a tree branch in odor-proof bundles, making sure that the packages hang at least 10 feet above the ground and well away from the tree's trunk. Bears are smart animals and have been known to retrieve these caches, so it is advisable to use a tree branch far away from your tent. There is a trend among parks to supply metal bear-proof lockers to campers, and you should use these if they are available.

If a bear should come into camp, banging pots will sometimes scare the animal away. Remember, though, that a human is smaller than a bear—males usually weigh between 135 and 350 pounds.

Information and advice on black bears is available on the New Jersey Division of Fish and Wildlife Web site at www.njfishandwildlife.com. Click on the Black Bear link in the Education pane.

Because rodents have sharp teeth and are good climbers, they can cause much damage to packs and tents if they detect food smells, so similar precautions should be taken to store food items away from camp.

MOUNTAIN BIKES

When this book was first published in 1987, there were no bicycles on New Jersey trails. But modern technology has produced a rugged bicycle that can withstand trail use, and today's mountain bikes can traverse terrain once reserved for the hiker alone. The popularity of these new bicycles has grown steadily, and by the early 1990s, many New Jersey trails had experienced sharp increases in use. User conflicts soon arose and continue to be a problem in many places. Mountain bike riders assumed that the trails made and maintained by hikers were there for them to share. Hikers resented the encroachment and trail destruction mountain bikes can cause—though mountain-biking proponents often deny these problems—and fought to have them banned or limited in parks and forests, because mountain bikes create many erosion problems and intrude on the tranquility that many hikers seek. Equestrians resented the speed at which some bikers travel along trails, which scares their horses. These problems are still with us, and policies are constantly being shaped and reshaped. If mountain biking is of concern to you, you may wish to contact the park or forest where you will be hiking for information on policies and complaints, or to express your opinion.

PARKING FEES

Many state parks and forests charge moderate fees for parking, normally between Memorial Day weekend and Labor Day weekend. In most cases, weekday rates are lower than weekend rates. A New Jersey State Park Pass is available, which provides free entry to all parks for 1 year. State residents older than 62 can obtain a free parking pass, good at any time. Passes can be purchased at any park or forest office.

HUNTING

New Jersey has a short deer hunting season, usually in December. Avoid hiking in hunting areas during firearms season. Check with the local park office, the New Jersey Department of Environmental Protection, or the New York–New Jersey Trail Conference for specific dates. As of this writing, there is no hunting in New Jersey on Sundays.

TRAIL ETIQUETTE

There is a certain etiquette to hiking. Two of the most important phrases to remember are the familiar "take only photographs, leave only footprints" and "carry out what you carry in." If every user of our woods followed these guidelines, litter would not be a problem. Many concerned hikers carry empty garbage bags in their packs, picking up litter they find along the trails and carrying it out.

Some trails border or cross private property. "No trespassing" signs should be honored, and care should be taken to respect the rights of private landowners. A few thoughtless walkers can damage good relations built up over the years with trail neighbors.

On the trail, give way to the person walking uphill. If there are trail registers, carefully fill out the first register on your hike and sign out at the last.

On overnights at existing shelters, remember that lean-tos should be available for all who need to use them. On those wet and windy nights, cheerfully make room for latecomers. Pack away all evidence that you have been there, and leave the shelter exactly as you would wish to find it on arrival.

Before beginning your backpacking hike, check whether fires are permitted in the area. Where fires are permitted, no live trees should be cut for firewood, and the fire should be contained in the fireplace provided at many shelters. It is courteous to gather enough dead wood so that the next occupant can at least get another fire started. Wood is in short supply in frequently camped areas. Whether you build them for atmosphere or for smudge (keeping mosquitoes away), keep fires small and safe. A small, lightweight backpacking stove is preferable for cooking. These are inexpensive, cook food quickly, and, unlike fires, keep pots from blackening.

There are certain areas in the United States—on the beaches of the Colorado River in the Grand Canyon, for instance—where human body waste has become such a problem that now it is required that all human excrement be carried out. With the increasing number of people using New Jersey trails, it is not unthinkable that in the future we might all be required to carry out our personal waste. To avoid this inconvenience, use the outhouse where one is provided, and otherwise be a "copycat"—act as a feline does. Choose a spot far away from any water and the trail, remove the layer of leaves and twigs, dig a hole at least 3 inches deep in the soil with either a rock or a sturdy stick (some hikers carry a special trowel for this purpose), take care of your business, and cover the whole mess over so that no disturbance is apparent.

HIKING ORGANIZATIONS

The umbrella organization for hiking in New Jersey is the New York–New Jersey Trail Conference (NY–NJTC), a nonprofit federation of 10,000 individuals and 100 hiking and environmental organizations working to build and maintain trails and to preserve open space. Its trail network includes more than 2,000 miles of foot trails. Formed in 1920, the Conference built the first section of the Appalachian Trail in 1923.

The Conference is supported by dues, publication sales, and donations—along with thousands of hours of volunteer time. Members receive the quarterly news journal *Trail Walker*, and can purchase maps and guides at a 25 percent discount, avail themselves of the Conference library, and obtain a 10 percent discount on purchases at many outdoors stores. At present, dues are $40 for individuals and $35 for seniors. A single life membership is $1,000; a joint life membership (for two adults residing at the same address) is $1,500.

We encourage you to support the people who maintain the trails. The NY–NJTC office is located at 600 Ramapo Valley Road (on US 202 about 2 miles south of NJ 17), Mahwah, NJ 07430. You can also call 201-512-9348, or visit their Web site, www.nynjtc.org.

There are also many fine hiking clubs in New Jersey, catering to all grades of hikers, in many areas of the state. These clubs provide an excellent way to meet people who share your love of the outdoors. The clubs are your ticket to the special natural sections of your area and will help you learn the ins and outs of hiking in the Northeast. For a listing, go to the Trail Conference's Web site, www.nynjtc.org.

Volunteers maintain many of the trails described in this book. Respect their work and their tender loving care, and do not cut corners on switchbacks or otherwise erode the trail unnecessarily. If you'd like to help maintain a trail, contact the New York–New Jersey Trail Conference.

MAPS

USGS: Free USGS topo maps are available online: store.usgs.gov.

NY–NJTC: The New York–New Jersey Trail Conference publishes and sells waterproof, color topographic maps, usually in sets. Four map sets cover trails in New Jersey: Hudson Palisades, North Jersey, Kittatinny, and Jersey Highlands. About half of the hikes in this book can be found on these maps, which are printed on nearly indestructible Tyvek. To obtain copies of these maps, contact the Trail Conference at 600 Ramapo Valley Road, Mahwah, NJ 07430, call 201-512-9348, or find them on the Web at www.nynjtc.org.

DEP: Free maps are available from the various state park and forest offices. Or, write to the New Jersey Department of Environmental Protection, Division of Parks and Forestry, P.O. Box 402, Trenton, NJ 08625; call 1-800-843-6420: or go to www.njparksandforests.org. The quality of these maps varies, and some of them do not clearly show hiking trails.

NPS: National Park maps, usually free, are available from individual park offices. Addresses are in the hike text. They are also available online at www.nps.gov.

MAP LEGEND

———	Described trail	≡≡≡	Interstate highway
- - - -	Important trail	≡≡≡	Secondary highway
◄———	Hike direction arrow	———	Minor highway, road, street
———	Perennial stream	- - - -	Unpaved road, trail
- - - -	Intermittent stream	++++	Railroad
———	Major contour line	—··—	International border
———	Minor contour line	--—--	State border
	National/state park, wilderness	**P**	Parking area
	National/state forest, wildlife refuge	**🚶**	Trailhead
	Perennial body of water	•	City, town
	Intermittent body of water	))⩽	Overlook, scenic view
	Swamp, marsh	Å	Campground, campsite
	Wooded area	⋔	Shelter
		×	Mountain peak
		▪	Place of interest

I.

RIDGE AND VALLEY

South of High Point

TOTAL DISTANCE: 6.3 miles

HIKING TIME: 4 hours

VERTICAL RISE: 500 feet

RATING: Moderately strenuous

MAPS: USGS Port Jervis South; NY–NJTC Kittatinny Trails #123; DEP High Point State Park map

TRAILHEAD GPS COORDINATES:
N 41° 18' 10" W 74° 40' 04"

South of High Point Monument and the popular Lake Marcia is a section of High Point State Park (1480 State Route 23, Sussex, NJ 07461; 973-875-4800; www .njparksandforests.org) that is wild, expansive, scenic, and lightly used. In contrast, the portion of the park north of NJ 23 is heavily used. The Appalachian Trail (AT) passes through this southern section, and the Rutherford Shelter, one of the few New Jersey AT trail shelters, is also found here. A warning is in order. If you have not had any experience with this section of the AT, or if your feet are particularly sensitive, be prepared for a rocky path that will test your boots. The first 2 miles of this hike will be demanding on your feet and on your balance. Most people prefer to do the hike in the direction described below, because the second leg of the hike is on a flat woods road. That way, you can do the more challenging portions of the hike first and then return on a relatively easy route.

GETTING THERE

The trailhead is just east of the High Point State Park Visitor Contact Station in Sussex County. Take NJ 23 to the visitor center at the top of Kittatinny Ridge, on the south side of the highway. Stop in at the office for a map (or a permit if you are camping and leaving your car overnight). Park at the AT parking area, which is on the same side of NJ 23, about 0.2 mile east of the visitor center. (It is the second active driveway when heading east on NJ 23 from the visitor center.)

THE HIKE

From the kiosk at the southwest corner of the parking area, follow a blue-blazed

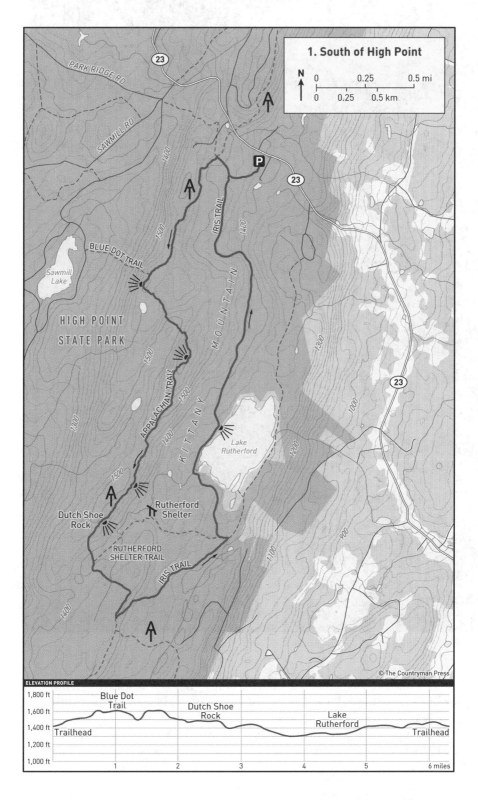

1. South of High Point

N

| 0 | 0.25 | 0.5 mi |
| 0 | 0.25 | 0.5 km |

PARK RIDGE RD

23

SAWMILL RD

1400

IRIS TRAIL

1500

1400

BLUE DOT TRAIL

Sawmill Lake

HIGH POINT STATE PARK

M O U N T A I N

1500

1300

APPALACHIAN TRAIL

1500

1400

K I T T A N Y

1300

1000

1200

Lake Rutherford

1500

900

Dutch Shoe Rock

Rutherford Shelter

RUTHERFORD SHELTER TRAIL

1100

1400

IRIS TRAIL

23

© The Countryman Press

ELEVATION PROFILE

1,800 ft						
1,600 ft	Blue Dot Trail	Dutch Shoe Rock		Lake Rutherford		
1,400 ft	Trailhead					Trailhead
1,200 ft						
1,000 ft	1	2	3	4	5	6 miles

A ROCKY SECTION OF THE AT

trail that leads uphill for about a quarter of a mile to the red-on-white-blazed Iris Trail. Turn right and follow both blue and red-on-white blazes for a short distance to a junction with the AT at a 4-foot-high drainpipe. Turn left at this junction and begin to follow the white-blazed AT.

After a short distance, the AT begins to climb, passing a large cliff on your right. The AT continues ahead on an old woods road, then bears right and climbs to the ridge of Kittatinny Mountain. The next section of the AT along the ridge is a beautiful stretch of trail. The trail follows the eastern side of a ridge for a while, then swings over to the western side. Your feet will notice that the rocks are particularly jagged in this section, a characteristic of the AT in Pennsylvania and New Jersey.

About a mile from the start, you'll reach a junction with the Blue Dot Trail, which descends steeply to the right and reaches Sawmill Lake below in about 0.5 mile. Continue ahead on the AT. A short distance beyond, you'll reach a west-facing viewpoint, with Sawmill Lake visible below. The trail now turns left and descends on a rocky footpath to a valley between the two ridges of the mountain. It then climbs very steeply to the eastern ridge (this is the steepest climb that you'll encounter on the hike). At the top of the climb, there are views to the right over the western ridge. The trail then moves to the eastern ridge and passes a limited east-facing viewpoint, with the views largely obscured by vegetation.

The AT now heads south along the ridge, descending gradually. It passes through a scrub oak/pitch pine forest and then an oak-and-maple woods.

In about a mile, you'll come out on a panoramic east-facing viewpoint from a long, glacially polished rock slab of Silurian sandstone to the left of the trail. Lake Rutherford and a large marsh are to the left, with the rural Wallkill Valley beyond. In the distance are Pochuck Mountain and Wawayanda Mountain, both traversed by the AT farther north.

You'll immediately pass another viewpoint, after which the trail goes back into the woods. In another 0.2 mile, you'll reach another east-facing viewpoint from open rocks on the left. This viewpoint, known as Dutch Shoe Rock, offers a broad view over the Wallkill Valley, but Lake Rutherford is not visible.

Continue following the AT south for another 0.3 mile to a junction with a blue-blazed side trail that leads northeast for 0.4 mile to the Rutherford Shelter. If you would like to take a detour to the shelter, it's a good place to stop for lunch. Otherwise, continue ahead on the AT for another 0.4 mile to its junction with the red-on-white-blazed Iris Trail. Turn left here and follow the Iris Trail along an old woods road that will feel positively soft after those first few miles on the jagged rocks of the AT. Keep left at a junction, staying with the red-on-white markers, then bear right at the next fork, and soon you will arrive at the west shore of Lake Rutherford.

Just before the trail bears left, away from the lake, a side trail on the right leads down to the lake. This is a good spot to take a break and enjoy the views over the scenic lake. Lake Rutherford is quite large and has only a few traces of civilization on its shores, Unfortunately, swimming is not permitted because the lake serves as the municipal water supply for the town of Sussex.

From the lake, continue northward on the Iris Trail, which climbs gradually. Along the way, you'll notice some interesting rock outcrops on both sides of the trail. In a mile and a half, after crossing a small brook on a footbridge, the Iris Trail reaches a junction with the blue-blazed trail that leads to the parking area. Turn right here and follow the blue blazes back to your car.

Blue Mountain Loop Trail

TOTAL DISTANCE: 8.5 miles
HIKING TIME: 5 hours
VERTICAL RISE: 950 feet
RATING: Moderate
MAPS: USGS Flatbrookville; NY–NJTC Kittatinny Trails #122; NY–NJ Appalachian Trail Guide map #4
TRAILHEAD GPS COORDINATES: N 41°13'33.5" W 74°45'23.0"

For many years, Stokes State Forest had a network of short, disconnected hiking trails. In 2015, the Park Superintendent decided to combine sections of several existing trails with newly constructed trail sections to form the 15-mile-long Blue Mountain Loop Trail, blazed with blue-dot-on-white blazes. The loop is bisected by the yellow-blazed Tinsley Trail, making it possible to divide it into two sections, each of which makes an attractive day hike.

This hike follows the northern section of the Blue Mountain Loop Trail, which climbs to two west-facing viewpoints and includes a 2-mile stretch where the trail closely parallels the cascading Big Flat Brook.

GETTING THERE

Take I-80 to Exit 34B and continue north on NJ 15 for about 17 miles. When NJ 15 ends, continue ahead on US 206 North for 8.6 miles and turn right onto Flatbrook Road. In 1 mile, turn sharply right to continue on Flatbrook Road. Continue for another 2.4 miles and turn right onto Skellenger Road at a sign for the New Jersey School of Conservation. Proceed ahead for another 0.6 mile, crossing a stone-faced bridge over the Big Flat Brook along the way. Just before a "Dead End" sign, turn right onto a gated dirt road, and park in a small parking area on the right (if this small parking area is full, you may be able to park along the shoulder of Skellenger Road).

THE HIKE

From the parking area, walk around the locked gate and proceed southeast on the yellow-blazed Tinsley Trail, which follows a woods road. Several marked trails maintained by the New Jersey

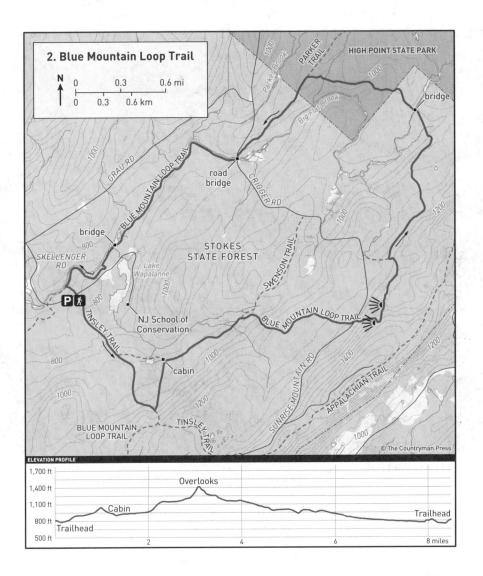

State School of Conservation branch off to the left, and one of these trails (the Purple Finch Trail) is co-aligned with the Tinsley Trail for some distance.

After descending to a wetland, the Tinsley Trail begins a gradual climb. About half a mile from the start, you'll reach a fork, where you should bear right to continue along the Tinsley Trail. The trail now levels off, but it soon resumes its climb.

At the next junction, turn left, leaving the Tinsley Trail, and follow the blue-dot-on-white blazes of the Blue Mountain Loop Trail, which descends on a rocky footpath. You will be following the Blue Mountain Loop Trail for the remainder of the hike.

In a third of a mile, you'll reach an open area with a locked cabin and an adjacent picnic table. Continue ahead on the Blue Mountain Loop Trail, which follows a level woods road. In about half a mile, after crossing several branches

THE CASCADING BIG FLAT BROOK

of a stream, follow the Blue Mountain Loop Trail as it turns right, leaving the woods road.

The Blue Mountain Loop Trail climbs on a footpath, paralleling a stream on the left. After crossing the stream on rocks, the trail levels off. Soon, it crosses another stream and continues through a dense understory of ferns. It then climbs a little more to cross the paved Sunrise Mountain Road. The climb steepens on the other side of the road, and, in a short distance, the trail reaches a panoramic west-facing viewpoint from an open rock ledge, with several pine trees. This is a good spot to take a break.

After climbing a little more, you'll come to another junction. Here, a side trail with black/blue blazes begins, but you should turn left, continuing to follow the blue-dot-on-white blazes of the Blue Mountain Loop Trail. Soon, you'll come to another west-facing viewpoint from an open rock ledge.

In another quarter mile, follow the Blue Mountain Loop Trail as it turns left onto an eroded woods road. After descending some more on this road, the Blue Mountain Loop Trail turns right onto an intersecting woods road. Just beyond, the gray-on-white-blazed Howell Trail begins on the left.

The Blue Mountain Loop Trail now descends gently. In about a mile, it crosses a few short wooden bridges and then a longer bridge over the Big Flat Brook. It continues to descend a little, but after crossing a stream on rocks, the trail begins to climb. After leveling off, the trail descends gradually. It then crosses a wet area on puncheons. Soon, it reaches a grassy woods road, where the blue-blazed Parker Trail begins on the right.

Turn left onto the road. In about half a mile, follow the blue-on-white blazes as they turn left, leaving the road, and descend on a footpath. Soon, you'll reach the paved Crigger Road, with a piped spring on the opposite side of the road. Turn left onto the paved road, continuing to follow the blue-on-white blazes of the Blue Mountain Loop Trail. The trail crosses the Big Flat Brook on the road bridge, then turns right, leaving the paved road, and continues on a footpath.

For the next 2 miles, the trail proceeds through a hemlock forest, closely paralleling the cascading Big Flat Brook. This is the most interesting and beautiful portion of the hike, and you'll want to take your time to enjoy this trail section.

After about 1.2 miles of pleasant walking along the brook, you'll traverse an open grassy area, with a fenced-in area on the left. A short distance beyond, the Blue Mountain Loop Trail turns right and crosses an impressive wooden footbridge over the outlet of Lake Wapalanne. Just beyond, you'll pass the ruins of a stone fireplace, and the Brown Creeper Trail joins from the left.

Soon, the Blue Mountain Trail turns left, away from the brook. With a parking area and buildings of the New Jersey School of Conservation visible ahead, the Blue Mountain Trail turns right and continues high above the brook. In a short distance, joined by the Orange Wood Lily Trail, it descends to the level of the brook, which it follows around a bend.

Be alert for a yellow blaze which marks the start of the Tinsley Trail. At this junction, turn left, leaving the Blue Mountain Loop Trail, and follow the Tinsley Trail up a steep rise. Just ahead, the Tinsley Trail crosses Skellenger Road and reaches the parking area where the hike began.

Rattlesnake Swamp— Appalachian Trail Loop

TOTAL DISTANCE: 5.2 miles

HIKING TIME: 3 hours

VERTICAL RISE: 500 feet

RATING: Moderate

MAPS: USGS Flatbrookville; NY–NJTC Kittatinny Trails #121; NPS Millbrook Area Trails map; NY–NJ Appalachian Trail Guide map #4

TRAILHEAD GPS COORDINATES: N 41° 03′ 29″ W 74° 57′ 54″

This loop hike in the heart of the Kittatinnies skirts the edge of a swamp, passes a lake, and then climbs to a panoramic overlook from the ridge. The area is not heavily used, and if you are hiking during the week, your chance of encountering others is minimal. Though you probably will not see any rattlesnakes (which are on the endangered species list), prepare for a very rocky trail by wearing sturdy boots with good ankle support. An overnight option is the AMC's Mohican Outdoor Center.

The Appalachian Mountain Club (AMC) is a Boston-based hiking club that has a strong presence in the White Mountains of New Hampshire and several other areas in New England. The club was founded in 1876 and was a model for the Sierra Club, founded in 1892. The AMC's Mohican Outdoor Center (formerly Camp Mohican) might be called a guide center: It is part nature center, part hotel, and part conference center. Workshops are held on weekends, covering topics such as backpacking, canoeing, and birding. Hikers may stay overnight in one of their cabins or at a walk-in campsite for a fee. The Mohican Outdoor Center is at 50 Camp Mohican Road, Blairstown, NJ 07825-9655. Call 908-362-5670, or check their Web site, www.outdoors.org/lodging-camping/lodges/Mohican. Call ahead for rates and availability if you plan to stay overnight.

GETTING THERE

Take I-80 to Exit 12 (Blairstown, Hope) and proceed north on County Route 521, following the sign to Blairstown. After about 5 miles, you'll come to a junction with NJ 94. Make a left here and, in another 0.2 mile, turn right at the light. Continue straight ahead on

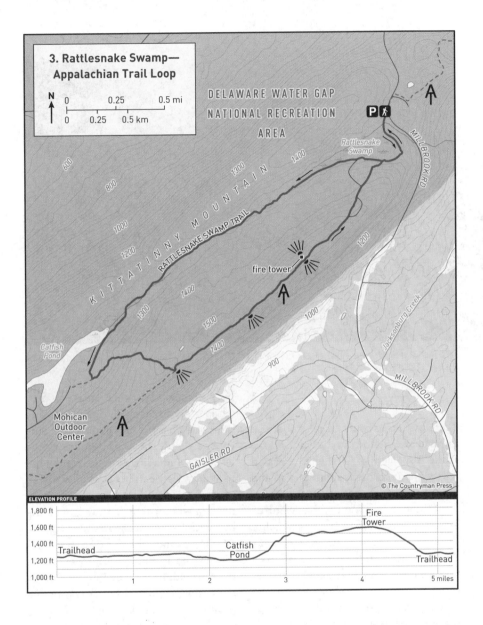

3. Rattlesnake Swamp—Appalachian Trail Loop

N
0   0.25   0.5 mi
0   0.25   0.5 km

DELAWARE WATER GAP
NATIONAL RECREATION
AREA

Rattlesnake Swamp

MILLBROOK RD

KITTATINNY MOUNTAIN

RATTLESNAKE SWAMP TRAIL

fire tower

Catfish Pond

Jacksonburg Creek

MILLBROOK RD

Mohican Outdoor Center

GAISLER RD

© The Countryman Press

ELEVATION PROFILE

1,800 ft
1,600 ft
1,400 ft
1,200 ft
1,000 ft

Trailhead

Catfish Pond

Fire Tower

Trailhead

1   2   3   4   5 miles

Bridge Street. (Do not make the sharp right onto County Route 521.) When you reach the end of Bridge Street at the top of a sharp rise, turn sharply right onto Millbrook Road and then make the next left. You are now on Millbrook-Blairstown Road (County Route 602). Continue ahead for 6.2 miles to the top of the ridge, where the Appalachian Trail (AT) crosses the road. You'll see the ridge and the fire tower looming in front of you about a mile before you reach the crest of the ridge. Parking for a few cars can be found near the gate on the left side of the road (don't block the gate). Additional parking is located on the right, about 150 yards west in a small area just off the road.

EAST-FACING VIEW OVER THE GREAT VALLEY FROM ROCK LEDGES AT THE JUNCTION OF THE APPALACHIAN TRAIL WITH THE RATTLESNAKE SWAMP TRAIL

THE HIKE

Begin by hiking south from the gate on a gravel road, following the white blazes of the Appalachian Trail (AT). Pass an AT trail sign, cross a small brook, and proceed through a dense rhododendron thicket. In 0.4 mile, the AT turns left off the gravel road and heads uphill through the rhododendron. Continue straight ahead on the gravel road, past this junction and Rattlesnake Spring (50 feet ahead on the left). About 300 feet beyond, a sign and a triple-orange blaze mark the start of the Rattlesnake Swamp Trail. Bear right, leaving the gravel road, and continue on a footpath. The footing, typical of trails on the Kittatinny Ridge, is quite rocky.

The Rattlesnake Swamp Trail continues to the left of and slightly above Rattlesnake Swamp, with its hemlocks, ferns, mosses, and skunk cabbage. Some sections are deep and dark, dominated by hemlock and other shade plants, while other areas, with dead trees and high ostrich ferns, are open to the sun. At one point, the trail detours to the left, climbing a little farther up the hill to avoid a wet section of the former trail route. As you leave the swamp, the trail, now traversing a thick growth of mountain laurel, enters a deep hemlock grove. Farther along, the footing becomes mossy and in places quite wet. Cross over a small brook (the inlet of Catfish Pond) and begin to climb toward higher ground and more open forest.

After a stretch of less dense woods, the trail descends and crosses the brook three more times. Soon after the last crossing of the brook, you'll approach the shore of Catfish Pond, which is visible on the right during leaf-off season.

As you walk past the northern end of the pond, the trail follows a rocky old road lined with both low- and highbush blueberries. The highbush blueberries, ripe in late July and early August, are particularly delicious. Catfish Pond is adjacent to Mohican Outdoor Center, the site of a former Boy Scout camp. The federal government acquired the camp in the 1960s as part of the Tocks Island dam project. After the project was abandoned, the camp was leased to the Appalachian Mountain Club, which now operates it as the Mohican Outdoor Center.

The Rattlesnake Swamp Trail gradually veers away from the pond and soon reaches a junction—just past a concrete slab—where a sign indicates that the Rattlesnake Swamp Trail turns left. (A right turn here leads to the Mohican Outdoor Center.) To continue the hike, turn left, following the orange blazes. The trail now begins a gradual climb of the Kittatinny Ridge on a woods road. After a while, the grade steepens, and the trail narrows to a footpath. Rock steps have been placed for assistance as you climb. Soon, there is a temporary respite where the trail levels off before it resumes climbing, this time not so steeply. After meandering through another level section, the trail climbs once more, leading to the summit of the Kittatinny Ridge. The Rattlesnake Swamp Trail then descends briefly and ends at a junction with the AT. Here, to the right, there is a magnificent east-facing view over the Great Valley from open rock ledges.

After resting from the climb and enjoying the spectacular view, head north, now following the white blazes of the AT. The trail winds along the east face of the broad summit through a park-like, open area of trees and grass. To the right are vistas out to the eastern horizon. After a mile of walking, you'll arrive at the Catfish Pond fire tower, which is operational during the fire season.

CATFISH FIRE TOWER

Climb the tower for views in all directions. On a clear day, even the distant Catskills to the north are visible.

Continue straight ahead on the AT, which now follows the service road that provides vehicular access to the fire tower. Watch for a turn where the AT heads left, leaving the road, and descends a little more steeply through bushes and ferns. The AT rejoins the road, now gravel, for a few hundred feet before turning right, back into the woods on a footpath. After descending on a rocky trail under a power line, you'll reach another junction where the AT joins the gravel road once again—this time near Rattlesnake Spring, which you passed toward the beginning of the hike. Turn right and follow the AT along the gravel road back to your car.

Mount Tammany

TOTAL DISTANCE: 3.5 miles

HIKING TIME: 3 hours

VERTICAL RISE: 1,200 feet

RATING: Moderately strenuous

MAPS: USGS Portland, Bushkill; NY–NJTC Kittatinny Trails #120; NPS Kittatinny Point Area Trails map; NY–NJ Appalachian Trail Guide map #4

TRAILHEAD GPS COORDINATES:
N 40° 58′ 17″ W 75° 07′ 31″

Overlooking the Delaware River, on the New Jersey side of the Delaware Water Gap, stands Mount Tammany. This mountain, at the southern tip of the Kittatinny Ridge and located within Worthington State Forest and the Delaware Water Gap National Recreation Area (Bushkill, PA 18324; 570-426-2452; www.nps.gov/dewa), offers one of the steepest climbs in all of New Jersey, as well as spectacular views from its summit. Because of its easy access from I-80, the trail to the summit is heavily used year-round, especially in summer. Also in the area are Dunnfield Creek, with its many falls and cascades, the Appalachian Trail (AT), and Sunfish Pond, making this location a major natural area in the state.

The Delaware Water Gap, certainly one of the scenic wonders of New Jersey, is a 1,200-foot-deep gorge carved by the waters of the Delaware River through the long, wall-like Kittatinny Ridge. Back in Cretaceous times, roughly 100 million years ago, the water gap did not exist. The entire area, which was once very mountainous, had been worn down by erosion to a flat plain that sloped gently toward the Atlantic Ocean some 40 miles away. The streams that drained the land meandered through this landscape on their way to the sea. In the late Cretaceous Period the land began to rise, and the streams began cutting deeper channels.

As the land rose, the ancestral Delaware River found itself confronted with a major barrier—the relatively resistant rock that makes up the Kittatinny Ridge. This rock, made of the tough sandstone and conglomerate of the Shawangunk Formation, dips to the north at the entrance to the gap. These rocks, as well as the red rocks that overlie them, are warped into many folds.

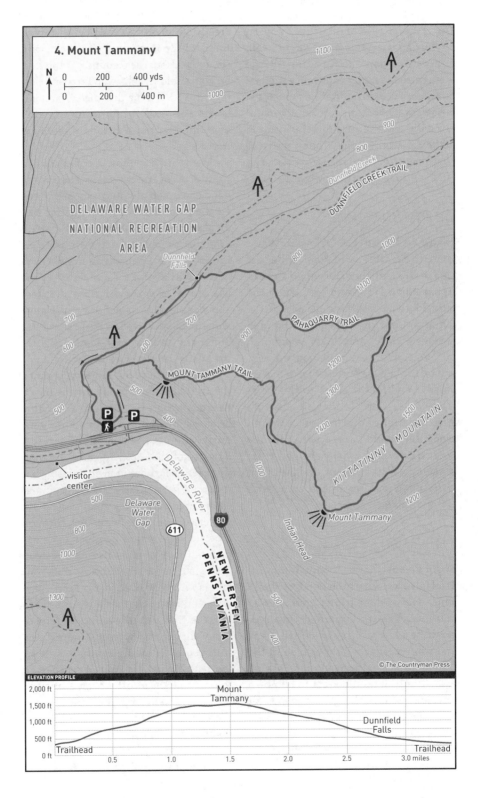

4. Mount Tammany

N

| 0 | 200 | 400 yds |
| 0 | 200 | 400 m |

1100

1000

900

800

DELAWARE WATER GAP
NATIONAL RECREATION
AREA

Dunnfield Creek

DUNNFIELD CREEK TRAIL

1000

Dunnfield
Falls

800

1100

PAHAQUARRY TRAIL

700

700

900

600

1200

MOUNT TAMMANY TRAIL

1300

500

500

1500

P P

400

1400

KITTATINNY MOUNTAIN

visitor
center

Delaware River

500

1000

Delaware
Water
Gap

1200

611

80

Indian Head

Mount Tammany

800

NEW JERSEY
PENNSYLVANIA

1000

550

1300

400

© The Countryman Press

ELEVATION PROFILE

Mount
Tammany

Dunnfield
Falls

Trailhead   Trailhead

2,000 ft
1,500 ft
1,000 ft
500 ft
0 ft

0.5   1.0   1.5   2.0   2.5   3.0 miles

The cross-section of the ridge exposed by the gap is a geology lesson in itself. Right at the gap, the Kittatinny Ridge is fractured, its long continuity broken. Because of this structural weakness, the Delaware River has successfully maintained its course through this section of the Kittatinny Ridge. Today, the river continues to cut and remove rock as the land continues to rise slowly.

GETTING THERE

Take I-80 west to the Delaware Water Gap. Immediately beyond milepost 1, take the exit for "Dunnfield Creek/ Appalachian Trail" and bear left at the fork. Continue past the underpass on the left and turn right into a parking area at signs with "P" and "hiker" symbols.

If you miss the turnoff, take the next exit off the highway—the last exit in New Jersey—and follow signs to the Delaware Water Gap National Recreation Area Kittatinny Point Visitor Center. To reach the parking area where the hike begins, go past the visitor center, cross back under I-80, bear left, and then turn right into a parking area at signs with "P" and "hiker" symbols.

THE HIKE

Begin the hike on the Mount Tammany Trail (also known as the Red Dot Trail), which leaves the parking area near its entrance. The trail, marked with red-on-white blazes, climbs wooden steps and soon merges with a branch of the trail that leads up from another parking area. The trail then begins to climb—a foreshadowing of things to come. After this brief elevation gain, the trail levels off, briefly paralleling Dunnfield Creek, well below you on the left. Where the trail turns sharply right, it begins a steady climb on a well-used, rocky path lined with evergreens, hemlocks, and rhododendrons. The sounds of the falls on Dunnfield Creek, even farther below now, are still in the distance. Watch for where the trail turns right, climbing over tilted but parallel beds of sedimentary rock.

After this last climb, you'll arrive at the first of several overlooks. Here, at the edge of a steep cliff and exposed to the elements, cedar trees struggle for survival. Below, looking south, the Delaware Water Gap opens in front of you. Mount Minsi on the Pennsylvania side is to the right and Mount Tammany is to the left. Mount Minsi, which rises 1,463 feet above sea level, is named after the Native Americans who lived in the area. Mount Tammany, at 1,527 feet, is named after the Lenni-Lenape chief Tamenund.

After skirting a few more viewpoints, the trail crosses a brook and passes a reliable spring on the left. After this brief respite, it once again begins seriously climbing the mountain ridge. Because of the rocky terrain, climbing this section is difficult in any season, but it can be particularly challenging and even dangerous in icy conditions. First you cross a boulder field; then, through a beautiful forest of hemlock and rhododendron, you must navigate a steep rock slab. Use both your feet and your hands when you need to, while still paying attention to the markers so as not to lose the trail. After leveling off temporarily through a more open forest, the trail begins climbing again on a rocky footpath high on the ridge. From here to the summit, the forest is sparse, offering little protection from the winds. Along the way, you will find a cedar-lined viewpoint on the right.

Just before you reach the summit, notice that the forest to the left is more

DELAWARE RIVER FROM VIEWPOINT ON THE MOUNT TAMMANY TRAIL

open; a fire burned this area some years ago. Thick laurel is replacing the former oak forest. Finally you reach the summit. Here the oak forest stops at the edge of a 1,200-foot cliff overlooking the Delaware River. Only scrub oak and pitch pine survive in this rocky, exposed environment. At the summit area, walk to the right and down over the exposed rocks, which offer you an expansive view west to Mount Minsi and the Blue Mountain Ridge behind it. The Pocono Plateau of Pennsylvania stretches north to the horizon. To the south you see the plains of the Great Valley, and beyond that, the Reading Prong section of the Highlands extends to the horizon. If you walk down the exposed rocks of the summit you will see the Indian Head profile—located on a portion of the cliff below and to the north (upriver) of the viewpoint—staring out over the river.

When you're rested from the climb, retrace your steps to the trail. Just ahead, you'll see a triple-blue blaze that marks the start of the Pahaquarry Trail (also known as the Blue Dot Trail). Follow this trail, which heads northeast along the ridge of Mount Tammany on a rocky but relatively level path. Upon reaching the actual summit (1,549 feet), it turns sharply left at a wooden sign for the Blue Trail and soon begins a rather steep descent on a rocky, eroded woods road.

After a long, steady descent from the ridge over rocks, the trail swings to the left and finally reaches a junction with the green-blazed Dunnfield Creek Trail. Turn left and follow the joint blue

VIEW FROM THE SUMMIT OF MOUNT TAMMANY

and green blazes parallel to Dunnfield Creek. Just ahead, you'll notice an open area on the right with a bench that overlooks an attractive waterfall. Continue ahead a short distance until you reach a wooden footbridge that spans the creek. Here, a short unmarked trail on the right leads to the base of the waterfall.

When you're ready to continue, cross the footbridge and follow along the trail, which parallels the creek on a wide path. Here, in this dark hemlock gorge, are numerous cascades and plunge pools, the white water creating a sharp contrast to the dark rock it glides over. Along with some spectacular rock, water, and plant scenery, you may encounter many people, including families with small children, who have stopped in their travels along I-80 to explore this scenic ravine. For some, this may be their first experience with a natural area.

In another quarter-mile, the Pahaquarry and Dunnfield Creek Trails end, and you continue ahead along the creek, now following the white-blazed Appalachian Trail. Soon, the trail bears left, leaving the wide path, and crosses Dunnfield Creek on a steel bridge with a wooden deck. Just ahead, you'll reach the parking area where the hike began.

II.

HIGHLANDS

5

Ramapo Valley County Reservation

TOTAL DISTANCE: 3.8 miles	

TOTAL DISTANCE: 3.8 miles

HIKING TIME: 2.5 hours

VERTICAL RISE: 650 feet

RATING: Moderate

MAPS: USGS Ramsey; NY–NJTC North Jersey Trails #115. Sketch map available at www.nynjtc.org/map/ramapo-valley -county-reservation-brochure-map

TRAILHEAD GPS COORDINATES: N 41° 02' 52" W 74° 15' 06"

The land that eventually became Ramapo Valley County Reservation was purchased from the Native Americans in 1720 by Samuel Laroe. Though the principal use of the land was for farming, it also housed a gristmill, a sawmill, and later a bronze foundry. The land changed hands several times before its 1872 purchase by Alfred B. Darling, a native of Burke, Vermont, and owner of many other properties, including the Fifth Avenue Hotel in Manhattan. Darling made it his country estate, and the area became known as Darlington. The name Ramapo means "round ponds."

Ramapo Valley County Reservation is a popular place for local residents to walk. Many visitors to the reservation are content to take a short walk around Scarlet Oak Pond, while others climb to the MacMillan Reservoir. Some choose a more challenging hike.

Historically, the blazing of the network of trails in Ramapo Reservation was geared to those who wanted longer hikes. Some hikers followed the trails with the expectation that they would lead back to their starting point and would call for help when they realized that they were deep in the woods and did not know how to return to the trailhead.

In 2016, with the encouragement of park officials, the New York-New Jersey Trail Conference redesigned the trail system at the Ramapo Reservation. To make the hiking experience more user-friendly, the North Jersey Trails Committee, under the leadership of Chris Connolly, created several loop trails that can be followed easily. This hike follows the most popular of these trails—the yellow-blazed Vista Loop Trail, built in the summer of 2016 by Trail Conference volunteers. Incorporating portions of

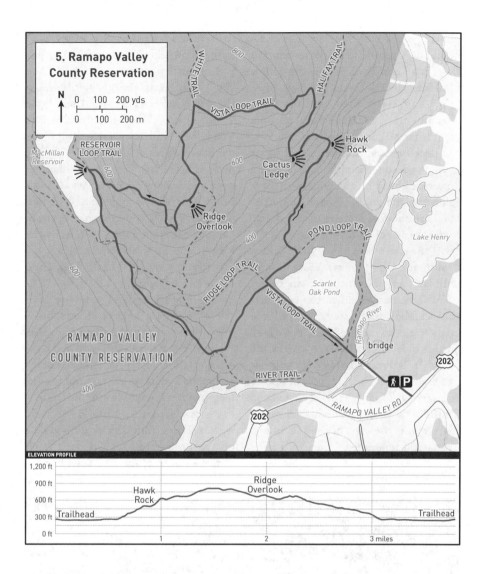

ELEVATION PROFILE

existing trails, as well as several newly blazed sections, this trail has been designed to enable the hiker to visit three panoramic viewpoints, as well as other scenic features of the Ramapo Reservation.

For more information on Ramapo Valley County Reservation, contact Bergen County Parks, One Bergen County Plaza, Hackensack, NJ 07601; 201-336-7275 (main office) or 201-327-3500 (park office); www.co.bergen.nj.us/parks.

GETTING THERE

Take NJ 17 to US 202 in Mahwah. Turn left at the bottom of the ramp, proceed south on US 202 for 2 miles, and turn right into the Ramapo Valley County Reservation parking area.

THE HIKE

The hike begins at a kiosk in the southwest corner of the parking area. Just ahead, you'll notice a triple-yellow blaze on a tree, which marks the start of the Vista Loop Trail. Follow the yellow blazes as they descend wooden steps, join a wide dirt road, and continue ahead to cross the Ramapo River on a steel truss bridge. In another 250 feet, the green-dot-on-orange-blazed River Trail begins on the left, but you should continue ahead on the wide dirt road, following the yellow blazes along the southern shore of Scarlet Oak Pond (formerly the site of a gravel quarry).

At the end of the pond, you'll notice a sign for the "Yellow Vista Loop," with arrows pointing in both directions. Continue ahead on the wide dirt road to follow the Vista Loop Trail in a counter-clockwise direction. In 100 feet, a triple-blue blaze marks the start of the Ridge Trail. Proceed ahead for another 125 feet, then turn right, continuing to follow the yellow blazes of the Vista Loop Trail. Just ahead, a triple silver-on-white blaze marks the start of the Pond Loop Trail. Continue ahead, parallel to the

western shore of the pond, now following both yellow and silver-on-white blazes.

In 500 feet, follow the Vista Loop Trail as it turns sharply left, leaving the wide dirt road and the Pond Loop Trail, to cross a wooden footbridge. The Vista Loop Trail now begins to climb on a moderately steep grade. After a short level stretch, followed by a brief climb over a rock outcrop, it arrives at Hawk Rock. This east-facing ledge offers an expansive view over much of Bergen County, with Ramapo College in the foreground on the left. Lake Henry is directly ahead, with Scarlet Oak Pond to the south (right).

The Vista Loop Trail now bends to the left and continues to ascend, bearing left at a fork just ahead. After a steep, rocky climb, the trail levels off and soon emerges on an open rock ledge, known as Cactus Ledge, with a panoramic east-facing view. The view from this ledge is even broader than that from Hawk Rock, with the New York City skyline visible on the horizon on a clear day. You'll notice several clumps of prickly pear

PRICKLY PEAR CACTUS AT CACTUS LEDGE

VIEW OF THE NEW YORK CITY SKYLINE FROM CACTUS LEDGE

cactus—the only native American cactus that grows east of the Rocky Mountains. You've climbed about 400 vertical feet to reach this spectacular viewpoint, so you'll want to take a break here.

When you're ready to continue, follow the yellow blazes as they turn right and reenter the woods at the southern end of the viewpoint. Soon, the Vista Loop Trail joins another footpath that comes in from the right. A short distance ahead, you'll reach a junction. Here, a triple-green-on-white blaze marks the start of the Halifax Trail, which begins on the right, but you should bear left to continue on the Vista Loop Trail.

The Vista Loop Trail continues to climb gradually. Near the crest of the rise, the trail briefly joins an old woods road. It bears right, climbs a little more, then levels off, with some minor ups and downs.

In half a mile, after crossing a low stone wall, the Vista Loop Trail reaches a T-intersection with a woods road. Here, the White Trail begins on the right, but you should turn left to continue on the yellow-blazed Vista Loop Trail. In 500 feet, the blue-blazed Ridge Trail joins from the right. Follow the co-aligned yellow and blue trails for another 500 feet, then turn right to continue on the yellow-blazed Vista Loop Trail.

In 200 feet, the Vista Loop Trail turns right, but you should bear left and continue on a wide path, blazed with green-dot-on-yellow blazes, that leads a short distance to a panoramic southeast-facing viewpoint from a rock ledge. Campgaw Mountain may be seen in the foreground to the right, and the New York City skyline is visible in the distance on a clear day.

After taking in the view, retrace your steps to the yellow-blazed trail and turn left, following the trail as it descends steadily. Just before reaching a large pile of boulders, the trail turns right and climbs to a rocky outcrop, from which Matty Price Hill is visible ahead. The trail now descends toward the MacMillan Reservoir, passing a rocky outcrop (with another view of Matty Price Hill) along the way.

SCARLET OAK POND

Soon, you'll emerge onto a large expanse of open rock that overlooks the reservoir. Here, the pink-blazed Reservoir Loop Trail joins from the right. You should turn left and head southeast, following both yellow and pink blazes parallel to the shore of the reservoir. You'll pass the concrete dam at the southeast corner of the reservoir and continue downhill to reach a junction with the main park road, where the pink-blazed Reservoir Trail ends and the blue-blazed Ridge Trail joins from the right.

Continue ahead and proceed downhill along the road, now following both blue and yellow blazes. Just before reaching a wide bridge over a stream (the outlet of the reservoir), at a sign for the "waterfall," follow the Vista Loop Trail as it turns right, leaving the road (the blue-blazed Ridge Trail continues ahead on the road).

The yellow-blazed trail now begins to parallel the stream, with its attractive cascades and pools. Soon, it begins to descend on stone steps, passing an attractive waterfall along the way. This beautiful trail section was built in 2017–18 by an AmeriCorps trail crew of the New York-New Jersey Trail Conference. At the base of the descent, the Vista Loop Trail turns left and crosses the stream on a wooden footbridge.

Just ahead, the Vista Loop Trail bears left, as the green-dot-on-orange-blazed River Trail begins on the right. Follow the yellow-blazed trail for another quarter mile to a wide dirt road, where the loop ends. Turn right and continue along the wide dirt road parallel to the southern shore of Scarlet Oak Pond, then proceed across the bridge over the Ramapo River and climb steps to reach the parking area where the hike began.

Ramapo Lake and the Van Slyke Castle

TOTAL DISTANCE: 5.5 miles	
HIKING TIME: 3.5 hours	
VERTICAL RISE: 700 feet	
RATING: Moderate	
MAPS: USGS Wanaque; NY–NJTC North Jersey Trails #115	
TRAILHEAD GPS COORDINATES: N 41° 01′ 57″ W 74° 15′ 08″	

The 3,000-acre Ramapo Mountain State Forest is part of a rugged ridge straddling the Bergen–Passaic County boundary. Added to New Jersey's public lands in the mid-1970s, much of it had been the estate of the late William MacEvoy, a wealthy public works contractor. The centerpiece of the forest is the attractive Ramapo Lake, formerly known as Lake LeGrande, and before that as Rotten Pond. Swimming is not permitted, but fishing is a popular pastime. A few privately owned inholdings remain; their owners use several dirt access roads which are closed to public vehicular use (but open to hikers and bicyclists).

Miles of marked hiking trails lace the forest and lead to viewpoints and rock outcrops. This hike climbs to one of the best of these outcrops and continues to the interesting remains of a large stone mansion. Parking areas can fill up early on weekend days. However, on weekdays the area is often an island of tranquility—just a stone's throw from busy I-287. Ramapo Mountain State Forest is administered by Ringwood State Park (1304 Sloatsburg Road, Ringwood, NJ 07456; 973-962-7031; www.njparksand forests.org).

GETTING THERE

To reach the upper parking area on Skyline Drive in Oakland, take I-287 to Exit 57. If you are coming from the north (heading south), bear right at the fork on the exit ramp to proceed onto Skyline Drive. If you are traveling from the south, make a left at the bottom of the exit ramp and continue under I-287 onto Skyline Drive. Follow Skyline Drive rather steeply uphill to the upper parking area for Ramapo Mountain State

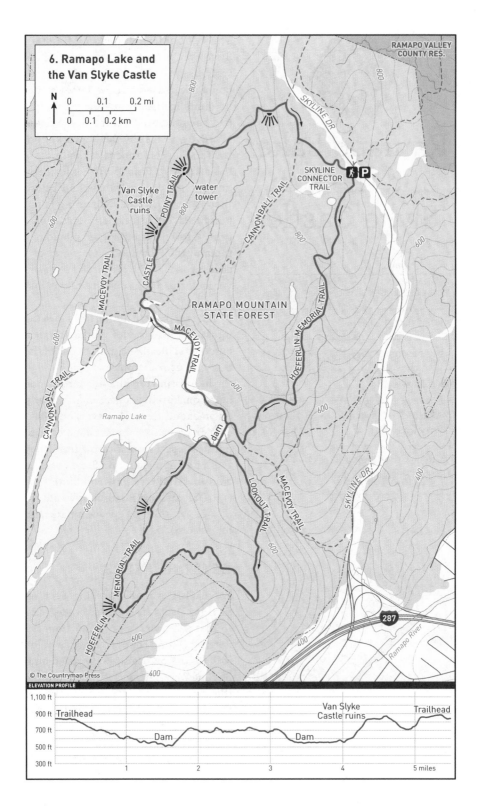

6. Ramapo Lake and the Van Slyke Castle

N

| 0 | 0.1 | 0.2 mi |
| 0 | 0.1 | 0.2 km |

RAMAPO VALLEY COUNTY RES.

SKYLINE DR

SKYLINE CONNECTOR TRAIL

water tower

Van Slyke Castle ruins

POINT TRAIL

CASTLE

CANNONBALL TRAIL

RAMAPO MOUNTAIN STATE FOREST

HOEFERLIN MEMORIAL TRAIL

MACEVOY TRAIL

MACEVOY TRAIL

Ramapo Lake

dam

LOOKOUT TRAIL

MACEVOY TRAIL

SKYLINE DR

CANNONBALL TRAIL

MEMORIAL TRAIL

HOEFERLIN

287

Ramapo River

© The Countryman Press

ELEVATION PROFILE

1,100 ft					
900 ft	Trailhead			Van Slyke Castle ruins	Trailhead
700 ft					
500 ft		Dam		Dam	
300 ft					
	1	2	3	4	5 miles

THE WATER TOWER FOR THE VAN SLYKE CASTLE

Forest—on the left side of the road at the top of the hill, just beyond milepost 1.4.

THE HIKE

At the northwest end of the parking area, you will see a yellow blaze of the Hoeferlin Memorial Trail, as well as a triple red-and-white blaze, which marks the terminus of the Skyline Connector Trail. You will be returning to the parking area on the Skyline Connector Trail, but the Hoeferlin Trail will be your route for the first part of the hike.

Head into the woods and immediately turn left, following the yellow blazes, then bear right onto a footpath parallel to a gravel road. After passing a small pond on the right, follow the yellow blazes as they briefly turn right onto the road (this portion of the road is paved), then turn left onto another woods road. After passing an interesting rock outcrop on the right,

you'll come to a Y-intersection, where the yellow-blazed trail bears right and begins to descend.

Soon, the gravel road briefly reappears to the right, but bear left to stay on the yellow-blazed trail, which follows a rocky woods road over undulating terrain. The road eventually narrows to a footpath and crosses an intermittent stream. After descending on a winding route and once again briefly approaching the gravel road, the Hoeferlin Trail heads down to a woods road—the route of the blue-blazed MacEvoy Trail. Turn right, now following both yellow and blue blazes. Soon, the trail bears left and descends a short pitch to the dam of Ramapo Lake (just to the left). Here, the blue-blazed MacEvoy Trail continues ahead onto North Shore Drive, but you should turn left and follow the yellow-blazed Hoeferlin Memorial Trail, which crosses the concrete dam and spillway.

About 100 feet beyond the dam, the

RUINS OF THE VAN SLYKE CASTLE

red-blazed Lookout Trail begins on the left. Turn left onto the Lookout Trail, which heads away from the lake, following a rocky footpath along a stream. Soon, the trail bears right and begins a steady climb up the ridge. Near the crest of the rise, the trail levels off and passes a huge boulder on the left.

A short distance beyond, the trail turns sharply right. Continue along the trail as it meanders up and down, sometimes steeply, for less than a mile to a T-junction with the yellow-blazed Hoeferlin Memorial Trail. The hike continues by turning right and following the joint Lookout/Hoeferlin Memorial Trail (yellow and red blazes). However, before continuing, take a moment to wander over to the left of the junction. This is a particularly scenic place to rest—a large rock ledge with a splendid pitch pine and a nice view across the Wyanokies.

Return to the trail, follow the yellow and red blazes across the ridge, and begin the descent back down to the lake. You'll pass several more viewpoints, with Ramapo Lake getting closer and looking more serene as you reach each spot.

When you reach the lake (where the Lookout Trail ends), turn right along the road and walk back across the dam. If you would like to shorten the hike, turn right and follow the yellow blazes back to your car. Otherwise, turn left and follow the blue MacEvoy Trail blazes along the lakeshore. You'll pass a large house on the right—one of the private inholdings previously mentioned—as well as an attractive cascade. A short distance beyond, a rock outcrop on the left offers a broad view over the lake.

At a trail junction at the northwest corner of the lake, a triple-white blaze marks the start of the Castle Point Trail. Turn right, uphill, now following both blue and white blazes and passing between two concrete posts. Soon, the blue trail turns left and leaves the road you've been following. Continue straight ahead along the road, but just ahead, as the road bends sharply to the right, follow the white blazes as they turn left, leaving the road, and continue uphill on a steep, rocky footpath.

Near the top of the ridge, a rock outcrop on the left affords a panoramic view of Ramapo Lake and the Wyanokies. Just beyond, the trail climbs over a stone wall on a stile and soon reaches the remains of the Foxcroft Estate, also known as Van Slyke Castle. The first ruin you'll encounter is the mansion itself, built about 1910 by William Porter, a stockbroker. He died soon after it was finished, but his widow occupied the house until her death around 1940. Sadly, it fell into ruin and was burned by vandals in the 1950s. A detailed history, including pictures, is available at www.atlasobscura.com/places/van-slyke-castle-ruins-2.

Continuing up the trail, you will pass the remains of an in-ground swimming pool. A short distance beyond, you'll pass a broad viewpoint on the left that looks over the Wyanokies. A bit later, you'll spot a massive stone tower. It appears to be a lookout tower, but it actually served as a water tower for the estate. Just beyond, another rock outcrop offers views of the Wyanokies to the west. After enjoying the view, continue on the Castle Point Trail, which begins to descend. Watch carefully as the trail briefly turns left onto a woods road, then immediately turns right just before reaching the route of a gas pipeline. It turns right again onto a woods road, turns left onto a footpath before reaching a wide gravel road, then turns right and follows the gas pipeline for 350 feet. After turning right and leaving the pipeline, the trail crosses a stream and climbs, first gradually, then rather steeply through mountain laurel thickets, to a rock ledge with a broad view. From the ledge, you may be able to see the stone tower you passed about half a mile back.

A short distance beyond, the Castle Point Trail reaches a paved road, with Skyline Drive just to the left. Here, the Castle Point Trail ends, and you turn right to continue along the Cannonball Trail (white-"C"-on-red blazes). The trail follows the road for 200 feet, then turns left onto a footpath through the woods. Soon, you'll reach a junction where the red/white-blazed Skyline Connector Trail begins on the left. Turn left and follow this red/white trail along a footpath roughly parallel to Skyline Drive until you reach the parking area where the hike began.

Ringwood Manor Circular

TOTAL DISTANCE: 3 miles

HIKING TIME: 2 hours

VERTICAL RISE: 250 feet

RATING: Easy

MAPS: USGS Greenwood Lake (NY/NJ); NY–NJTC North Jersey Trails #115; DEP Ringwood State Park

TRAILHEAD GPS COORDINATES: N 41° 08′ 21.5″ W 74° 15′ 13.5″

Ringwood Manor, part of Ringwood State Park, is located in northeast Passaic County. The history of the area is closely tied to the local iron industry, which started at Ringwood in 1740. The products of the forges and furnaces were of much importance to the colonies during the Revolutionary War. Troops were stationed here, and George Washington made Ringwood his headquarters on several occasions. Robert Erskine, manager of the mines, served General Washington as surveyor general and prepared many of the maps for the campaign against the British.

Peter Cooper purchased the property in 1853. Cooper, a New York philanthropist, is best known as the founder of Cooper Union for the Advancement of Science and Art. Abram Hewitt, a family friend of the Coopers who later married their daughter Sarah Amelia, became a business partner of Peter Cooper, and the firm became known as Cooper, Hewitt & Co. It was always a summer house; the family spent winters in New York City.

The greatest part of the present manor house was built between 1854 and 1910, during the Hewitt period. However, the earliest part of the house dates to 1807, when it was owned by the Ryerson family.

In 1936, Abram Hewitt's son Erskine Hewitt donated the manor house and 95 acres to the State of New Jersey. His nephew, Norvin Green (namesake of nearby Norvin Green State Forest), made an additional gift to bring the total to 579 acres. Later purchases, using Green Acres funds, continued until as recently as 1978. The park now extends east into Bergen County, connecting with Ramapo Mountain State Forest and Ramapo Valley County Reservation to form a large network of public

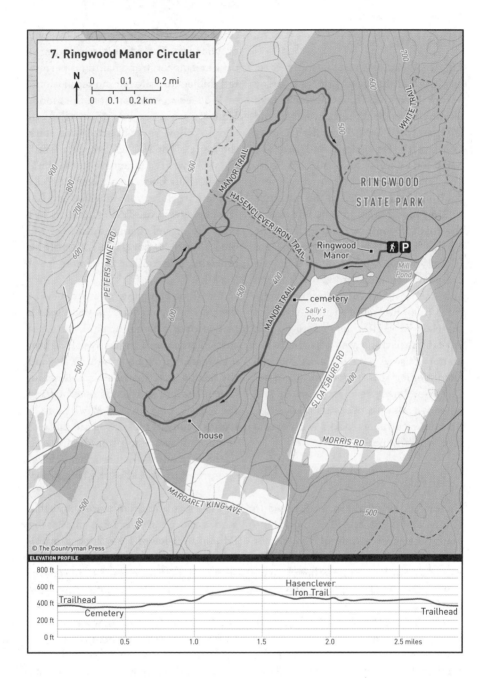

7. Ringwood Manor Circular

N

| 0 | 0.1 | 0.2 mi |

| 0 | 0.1 | 0.2 km |

MANOR TRAIL

HASENCLEVER IRON TRAIL

WHITE TRAIL

RINGWOOD
STATE PARK

Ringwood
Manor

PETERS MINE RD

MANOR TRAIL

cemetery

Sally's
Pond

Mill
Pond

SLOATSBURG RD

house

MORRIS RD

MARGARET KING AVE

© The Countryman Press

ELEVATION PROFILE

800 ft						
600 ft				Hasenclever		
400 ft	Trailhead			Iron Trail		Trailhead
200 ft	Cemetery					
0 ft		0.5	1.0	1.5	2.0	2.5 miles

lands. Volunteers coordinated by the New York–New Jersey Trail Conference developed an extensive network of trails in the area in the 1970s.

For more information on the park, contact Ringwood State Park, 1304 Sloatsburg Road, Ringwood, NJ 07456; 973-962-7031; www.njparksandforests.org. For more information on Ringwood Manor, go to www.ringwoodmanor.com.

GETTING THERE

Ringwood Manor is on Sloatsburg Road, just south of the New York-New Jersey border. If coming from the south, take Skyline Drive to its northwestern end at Greenwood Lake Turnpike (County Route 511). Turn right and proceed north for 1.5 miles to Sloatsburg Road. Turn right onto Sloatsburg Road and continue for 2.4 miles to the entrance to Ringwood Manor, on the left side of the road. If you are coming from the north, take NY 17 to Sterling Mine Road (County Route 72), just south of Sloatsburg, and continue for 4.5 miles to the entrance to Ringwood Manor, on the right (the entrance is 1 mile south of the New York–New Jersey state line). Park in the parking area adjacent to the manor house. A parking fee is charged from Memorial Day weekend to Labor Day. New Jersey residents ages 62 and older can obtain a pass that allows free parking at all state parks and forests (see the Introduction).

THE HIKE

History is everywhere at Ringwood Manor, and it is a fine idea to combine your hike with a tour of the manor house. Call ahead (973-962-2240) to determine the house tour schedule, usually Wednesday through Sunday, except in the winter.

The hike commences at the park office, where maps and brochures are usually available. Walk around the front of the manor house. You'll notice a pair of wrought-iron gates in front of the porch. Walk through these gates and continue to the western end of the porch, where you'll notice another pair of wrought-iron gates standing by themselves on the lawn below. Head down to

these gates, with the large Sally's Pond on your left. The pond is stocked with bass and pickerel, and fishing is permitted, subject to state fishing regulations.

Proceed west (away from the Manor House) across the lawn. Initially, you should follow yellow blazes that mark the route of the Hasenclever Iron Trail, but when you reach a gravel road, you'll notice a blue blaze on a telephone pole to the left. Here, you should leave the Hasenclever Iron Trail and turn left onto the gravel road, the route of the blue-blazed Manor Trail. You will be following this trail for the remainder of the hike.

Continue along the gravel road, with the pond on your left. As you cross a bridge over a small stream, note the rust-colored rocks, indicative of the iron ore present throughout the area. Beyond the bridge, you'll notice a small cemetery on the left, with headstones bearing the Morris, Erskine, and Hewitt family names. Many of the graves are those of small children, who often died young in the 18th and 19th centuries. Several evergreen trees add to the tranquility of the area.

The large Victorian mansion visible across the pond was built in 1861 by Edmund Miller of New York, a prominent farmer and politician. In 1878, Abram Hewitt purchased the property and gave it to his daughter Amy as a wedding present when she married Dr. James O. Green. Their son Norvin Green donated the property to the Capuchin Sisters in 1930, and it served as the Mount St. Francis Retreat Center until its closing in 2011.

After passing the stone dam and spillway at the southern end of Sally's Pond, the trail goes around a gate. Just beyond, you'll come to a fork in the road. Bear right and follow the blue blazes

SALLY'S POND

uphill on a gravel road. In a short distance, you'll pass a house on the left. Beyond the house, the road becomes rougher, and the sounds of traffic become louder. At the next fork, bear right again (the road to the left, blocked by boulders and fallen trees, leads out to Margaret King Avenue).

As the trail continues to head uphill on a woods road, first rather steeply, then more gently, the sounds of traffic gradually disappear. Note the rusted cables embedded in the trailbed. Park historians surmise that they may have been used as part of a conveyor system to transport iron ore from nearby mines, but they don't know for sure. In spring, flowers abound: jack-in-the-pulpit, rue anemone, spring beauty, and trout lily, to name just a few.

At the top of the climb (about 45 minutes into the hike), you'll see a power line ahead. The marked trail turns right before reaching the power line, but you might want to take the short jog out to the power line for this hike's only view. The valley below was the site of several iron mines, including the Hope and Peters Mines.

Return to the trail, bear left at the fork, then immediately turn left again onto a narrower route. The trail now descends steadily to a lovely stream. It turns right, follows along the stream for a short distance, then turns left and crosses it on rocks. The stream crossing can be a little tricky when the water is high.

In a few minutes, you'll come to a junction with the yellow-blazed Hasenclever Iron Trail. You've now hiked about 2 miles. A right turn onto this yellow-blazed trail will take you directly back to the manor house and shorten your hike. But the route of the hike continues ahead on the blue-blazed Manor Trail, which follows a pleasant, relatively level footpath through the woods. There is little evidence of civilization in this isolated area.

The trail descends to skirt a wet area

RINGWOOD MANOR

and continues along undulating terrain, with some minor ups and downs. In about 15 minutes from the junction with the Hasenclever Iron Trail, you'll pass a large water-filled depression—an old mine pit—on the left. Just beyond, the trail crosses a wide stream on rocks. Soon, you'll parallel another stream for a short distance and then cross it (and a tributary) on rocks. (If the water is high, the stream can be more easily crossed a short distance upstream.)

The trail now joins a wide woods road and passes through an area where the thick vegetation forms a canopy overhead. After a short climb, you'll reach a T-intersection with another woods road. The White Trail begins on the left and can be used as an alternative return route that adds about 0.7 mile to the hike (it ends at the Ramapo River, just upstream of the manor house). But to continue on the route of the hike, bear right at the junction and follow the blue blazes downhill.

At the next junction, the blue blazes head in both directions. Turn left, and you'll soon pass behind the manor house. Continue ahead to the parking lot where the hike began.

8

Skylands Manor

TOTAL DISTANCE: 8.5 miles

HIKING TIME: 5 hours

VERTICAL RISE: 1,200 feet

RATING: Moderate

MAPS: USGS Ramsey; NY–NJTC North Jersey Trails #115

TRAILHEAD GPS COORDINATES:
N 41° 08' 10" W 74° 13' 56"

This hike combines portions of the Crossover (white), Halifax (green), Ringwood-Ramapo (red), and Blue and Hoeferlin Memorial (yellow) Trails. Many of the trails in the park are multi-use, and at most trailheads there are signs indicating the trail's designated use. For more information, contact Ringwood State Park, 1304 Sloatsburg Road, Ringwood, NJ 07456; 973-962-7031; www.njparksandforests.org.

The hike begins at Skylands Manor, the site of the New Jersey State Botanical Garden. This was originally a working farm assembled from pioneer farmsteads by Francis Lynde Stetson, a prominent New York lawyer. In addition to a mansion, outbuildings and gardens, it included a vast lawn used as a nine-hole golf course. Many famous people—including President Grover Cleveland, actress Ethel Barrymore, industrialist Andrew Carnegie, and financier J. P. Morgan—were guests at Skylands Farms.

The estate was sold in 1922 to Clarence McKenzie Lewis, an investment banker and a trustee of the New York Botanical Garden, who demolished the mansion built by Stetson and replaced it with the Tudor mansion now on the site, designed by John Russell Pope and built of stone quarried from Pierson Ridge. The building's weathered facade and the sags and ripples in its slate were deliberately introduced to make it appear older. Clarence Lewis collected plants from all over the world (including New Jersey roadsides), resulting in the fine collection now in the botanical garden. He also planted most of the trees framing the house.

The state of New Jersey bought Skylands Gardens in 1966. This property was the first purchased under the Green

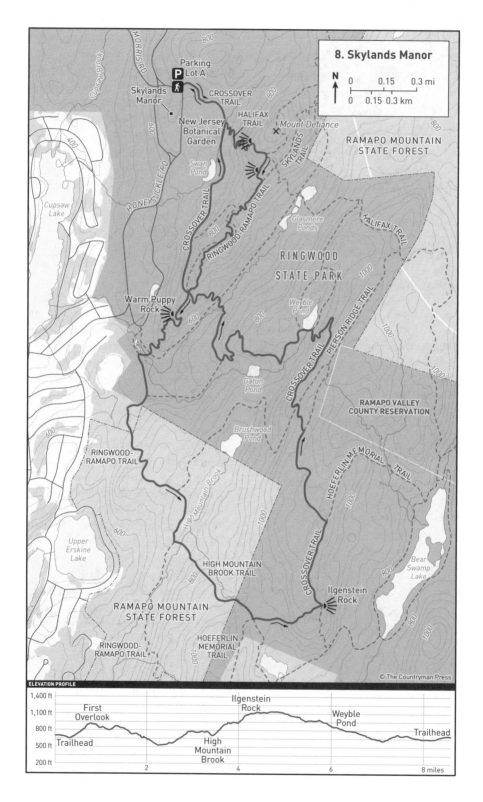

8. Skylands Manor

N

| 0 | 0.15 | 0.3 mi |
| 0 | 0.15 | 0.3 km |

MORRIS RD

CHESTER BROOK

Parking
Lot A

P

Skylands
Manor

CROSSOVER
TRAIL

HALIFAX
TRAIL

× Mount Defiance

SKYLANDS TRAIL

RAMAPO MOUNTAIN
STATE FOREST

New Jersey
Botanical
Garden

HONEYSUCKLE RD

Swan
Pond

Cupsaw
Lake

CROSSOVER TRAIL

RINGWOOD-RAMAPO TRAIL

Glasmere
Ponds

HALIFAX TRAIL

RINGWOOD
STATE PARK

Warm Puppy
Rock

Weyble
Pond

PIERSON RIDGE TRAIL

Gatun
Pond

CROSSOVER TRAIL

RAMAPO VALLEY
COUNTY RESERVATION

Brushwood
Pond

RINGWOOD-
RAMAPO TRAIL

High Mountain Brook

HOEFERLIN MEMORIAL TRAIL

Upper
Erskine
Lake

HIGH MOUNTAIN
BROOK TRAIL

Bear
Swamp
Lake

RAMAPO MOUNTAIN
STATE FOREST

CROSSOVER TRAIL

Ilgenstein
Rock

RINGWOOD-
RAMAPO TRAIL

HOEFERLIN
MEMORIAL
TRAIL

© The Countryman Press

ELEVATION PROFILE

		Ilgenstein Rock		
1,400 ft				
1,100 ft	First Overlook		Weyble Pond	
800 ft				Trailhead
500 ft	Trailhead	High Mountain Brook		
200 ft				
	2	4	6	8 miles

Acres program and was later designated the state's official botanical garden.

The manor house is open to the public for tours one Sunday each month. Sixty gardeners worked here during Mr. Lewis's ownership, but volunteers now help out. The New Jersey Botanical Garden/Skylands Association is a nonprofit organization founded in 1976 to assist with the preservation and restoration of the gardens and the manor house. For information on volunteering and membership, or for information on tours of the manor house, call 973-962-9534, or go to www.njbg.org.

GETTING THERE

Take I-287 to Exit 57 and proceed north on Skyline Drive. At the end of Skyline Drive, turn right and follow Greenwood Lake Turnpike north for 1.5 miles to Sloatsburg Road. Turn right and follow Sloatsburg Road for 2.1 miles to Morris Road, then turn right and follow Morris Road for 1.4 miles to its end at the Skylands Manor section of Ringwood State Park. Pass between two stone eagles and turn left into Parking Lot A. During the summer season, a parking fee may be charged.

THE HIKE

From the parking area, turn left onto a paved park road, the route of the white-blazed Crossover Trail. The trail proceeds through the New Jersey Botanical Garden, which features various exotic trees, and passes by outbuildings of Skylands Manor. You'll pass to the right of a greenhouse and an English Tudor guest house with a sundial clock on its chimney.

A short distance beyond, follow the Crossover Trail as it turns left onto an unpaved carriage road that follows the western base of Mount Defiance. In about a quarter mile, you'll cross a stream and pass between two concrete posts. Just beyond, the green-on-white-blazed Halifax Trail begins on the left. Turn left onto the Halifax Trail, which climbs Mount Defiance on gentle switchbacks, following the route of an old carriage road, which has narrowed in places to a footpath. As you reach the crest of the ridge, you'll notice an unmarked trail on the left. Follow this trail, which heads slightly uphill to a panoramic west-facing viewpoint. Skylands Manor may be seen directly below, surrounded by the exotic trees of the New Jersey State Botanical Garden. The Monksville Reservoir is directly ahead, and the Wanaque Reservoir is visible to the left (south) through the trees.

After taking in the view, return to the Halifax Trail and turn left. In about 500 feet, you'll reach a junction (marked by a cairn) with the red-on-white-blazed Ringwood-Ramapo Trail. Turn right onto the Ringwood-Ramapo Trail, which you'll be following for the next 2.5 miles. In about 350 feet, you'll notice a large rock outcrop on your right, studded with cedar trees. Climb the outcrop to reach another panoramic west-facing view. The view of Skylands Manor is largely obscured by trees, but you get a better view of the Wanaque Reservoir.

Continue south on the Ringwood-Ramapo Trail, which descends gradually on a winding footpath. Soon, it reaches a junction where the blue-triangle-on-white Skylands Trail begins on the left. Bear right to continue on the Ringwood-Ramapo Trail, which heads south along the ridge of Mount Defiance. After crossing a wide carriage road, the trail levels off and traverses open rock ledges. It recrosses the carriage road, passes

VIEW FROM MOUNT DEFIANCE

plant, rarely seen in the Ramapos. Just beyond, at a T-intersection, the trail turns left on a wide fire road, which it follows for 0.2 mile.

At a large brown trail marker, the Ringwood-Ramapo Trail turns right, leaving the fire road, and ascends on a footpath. After crossing a stream on a wooden plank bridge, it reaches a T-intersection, turns left, and climbs along a woods road. It soon bears left at a second T-intersection. A short distance beyond this point, it turns left, leaving the road, and continues to ascend on a footpath, with broad switchbacks. Near the crest of the ridge, it turns left, rejoining the woods road, then descends to cross a stream on a wooden bridge. Just beyond, the trail crosses a woods road and continues ahead into the woods on a footpath, which soon curves to the right.

After following along a ridge, with views over the valley below to the left, the Ringwood-Ramapo Trail descends into the valley. Near the base of the descent, three blue-on-white blazes on the left mark the start of the blue-blazed High Mountain Brook Trail.

Turn left, leaving the Ringwood-Ramapo Trail, and follow the blue-blazed trail, which descends to cross High Mountain Brook on a wooden bridge and begins to climb on a footpath. It soon turns left onto a woods road, which climbs gradually to the crest of the ridge. Near the top, you'll pass a small pond on the right, after which the grade briefly steepens, but the trail soon begins a slight descent. It crosses a stream on a wooden bridge and, a short distance beyond, reaches a junction with the yellow-blazed Hoeferlin Memorial Trail.

Turn left onto the Hoeferlin Memorial Trail. After a relatively level stretch, the trail crosses a stream on rocks and

a balanced boulder on the left, and descends gradually until it once again reaches the carriage road. The carriage road that you cross here is the route of the white-blazed Crossover Trail, which will be your return route. For now, though, continue straight ahead along the Ringwood-Ramapo Trail, which follows a rougher woods road, with many exposed rocks.

A short distance ahead, you'll reach an open rock ledge, with glacial striations, known as Warm Puppy Rock, which offers limited west-facing views. Here, the trail turns left and descends on a footpath, passing another rock ledge on the left with east-facing views. Near the base of the descent, the trail crosses a carriage road and descends to cross a stream on a flat rock. It then passes through a stand of bamboo—a non-native

AN ENGLISH TUDOR GUEST HOUSE WITH A SUNDIAL ON ITS CHIMNEY

climbs a rocky footpath to reach a panoramic view from Ilgenstein Rock. Bear Swamp Lake is below, with Drag Hill and Rocky Mountain in the background. On clear days, the New York City skyline may be visible on the horizon to the right, and you can even see the Verrazano-Narrows Bridge on the extreme right. Here, the white-blazed Crossover Trail joins from the right. You'll be following the Crossover Trail all the way back to the parking area.

Follow the joint yellow-and-white-blazed trails as they proceed north on a rocky footpath. In half a mile, the two trails split. Turn left, following the white-blazed Crossover Trail, which soon widens into a woods road. In another half mile, you'll reach a junction where the blue-blazed Pierson Ridge Trail begins. Follow the white blazes as they turn left, leaving the woods road, and begin to descend.

After crossing a carriage road, the Crossover Trail bears right and begins to follow a well-constructed footpath along the side of the hill. The next mile of the trail was built by the Jersey Off-Road Bicycle Association and was designed primarily for mountain bikes. It features very gentle grades and switchbacks that may seem excessively long to hikers (but are more pleasant to hike than the woods roads that they replaced).

The trail heads north for a third of a mile, then switches back to the left and begins a gradual descent toward Weyble Pond. When it reaches the pond, it turns left onto a carriage road that goes around the south side of the pond. The trail then bears left, leaving the road, and heads south on a path, with a stream below on the left. A short distance ahead, the trail crosses the road and begins to climb, continuing along the side of a hill, with Gatun Pond visible below through the trees. After a while, it switches back to the left and begins to descend. Along the way, it crosses a stream on rocks (as well as a woods road) and passes a balanced rock on the right.

At the base of the descent, the Crossover Trail briefly turns right onto a woods road. It follows the road over a stream, then turns left, reenters the woods on a path, and begins to climb. In a short distance, it crosses a wide gravel road and continues to climb on switchbacks.

At the crest of the rise, the Crossover Trail reaches a junction with the red-on-white-blazed Ringwood-Ramapo Trail, which you followed earlier in the hike. This marks the end of the trail section constructed by JORBA. Follow the white-blazed Crossover Trail, which bears left onto a wide woods road. It soon curves to the right and begins to head north. Continue to follow the white blazes along the base of Mount Defiance, then turn right onto a paved road at Skylands Manor and follow it back to Parking Area A, where the hike began.

Lake Sonoma and Overlook Rock

TOTAL DISTANCE: 4.5 miles

HIKING TIME: 3 hours

VERTICAL RISE: 700 feet

RATING: Moderate

MAPS: USGS Wanaque, Greenwood Lake (NJ/NY), Sloatsburg (NJ/NY); NY–NJTC North Jersey Trails #115

TRAILHEAD GPS COORDINATES: N 41° 05' 28" W 74° 19' 16"

This hike traverses the northwestern area of Norvin Green State Forest. It goes along Lake Sonoma and climbs to two panoramic viewpoints: Overlook Rock and Manaticut Point.

The area surrounding Lake Sonoma was once owned by Maitland B. Bleecker, an American inventor and author who was instrumental in modern helicopter design. In the late 1920s, he developed and constructed a prototype helicopter known as the Curtiss-Bleecker SX, which flew successfully. When he retired in 1945, he purchased 1,500 acres in West Milford, where he dammed a tributary of Burnt Meadow Brook to create Lake Sonoma, started a trout hatchery, and operated the Tapawingo Fishing Preserve.

Prior to his death in 2002 at the age of 99, Bleecker sold the property to the State of New Jersey, and it became a part of Norvin Green State Forest. Beginning in 2007, several trails were constructed in the area by the North Jersey Trails Committee of the New York–New Jersey Trail Conference, under the leadership of John Moran. Volunteers scouting out the trails discovered the spectacular Overlook Rock and routed the trails to pass this vista.

GETTING THERE

Take Skyline Drive to its northwestern terminus at Greenwood Lake Turnpike (County Route 511). Turn left and proceed south for 1.6 miles to West Brook Road. Turn right onto West Brook Road and cross the Wanaque Reservoir on a causeway.

At the next T-junction, turn left and proceed for 0.8 mile to Magee Road. Turn right onto Magee Road and take the first left onto Burnt Meadow Road. Continue for 0.9 mile and turn left at the second intersection with Crescent

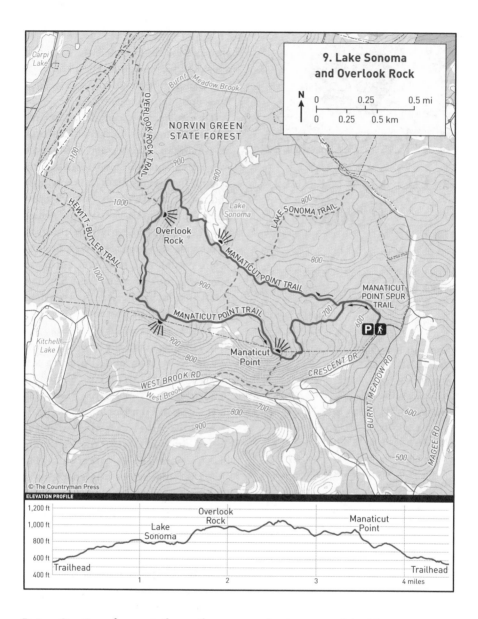

Drive. Continue for 0.2 mile until you reach a huge boulder and a kiosk on the right side of the road, just beyond a curve. Park along the side of the road.

THE HIKE

Between the boulder and the kiosk, a triple black-square-on-yellow blaze marks the start of the Manaticut Point Spur Trail. Head into the woods on this trail. Soon, you'll cross two branches of a stream on rocks, with several abandoned sections of concrete pipe adjacent to the stream, and pass by a huge fractured rock. A short distance beyond, you'll cross another stream.

After crossing a third stream below an

interesting inverted-V-shaped rock formation, the Manaticut Point Spur Trail ends at a junction with the yellow-blazed Manaticut Point Trail. Here, the yellow blazes head both to the left and straight ahead. Continue straight ahead, uphill, to follow the loop of the Manaticut Point Trail in the counterclockwise direction.

About a mile from the start, you'll pass the trailhead of the orange-blazed Lake Sonoma Trail on the right. A short distance ahead, you'll notice a triple yellow-orange blaze on the left, but continue ahead on the yellow-blazed Manaticut Point Trail, which descends to cross the inlet stream of Lake Sonoma at a woods road, immediately turns right, and soon reaches a viewpoint over the lake. The trail parallels the lake for a quarter mile, with views of the lake through the trees.

The Manaticut Point Trail recrosses the woods road, briefly parallels a stream, then crosses it below an attractive cascade. It immediately turns sharply left, crosses another woods road, and begins a steady climb. At the top, it bears left, briefly descends, then turns sharply left at a switchback and climbs gently to reach a junction with the white-blazed Overlook Rock Trail, which joins from the right.

Continue ahead, now following both yellow and white blazes. In 150 feet, both trails turn right at a double blaze. Here, you should turn left and make a short, steep climb up a rock ledge, emerging onto Overlook Rock—a massive exposed rock face. Overlook Rock affords a panoramic east-facing view over Lake Sonoma and Windbeam, Bear, and Board Mountains, with the

VIEW FROM OVERLOOK ROCK

CASCADE ALONG THE LAKE SONOMA TRAIL

and blue blazes. The trail descends briefly, then climbs steeply to the crest of the ridge. It heads southeast along the ridge, passing a viewpoint on the right over Saddle Mountain and then descending gradually. At the base of the descent, there is a small pond on private property to the right.

After climbing through a cleft in the rock, you'll pass on the left the southern end of the yellow/orange-blazed connector trail. Continue along the blue/yellow-blazed trail, which descends a little and then climbs steadily to a panoramic viewpoint from Manaticut Point—an open rock ledge (the best view is from the rock ledge to the right of the one traversed by the trail). Windbeam Mountain is directly ahead (east). To the south, you can see a quarry, with the New York City skyline visible on the horizon on a clear day.

The trail now descends very steeply. Watch carefully for a double blaze painted on a rock. Here, the blue-blazed Hewitt-Butler Trail turns right, but you should follow the yellow-blazed Manaticut Point Trail, which turns left and continues to descend more gradually. The trail soon bears left and climbs a little, goes through an interesting passage between rocks, then resumes a steady descent. After passing several rock formations on the left and crossing a stream, it reaches the junction where the loop of the Manaticut Point Trail ends. Bear right and follow the black-square-on-yellow blazes of the Manaticut Point Spur Trail, retracing your steps to the trailhead on Crescent Drive, where the hike began.

Ramapo Mountains in the background. You've now gone about 2 miles from the start, and you'll want to take a break and enjoy the spectacular view.

When you're ready to continue, descend from the rock and turn left onto the white/yellow-blazed trail. In half a mile, after crossing an intermittent stream and climbing gradually, you'll reach a junction (marked by a single cedar tree) with the blue-blazed Hewitt-Butler Trail at a limited viewpoint to the southwest.

Turn left, now following both yellow

10

Wyanokie Circular

TOTAL DISTANCE: 7.1 miles

HIKING TIME: 5.5 hours

VERTICAL RISE: 1,500 feet

RATING: Moderate to strenuous

MAPS: USGS Wanaque; NY–NJTC North Jersey Trails #115

TRAILHEAD GPS COORDINATES:
N 41° 04' 12" W 74° 19' 20"

The Wyanokie Ridge, which forms part of the New Jersey Highlands, dates back to the Precambrian Period, and many of the rocks in the area are more than 600 million years old. These hills were here long before there was a Wanaque Reservoir or a New York skyline to be seen from the viewpoints on this hike. Blue iron ore was abundant, and villages grew up around the iron mining operations and charcoal furnaces scattered throughout the area. Construction of the Wanaque Reservoir, which is visible from several high points in the area, was started in 1920, and the reservoir was filled by 1930. Wanaque and Wyanokie are both variants of the Native American word meaning "sassafras."

This hike offers spectacular views, pleasant walking in the woods, some rock scrambling, waterfalls on Blue Mine Brook, and two mines in rugged territory. Located in Norvin Green State Forest (c/o Ringwood State Park, P.O. Box 1304, Ringwood, NJ 07456; 973-962-7031), the hike traverses an area with one of the largest concentrations of trails in New Jersey.

In season, one attractive possibility is to swim after your hike in the freshwater Highlands Natural Pool, adjacent to the New Weis Center. A provisional membership is available. For more information, go to www.highlandspool.com.

GETTING THERE

Norvin Green State Forest is accessible from County Route 511, reached from the north by way of Skyline Drive or from the south by via I-287.

Turn west onto West Brook Road, which is 1.6 miles south of the western end of Skyline Drive. The road soon crosses the reservoir on a causeway, then parallels the reservoir on the left.

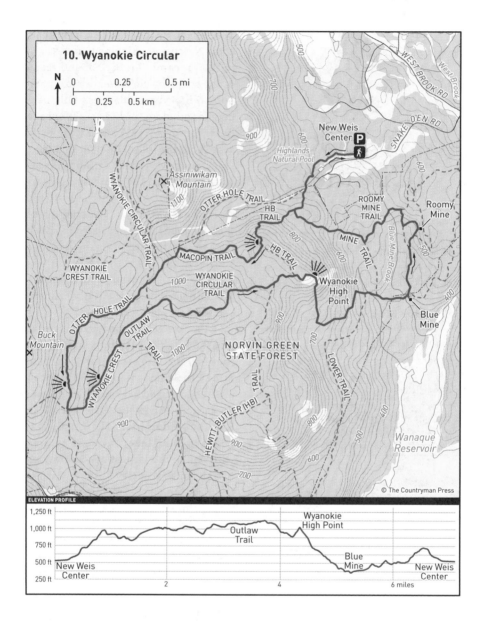

10. Wyanokie Circular

N

| 0 | 0.25 | 0.5 mi |
| 0 | 0.25 | 0.5 km |

New Weis Center P

Highlands Natural Pool

WEST BROOK RD

West Brook

SNAKE DEN RD

ROOMY MINE TRAIL

Roomy Mine

Assiniwikam Mountain

OTTER HOLE TRAIL

HB TRAIL

HB TRAIL

MINE TRAIL

Blue Mine Brook

WYANOKIE CIRCULAR TRAIL

MACOPIN TRAIL

WYANOKIE CREST TRAIL

WYANOKIE CIRCULAR TRAIL

Wyanokie High Point

Blue Mine

OTTER HOLE TRAIL

OUTLAW TRAIL

WYANOKIE CREST TRAIL

Buck Mountain

NORVIN GREEN STATE FOREST

LOWER TRAIL

HEWITT-BUTLER (HB) TRAIL

Wanaque Reservoir

© The Countryman Press

ELEVATION PROFILE

1,250 ft				Wyanokie High Point	
1,000 ft			Outlaw Trail		
750 ft					
500 ft	New Weis Center			Blue Mine	New Weis Center
250 ft		2	4		6 miles

At the end of the reservoir, you reach a junction with Stonetown Road. Bear left to continue on West Brook Road, and after about 0.5 mile, turn left onto Snake Den Road. In 0.3 mile, bear left at a fork, and continue for another 0.3 mile to a large dirt parking area on the right side of the road, just before the entrance to the New Weis Center.

THE HIKE

The hike begins at the western end of the parking area, where a gatepost with a triple light-green blaze marks the start of the Otter Hole Trail, which you will follow for the first part of this hike. Several short trails, such as the "L" Trail and the "W" Trail, are co-aligned for part of the way. The Otter Hole Trail turns left just before reaching a large field, and then, almost immediately, turns right. This pleasant entryway parallels Blue Mine Brook on the left, with a row of large Norway spruce trees on the right. Continue to follow the light-green blazes through a spruce grove, with Blue Mine Brook on the left. Soon, the trail bears right to skirt the Highlands Natural Pool. The trail briefly joins a dirt road, then bears left and ascends on a footpath, passing a waterfall and the weir that regulates the supply of water to the pool.

After crossing a footbridge over the brook, the Otter Hole Trail proceeds through a rocky area and reaches a wide woods road—the continuation of Snake Den Road. Here, the Otter Hole Trail turns right and follows the road, but you should cross the road at a kiosk and continue ahead on the joint Mine (yellow-on-white) and Hewitt-Butler (blue) Trails. The joint trails climb steeply through a rocky area, using stone steps constructed by volunteers.

The trails level off and reach a junction where they split. The Mine Trail turns left, but you should continue ahead, following the blue blazes of the Hewitt-Butler Trail. After a short level section, the trail begins a steady climb. Just before reaching the top, a rock outcrop to the right of the trail offers a west-facing view, with Assiniwikam Mountain visible to the right (northwest). There are more views from a rock outcrop at the top of the climb and, just beyond, the white-blazed Macopin Trail begins on the right. Turn right onto the Macopin Trail.

The Macopin Trail descends through mountain laurel, levels off, and descends some more. In half a mile, after crossing several branches of a stream on rocks, it ends at a junction with the light-green-blazed Otter Hole Trail. Turn left onto the Otter Hole Trail, which climbs along a woods road, goes through a valley, and continues past dense mountain laurel thickets. Along the way, it crosses the red-on-white-blazed Wyanokie Circular Trail (the junction is marked by a cairn). In about a mile, the Otter Hole Trail crosses a stream and climbs to a rock outcrop to the right of the trail that offers views across a valley toward Buck Mountain. The trail now descends and soon reaches a junction with the yellow-blazed Wyanokie Crest Trail.

Turn left and follow the Wyanokie Crest Trail, which crosses a stream on rocks and climbs rather steeply through dense mountain laurel thickets. At the crest of the rise, the trail emerges at a west-facing viewpoint that overlooks Buck Mountain (this viewpoint is higher than the one on the Otter Hole Trail and thus offers a broader view). After descending a little through a second-growth forest of deciduous trees, with an understory of blueberries and mountain laurel, the Wyanokie Crest Trail climbs to a junction (marked by a post) with the orange-blazed Outlaw Trail in an open area.

Turn left onto this short, level trail. In 0.2 mile, when the Outlaw Trail ends at a junction with the Wyanokie Circular Trail (marked by a large boulder), turn right onto this red-on-white-blazed trail. The Wyanokie Circular Trail climbs to an open rock outcrop with a view of a portion of the New York skyline between the trees and then descends to a junction with the blue-blazed Hewitt–Butler Trail (also the route of the teal-diamond-blazed Highlands Trail). Turn left, now following red-dot-on-white, blue-, and teal-diamond blazes.

After crossing a seasonal stream, the trails begin a short, sharp climb to another junction. Turn right (following

VIEW FROM WYANOKIE HIGH POINT

the sign to Hi-Point) and proceed steeply uphill, following both red-dot-on-white and teal-diamond blazes. The last part of the short climb is over bare rock; the trail is marked by blazes painted on the rock.

The summit of Wyanokie High Point offers a magnificent 360-degree view. The Wanaque Reservoir is to the southeast. Beyond the reservoir, you can see a long bridge carrying I-287 over a low area and, on a clear day, the New York City skyline may be seen on the horizon. To the north and west are Saddle, Assiniwikam, and Buck Mountains.

When the time comes to leave this superb viewpoint, find the trail that leads toward the reservoir and follow the red-dot-on-white and teal-diamond blazes as they descend steeply from the summit, passing more views of the reservoir along the way. Soon, the trail bears left and the grade moderates.

The trail eventually goes back into the woods and bears left, and the descent becomes less steep. At the base of the descent, the white-blazed Lower Trail begins on the right and the Wyanokie Circular/Highlands Trail crosses a stream on rocks. A short distance beyond, the yellow-on-white Mine Trail joins from the left. Proceed ahead, now following three different trail blazes:

right to see the entrance to the Blue Mine, so called because of the dark blue color of the local ore. Now filled with water, it was once known as the Iron Hill, London, or Whynockie Mine. Until 1855, most of the ore was processed at a hot-blast charcoal furnace called the Freedom Furnace. For a short period after the Blue Mine's reopening in 1886, the mine produced about 300 tons of ore per month. Water in the mine was obviously a problem, and the mine was "de-watered" several times. This operation was quite difficult. Mine workers stood on a raft that sank lower as the water was pumped out. Their job was to remove the debris left clinging to the walls of the mine and to shore up the timbers in the sides of the shaft, while keeping their balance on the raft. After another dewatering operation in 1905, the mine was not worked again. The concrete pad in front of the mine was once used as a base for steam-operated equipment. If you explore the surroundings you can detect other evidence of mining operations.

Return to the bridge (but do not cross it). Just beyond, the teal-diamond-blazed Highlands Trail diverges to the right, but you should continue ahead on the joint Mine (yellow on white) and Wyanokie Circular (red dot on white) Trails, which follow a rocky woods road. Bear left at a fork and continue ahead for about a quarter of a mile until the two trails separate. Here, you should turn right and follow the yellow-on-white blazes of the Mine Trail, which climbs on a narrow woods road, once used to access the Roomy Mine. At the top of a rather steep pitch, the Mine Trail turns sharply right, but you should continue ahead on the old road, now following the orange blazes of the Roomy Mine Trail.

At the top of the rise, the entrance

red-dot-on-white, teal-diamond, and yellow-on-white.

A short distance ahead, after bearing left and descending, you'll notice on the left the ruins of a stone shelter, constructed by members of the Green Mountain Club in the 1930s. The trail now approaches Blue Mine Brook. Just before reaching the brook, there is a circular mine pit to the right of the trail, with a small pile of tailings (discarded waste rock) to its left. The trail crosses the brook on a wooden footbridge, built as an Eagle Scout project in 2002, with the assistance of volunteers from the New York–New Jersey Trail Conference.

On the other side of the bridge, turn

of the Roomy Mine (formerly known as the Laurel or Red Mine) is on the right. Named for Benjamin Roome, a local land surveyor, the mine opened shortly after 1840 and was worked until 1857. The ore was compact and mostly free of rock. The vein was about 4 feet thick, with a pitch of 58 degrees, dipping sharply to the southeast.

To enter the mine (open only from April 15 to September 15), you first have to crawl through a short passage that is only about 2 feet high. That leads to a large chamber, with the horizontal shaft heading into the mine directly ahead. The shaft is about 6 feet high and leads 60 feet into the hillside, where it dead-ends. The temperature inside the mine is a constant 52 degrees, and the floor is usually wet.

Continue to follow the orange blazes of the Roomy Mine Trail along the mine road. Soon, the trail bears right onto another road (the red-on-white-blazed Wyanokie Circular Trail ends here). A short distance ahead, at a huge boulder marked with orange blazes, turn left and continue to follow the Roomy Mine Trail, which climbs over a rise and passes interesting rock outcrops.

After a jog to the right, the trail crosses Blue Mine Brook above a water-fall, briefly follows the brook, then turns left and continues to a junction with the yellow-on-white-blazed Mine Trail. Here, the Roomy Mine Trail ends, and you should turn right onto the Mine Trail. The trail is level at first, then climbs steadily. Near the top, you'll pass some interesting jumbled boulders and rock outcrops on the right.

At the top of the climb, turn right, joining the blue-blazed Hewitt-Butler Trail. Now following both blue and yellow-on-white blazes, descend steeply to a kiosk at Snake Den Road, here a dirt road. The Hewitt-Butler and Mine Trails end here, but you should cross the road and continue ahead on the green-blazed Otter Hole Trail, retracing your steps past the Highlands Natural Pool and along Blue Mine Brook and end-ing at the parking area where the hike began.

11

Carris Hill

TOTAL DISTANCE: 4 miles	
HIKING TIME: 4 hours	
VERTICAL RISE: 800 feet	
RATING: Moderately strenuous	
MAPS: USGS Wanaque; NY–NJTC North Jersey Trails #115	
TRAILHEAD GPS COORDINATES: N 41° 02' 45" W 74° 21' 02"	

Although this hike is less than 5 miles long, the rugged terrain and possibly difficult water crossings make for an exciting and challenging day hike. Carris Hill is not the highest point in Norvin Green State Forest (c/o Ringwood State Park, 1304 Sloatsburg Road, Ringwood, NJ 07456-1799; 973-962-7031; www.njparksandforests.org), but it offers spectacular views. Since the hike includes a strenuous climb and descent, good footwear is necessary, and you should take special care if you attempt this hike in winter—certain sections are on steep slopes of bare rock that could be difficult to navigate when covered with snow and ice. Posts Brook, which you will cross at the start of the hike, is usually easily crossed on rocks. After a snowmelt or heavy rain, however, it becomes a raging torrent and can present serious problems.

GETTING THERE

From I-287, take Exit 53 (Bloomingdale) and turn left onto Hamburg Turnpike. Upon entering Bloomingdale, the name of the road changes to Main Street. In 1.3 miles (from I-287) you will reach a fork in the road. Bear right, and in another 0.1 mile turn right (uphill) onto Glenwild Avenue, following the sign to West Milford. Continue ahead for 3.2 miles to a parking area on the right side of the road. If this lot is full, there is space for more cars a little farther down the road.

THE HIKE

For the first part of this hike, you will be following the blue-blazed Hewitt-Butler Trail, which heads north into the woods from the eastern end of the parking area. Soon you will arrive at Otter Hole, a small cascade and falls on Posts Brook.

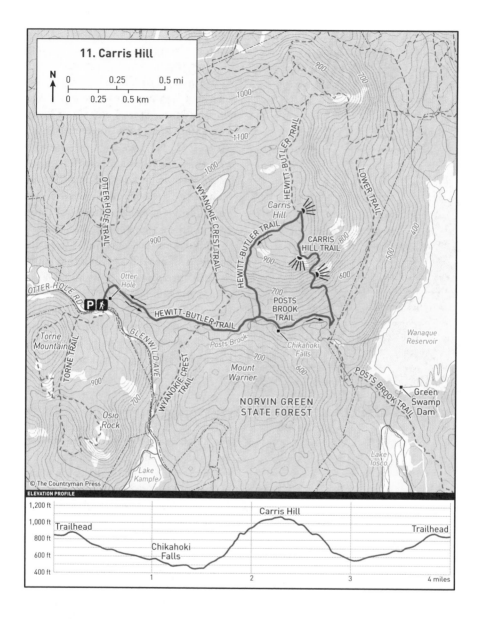

It is normally possible to cross the brook on large boulders, but if this is impractical or dangerous, you should abort this hike and try another one. (Just across the road, the Hewitt-Butler Trail ascends Torne Mountain and Osio Rock, with several fine views; see Hike #12.)

After crossing the brook, continue ahead to an intersection with the green-blazed Otter Hole Trail. Bear right to continue on the blue-blazed Hewitt-Butler Trail, which is joined by the teal-diamond–blazed Highlands Trail. You'll now head uphill, roughly parallel to Posts Brook, following a rocky woods road. The trail continues to ascend for a short distance and then begins a steady descent.

In about half a mile, the trail turns left, leaving the woods road, and continues to descend. Soon, the yellow-blazed Wyanokie Crest Trail joins from the right. The two trails run jointly for only 75 feet, and when the Wyanokie Crest Trail leaves to the left, continue ahead, following the blue and teal diamond blazes.

After leveling off and passing through a wet area, the trail approaches Posts Brook and then crosses a tributary stream on a log bridge. A short distance beyond this stream crossing, you'll reach a junction with the white-blazed Posts Brook Trail. Here, the Hewitt-Butler and Highlands Trails turn left, but you should continue ahead on the white trail, which closely parallels the cascading brook.

Soon, the trail reaches the top of Chikahoki Falls and descends to the brook, with a good view of the falls. The trail closely parallels the brook for a short distance, then bears left and heads uphill, away from the brook. After a while, it again descends to the brook.

A short distance beyond, you'll come to a junction with the Lower Trail, blazed with a black "L" on white. Turn left and follow the Lower Trail a short distance to a junction with the yellow-blazed Carris Hill Trail. Turn left again, now following the yellow blazes.

After traversing a level, rocky area, the Carris Hill Trail crosses a stream and begins a rather steep climb. The grade soon moderates, but after a third of a mile, it again climbs steeply over rocks, reaching a viewpoint to the southeast from a rock outcrop just to the right of the trail. The trail continues to climb to another rock outcrop, with a broader view. Here, it bears right and ascends to the left of a 40-foot-high massive rock face.

At the top of the ascent, a short detour to the right leads to a magnificent viewpoint to the east. The Wanaque Reservoir, contained by the Raymond, Wolf Den, and Green Swamp dams, is

CHIKAHOKI FALLS

WANAQUE RESERVOIR FROM CARRIS HILL

in the foreground, with the Ramapo Mountains beyond, and a long viaduct of I-287 is visible to the right. On a clear day, the New York City skyline may be seen on the horizon. This is a good place to pause and enjoy the spectacular view.

The yellow trail now climbs more gradually, soon reaching another viewpoint (partially blocked by trees), with a 6-foot-high balanced glacial erratic silhouetted against the sky. The trail curves to the right and traverses open rock ledges with views to the south. After going through dense mountain laurel thickets, it reaches a fifth viewpoint—this one to the southwest—with pitch pines and a large glacial erratic. The trail continues on a level footpath through laurel and blueberry bushes and climbs slightly to end on a rock outcrop with views to the north and west, at a junction with the blue-blazed Hewitt-Butler Trail and the teal-diamond-blazed Highlands Trail.

Turn sharply left here, following the sign for "O-H PRKG," and head southeast on the joint Hewitt-Butler/Highlands Trail (do *not* follow the route of these trails, marked by a sign pointing to "Weis," that heads north). After reaching another large rock outcrop, the trail begins a steady descent through blueberries and mountain laurel, finally leveling off on a woods road. It soon reaches the junction with the white-blazed Posts Brook Trail that you encountered earlier in the hike. Turn right at this junction and follow the blue and teal-diamond blazes westward, retracing the first part of the hike. Most of the way back is a gradual uphill climb. After about a mile, the teal-diamond blazes leave to the right. Continue ahead on the blue-blazed trail, cross Posts Brook on boulders, and you'll soon reach the parking area on Glenwild Avenue where you started the hike.

12

Torne Mountain— Osio Rock

TOTAL DISTANCE: 2.7 miles

HIKING TIME: 3 hours

VERTICAL RISE: 750 feet

RATING: Easy to moderate

MAPS: USGS Wanaque; NY–NJTC North Jersey Trails #115

TRAILHEAD GPS COORDINATES:
N 41° 02' 45" W 74° 21' 02"

Although this figure-eight, double-loop hike starts at a popular trailhead, most hikers head north into the main section of Norvin Green State Forest. This hike heads south into a less-used section of the forest, where you are likely to find greater solitude. It climbs Torne Mountain and Osio Rock, both of which offer panoramic views. Although it is less than 3 miles long, the hike will probably seem longer, given that it involves considerable ups and downs on rocky trails.

Members of the local chapter of the Green Mountain Club planned and constructed many of the trails in Norvin Green in the 1920s, and the trails were subsequently maintained by the Nature Friends. Their former camp is now the New Weis Center, a few miles to the north (see Hike #10, Wyanokie Circular, and Hike #11, Carris Hill).

For many years, there was only a single trail route up Osio Rock. In 2017, volunteers of the New York-New Jersey Trail Conference constructed an alternate route that makes this double-loop hike possible. Hikers are now able to climb both mountains without retracing their steps.

GETTING THERE

To reach the trailhead, take I-287 to Exit 53 (Bloomingdale) and turn left onto Hamburg Turnpike. Upon entering Bloomingdale, the name of the road changes to Main Street. In 1.3 miles (from I-287), you will reach a fork in the road. Bear right, and in another 0.1 mile, turn right (uphill) onto Glenwild Avenue (following the sign to West Milford). Continue ahead for 3.2 miles to a parking area on the right side of the road. If this lot is full, there is space for more cars a little farther down the road.

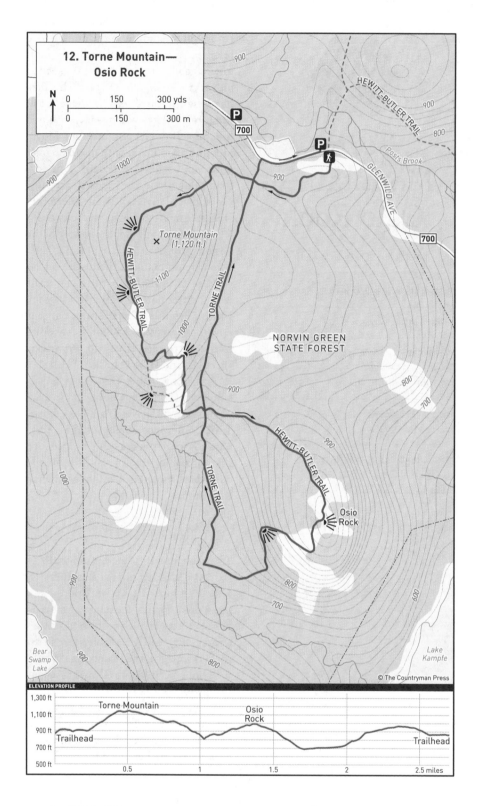

12. Torne Mountain— Osio Rock

N

| 0 | 150 | 300 yds |
| 0 | 150 | 300 m |

900

HEWITT-BUTLER TRAIL

900

800

P

700

P

Posts Brook

GLENWILD AVE

700

1000

900

900

Torne Mountain
(1,120 ft.)

HEWITT-BUTLER TRAIL

1100

1000

TORNE TRAIL

NORVIN GREEN
STATE FOREST

800

700

900

1000

HEWITT-BUTLER TRAIL

900

TORNE TRAIL

Osio
Rock

600

800

700

1000

900

Bear
Swamp
Lake

900

800

700

Lake
Kampfe

© The Countryman Press

ELEVATION PROFILE

1,300 ft			
1,100 ft	Torne Mountain	Osio Rock	
900 ft			
700 ft	Trailhead		Trailhead
500 ft			
	0.5	1	1.5	2	2.5 miles

THE HIKE

Cross the road at the eastern end of the parking area (at the sign "Welcome to Bloomingdale") and enter the woods at a blue-blazed post marked "HB." Follow the blue-blazed Hewitt-Butler Trail, which climbs on a rocky footpath. Soon, it will seem that you have left civilization behind—well, except for some road noise! After a short dip, the climb resumes, and then you descend a little into a ravine, where you cross the red-blazed Torne Trail, with Glenwild Avenue just to the right. Make a mental note of this spot, because you'll return to it after completing the loop.

Proceed straight ahead on the blue-blazed Hewitt-Butler Trail and begin a steady ascent of Torne Mountain, climbing steeply at times. After 15 minutes or so, you'll reach a large rock ledge with a vista to the west and north. If there are no leaves on the trees, you'll get a good view of Buck Mountain, just to the north.

VIEW FROM OSIO ROCK

Continue ahead, taking care to follow the blue blazes (there are a number of unmarked paths in this area) as the trail contours around the edge of Torne Mountain (1,120 feet). A short hike through the woods brings you to a second open area, marked by a cairn, which features a view to the west through the trees. Soon, you'll reach yet a third open area—this one marked by a larger cairn.

Continue to follow the blue-blazed trail along the crest of the mountain. Soon, you'll reach another open area, with two cedar trees and two balanced glacial erratics. There are views both to the west and to the south from here. You can see both Osio Rock and a peak covered with pine trees (known as the West Torne) to its right.

The trail now begins to descend.

Soon, you'll reach a junction with a black-dot-on-blue side trail. Here, you should turn left to stay on the blue-blazed trail. Just ahead, you'll come to a southeast-facing viewpoint over Osio Rock (the next peak you will climb), with the New York City skyline visible in the distance. After descending some more, you'll come to another view of Osio Rock. The trail now descends on switchbacks, with Osio Rock visible to the left along the way. After a steep descent on log steps, the trail levels off.

Just beyond, you'll pass the other end of the black-dot-on-blue side trail and descend into a ravine with an intermittent stream. The red-blazed Torne Trail crosses here. You'll be returning along this trail, but for now, turn right and continue to follow the blue-blazed

WEST-FACING VIEW FROM TORNE MOUNTAIN

Hewitt-Butler Trail, which climbs through dense thickets of mountain laurel, levels off, then resumes its climb.

After passing a jumbled formation of huge boulders on the right, the trail again briefly levels off, then resumes a steady climb to reach a limited east-facing viewpoint. A short distance beyond, it emerges onto a rock ledge—the summit of Osio Rock. This peak affords a spectacular 360-degree view. The large body of water visible in the distance on the left is the Wanaque Reservoir, and the curved elevated roadway on the right is I-287. This is a good place to take a break.

When you're ready to continue, follow the blue blazes as the trail descends from Osio Rock. On the way down, you'll pass a southeast-facing viewpoint over the private Lake Kampfe. The trail now descends more steeply on a rocky footpath, with a rocky peak studded with pines (the West Torne) visible ahead. After a short level stretch, the blue-blazed Hewitt-Butler Trail ends, just before a stream, at a junction with the red-blazed Torne Trail.

Turn right onto the Torne Trail, which heads north on a level footpath parallel to the stream, then begins to climb through a ravine. After passing an interesting cascade on the right, you'll once again cross the blue-blazed Hewitt-Butler Trail. Continue to follow the red-blazed Torne Trail, which climbs steeply through a boulder-filled ravine, paralleling a stream. You'll have to squeeze your way between some huge boulders to negotiate this stretch of the trail. The trail continues to ascend on a very gentle grade through an attractive valley.

After descending from the crest of the rise, the red-blazed Torne Trail again crosses the blue-blazed Hewitt-Butler Trail. When the Torne Trail ends at Glenwild Road, turn right onto the road and follow it for a short distance to the parking area where the hike began.

Terrace Pond

TOTAL DISTANCE: 4.5 miles	
HIKING TIME: 3.5 hours	
VERTICAL RISE: 350 feet	
RATING: Moderate	
MAPS: USGS Wawayanda, Newfoundland; NY–NJTC North Jersey Trails #116	
TRAILHEAD GPS COORDINATES: N 41° 08' 34.5" W 74° 24' 27"	

This hike in Wawayanda State Park (885 Warwick Turnpike, Hewitt, NJ 07421; 973-853-4462; www.njparksand forests.org) is on land called the Sussex Woodlands when it was owned by Fred Ferber, a Depression-era immigrant from Austria. Ferber was not a lover of state parks; he objected to hunting and to restaurants, toilets, and campsites—facilities normally found in state parks. His ambition was to keep his property as wilderness, untouched by such facilities. But gradually, as he ran into debt over the years, he sold portions of his land to the state. Bearfort Mountain, which contains Terrace Pond, was one of the last tracts sold, in 1973.

This hike uses portions of the yellow-blazed Terrace Pond South Trail, the Yellow Dot Trail, the Terrace Pond Red Trail, the white-blazed Terrace Pond Circular Trail, and the blue-blazed Terrace Pond North Trail. The terrain is varied, and all sections are superb. At first the hike is gentle, but the approach to Terrace Pond—the climax of the hike—may remind you of a roller coaster.

To make the hiking experience at Terrace Pond more user-friendly, it is anticipated that, during 2020, the approximate route of this hike will be marked in its entirety with yellow blazes, thus creating a single-color loop that can be easily followed to the pond and back. If you see only yellow blazes (no blue blazes) at the trailhead, the reblazing will have been completed, and you should follow the yellow blazes for the entire hike.

GETTING THERE

The trailhead is on the east side of Clinton Road, which runs north from NJ 23 to Warwick Turnpike. Look for it 1.7 miles south of the junction with Warwick

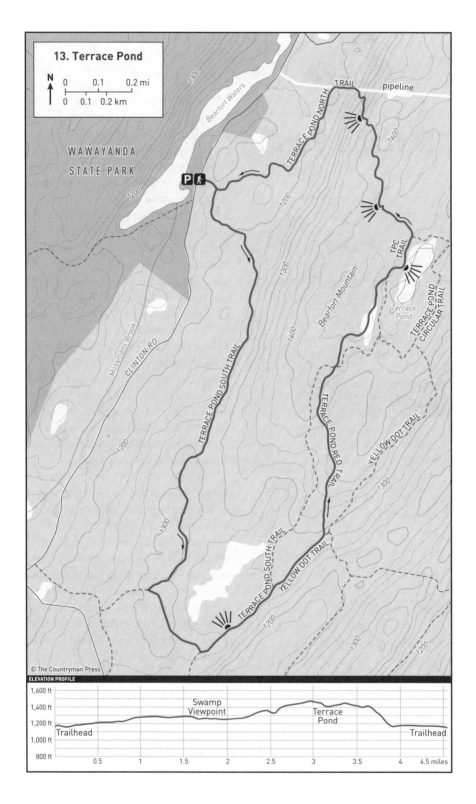

13. Terrace Pond

N

| 0 | 0.1 | 0.2 mi |
| 0 | 0.1 | 0.2 km |

WAWAYANDA
STATE PARK

Bearfort Waters

1300

1200

TERRACE POND NORTH TRAIL

pipeline

1400

TPC TRAIL

Terrace Pond

TERRACE POND CIRCULAR TRAIL

Bearfort Mountain

1300

1400

Mossmans Brook

CLINTON RD

1200

TERRACE POND SOUTH TRAIL

1300

TERRACE POND RED TRAIL

YELLOW DOT TRAIL

1300

TERRACE POND SOUTH TRAIL

YELLOW DOT TRAIL

1200

1300

1200

© The Countryman Press

ELEVATION PROFILE

1,600 ft					
1,400 ft		Swamp Viewpoint		Terrace Pond	
1,200 ft					
1,000 ft	Trailhead				Trailhead
800 ft					
	0.5	1	1.5	2	2.5	3	3.5	4	4.5 miles

Turnpike, or 7.3 miles north of NJ 23. There is a parking area on the west side of the road, just north of the entrance to the Wildcat Environmental Center (Project U.S.E.). This parking area is designated as P7 on the New York–New Jersey Trail Conference maps.

THE HIKE

Cross the road and enter the woods at a trailhead with a triple-blue blaze and a triple-yellow blaze. These blazes mark the start, respectively, of the Terrace Pond North Trail and the Terrace Pond South Trail. Follow the yellow blazes, which almost immediately bear right (the blue trail, which goes off to the left, will be your return route) and proceed over a small hill through mountain laurel and white pine, crossing several wet areas on puncheons and large rocks. Volunteers from the New York–New Jersey Trail Conference continue their work to improve the trail through wet sections by installing puncheons (bog bridges). Soon, the trail winds around a swampy area to the left, then parallels a small stream.

In about half a mile, the trail goes through a magnificent rhododendron grove, with the large rhododendrons forming an arch over the trail in places. Soon after you leave the rhododendron grove, the laurel and evergreens end, and you proceed through a second-growth forest of deciduous trees. A short distance beyond, the trail heads across an interesting whaleback rock and crosses two low stone walls. Before the walls, there is a pleasant place to take a break on a large rock to the left, which looks down over a tiny, elongated lake. Just beyond the stone walls, the yellow trail turns left onto a woods road. You'll be following woods roads, with gentle grades, for the next 1.3 miles.

Soon, the yellow blazes bear left again onto another woods road lined with barberry bushes, indicating that this area was once farmed. Then, after half a mile, take care to follow the yellow blazes as they bear very sharply left at a junction of woods roads. A short distance ahead, the yellow trail passes a swamp (with many dead trees) on the left. A quarter of a mile beyond the sharp turn, the yellow trail bears left at the top of a rise, with another woods road going off to the right.

The trail again begins to run along the swamp on the left, with much beaver activity visible in the swamp. Two miles into the hike, the yellow-blazed Terrace Pond South Trail goes off to the left, and three blazes resembling fried eggs (a yellow circle on a white background) indicate the beginning of the Yellow Dot Trail. Continue straight ahead on this wide woods road. In 0.2 mile, leave the Yellow Dot Trail—it continues straight ahead—and turn left onto the red-blazed Terrace Pond Red Trail, which follows a rugged, rocky footpath.

The trail flattens out briefly, but then climbs through more rugged terrain before descending into an attractive valley, where it crosses a stream. It crosses several low ridges and proceeds along the base of a large slab of puddingstone rock, which it climbs and continues across the top. After approximately 45 minutes walking on the Terrace Pond Red Trail, the footpath descends to a junction with the yellow-blazed Terrace Pond South Trail, which you followed at the start of this hike. For a short distance, you follow both red and yellow blazes, but when the yellow blazes leave to the right, bear left, continuing to follow the red blazes of the Terrace Pond Red Trail.

The Terrace Pond Red Trail climbs

TERRACE POND

along another rock outcrop, then steeply climbs over rocks to reach a seasonal viewpoint to the east, through the trees. Just beyond, Terrace Pond itself may be seen below to the right (when there are no leaves on the trees). Finally, the Terrace Pond Red Trail descends steeply over rocks to end at a junction with the white-blazed Terrace Pond Circular Trail. The Terrace Pond Circular Trail circles Terrace Pond, but if you make a right turn, you'll eventually have to cross

another rock scramble—you'll reach an open area along the lakeshore. This is a great spot to take a break and enjoy the beauty of this secluded glacial lake. In about a quarter of a mile, you'll come to a T-junction with the blue-blazed Terrace Pond North Trail. Here, you'll notice a triple white blaze (indicating that the Terrace Pond Circular Trail technically begins and ends here). Turn left and follow the blue blazes of the Terrace Pond North Trail, which crosses several wet areas on rocks and logs. After a short climb, you'll emerge onto a large open rock outcrop. Just to the left of the trail, there are panoramic west-facing views from the top of a rounded peak of conglomerate rock. This is another good spot for a break.

After refreshing your spirit with the beautiful panorama, continue on the blue-blazed trail, which passes alternately through woody, wet areas and rock outcrops. Some of the descents, although short, are steep and can be slippery. The main direction is downhill, but there are a few short climbs. Quite suddenly, the trail comes upon the ugly slash of a pipeline.

Turn left and follow the pipeline downhill for about 500 feet, keeping to the left of the gash on the hill and looking for the blue blazes to confirm that you are still on the trail. Just as the pipeline levels off, you will reach a very distinct, blue-blazed woods road. (If you miss it, follow the pipeline to Clinton Road, turn left, and walk 0.4 mile along the road to the parking lot.) Turn left, following the blue blazes, which follow a relatively level route for the next half mile, crossing several wet areas on rocks, and lead back to the trailhead. Cross the road to reach the parking area where the hike began.

the outlet of the pond, and this crossing is sometimes difficult to negotiate. So to continue along the route of the hike, turn left and follow the white blazes along the west side of Terrace Pond.

A short distance ahead—just beyond

14

Bearfort Ridge

TOTAL DISTANCE: 7 miles

HIKING TIME: 5.5 hours

VERTICAL RISE: 1,200 feet

RATING: Moderately strenuous

MAPS: USGS Greenwood Lake (NY/NJ); NY–NJTC North Jersey Trails #116; DEP Hewitt State Forest map

TRAILHEAD GPS COORDINATES: N 41° 09' 20.5" W 74° 21' 46"

This hike is in Abram S. Hewitt State Forest, administered by Wawayanda State Park (885 Warwick Turnpike, Hewitt, NJ; 973-853-4462; www.njparks andforests.org) as a day-use area; no camping or swimming is permitted. Bearfort Mountain, which this hike traverses, may still even have a few bears—they have been seen in nearby Wawayanda—and it is assumed that this is the derivation of the name.

GETTING THERE

From the large shopping center—which contains a post office and large Tractor Supply Co. store—on the southwestern shore of Greenwood Lake, where County Route 511 meets County Route 513 (just west of Browns Point Park in West Milford), continue west 0.1 mile on County Route 513 to a fork in the road. Take the right fork (Warwick Turnpike) going uphill. Cross a small concrete bridge and park on the right side of the road just after the bridge. If you reach a junction with White Road, you've gone too far.

THE HIKE

The trail begins on the north side of the road, just east of the bridge. Three white paint blazes indicate the start of the Bearfort Ridge Trail. You'll also notice a sign for the Jeremy Glick Trail, named to honor a local hero of the tragic events of September 11, 2011. Glick was one of the passengers who tried to regain control of Flight 93, which crashed in Pennsylvania. The trail (unofficially) named in his honor will be your return route.

Starting uphill through a pretty grove of hemlocks and rhododendrons, the trail briefly traverses the slope before joining a woods road. Following the white blazes, proceed left along the

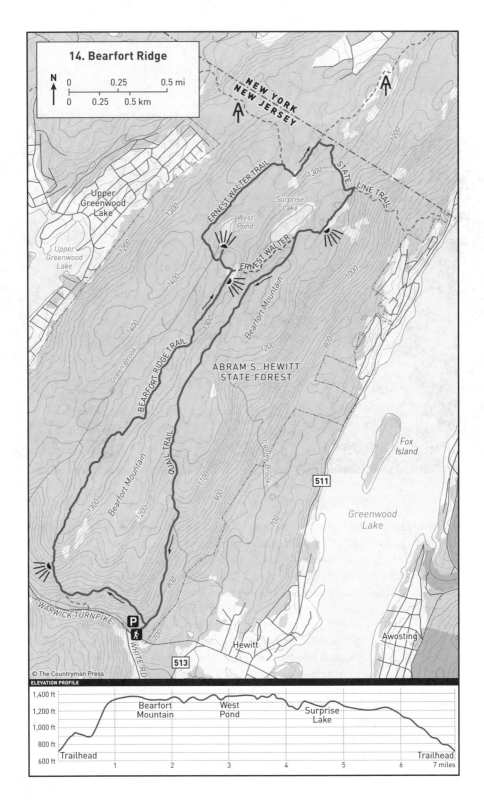

14. Bearfort Ridge

N

| 0 | 0.25 | 0.5 mi |

| 0 | 0.25 | 0.5 km |

NEW YORK
NEW JERSEY

ERNEST WALTER TRAIL

STATE LINE TRAIL

1300

1200

Surprise
Lake

West
Pond

ERNEST WALTER

Bearfort Mountain

1400

1300

1200

BEARFORT RIDGE TRAIL

Upper
Greenwood
Lake

Upper
Greenwood
Lake

Green Brook

1400

1300

ABRAM S. HEWITT
STATE FOREST

1000

800

QUAIL TRAIL

Bearfort Mountain

1300

1200

1100

900

800

700

Cooley Brook

700

Fox
Island

511

Greenwood
Lake

WARWICK TURNPIKE

P

WHITE RD

513

700

800

Hewitt

Awosting

© The Countryman Press

ELEVATION PROFILE

1,400 ft		Bearfort	West	Surprise		
1,200 ft		Mountain	Pond	Lake		
1,000 ft						
800 ft						
600 ft	Trailhead					Trailhead

1   2   3   4   5   6   7 miles

WEST POND

woods road, and, after a short distance, turn left again, uphill and off the road. The woods road, called the Quail Trail, is marked with orange blazes and continues northward to Surprise Lake. Note this spot, as it will be on your return route.

The Bearfort Ridge Trail is well marked with white blazes. It climbs moderately uphill, with some steep pitches, through a mixed hardwood forest consisting of red, black, and white oak, and some maple, ash, beech, and birch. The forests here were heavily timbered for charcoal production during the area's iron-producing period. This forest is therefore the second—or even third—growth of trees.

After crossing a stream in a small hollow, the trail continues ahead along the side of a slope. Except for some road noise from nearby Warwick Turnpike, there is a feeling of isolation in deep woods. You may or may not notice a blue-blazed side trail to the left, which is a short link to Warwick Turnpike and the Terrace Pond North trailhead. As you proceed, gaining elevation, the road noise quickly fades, and the real beauty of this area becomes evident. Passing through some tall and lush rhododendrons—magnificent in June when they bloom—the climb begins to steepen. After you ascend around rocks and along the base of a ledge, there is a good south-facing viewpoint off the trail to the right. The steep, bare-faced peak across the road is another part of this same mountain. Continuing ahead and upward, you soon reach the first of the pitch pines that dominate the main part of the hike.

As the trail turns right onto the ledge, a scramble up the large rock on the left of the trail yields another fine view. The water in the distance is a small section of Upper Greenwood Lake. This viewpoint is also a good place to take note of the rock formation that makes up much of Bearfort Ridge. A collection of white quartz pebbles embedded in a red puddingstone, it is considered similar to the Shawangunk conglomerate found in Mohonk and Minnewaska. These rocks generally provide secure footing, but, as usual, take extra care when they are wet or icy.

Continue on the trail as it climbs up onto the ledges. Once you reach the top of the ridge, the Bearfort Ridge Trail follows a relatively level route along puddingstone conglomerate outcrops, with several dips back into the woods to cross small hollows and streams. There are some sudden but well-marked turns; if you lose the white blazes, retrace a short way back and pick up the turn. The elevation is generally 1,300 feet or more, and the climb up has been more than 600 feet. The views from this section of the Bearfort Ridge Trail are not as sweeping as those behind you or to come, but the charm of the landscape surrounds you. Note the fine array of mosses along—and occasionally even in—the footpath, indicative of the surprisingly light use this trail receives. The boulders strewn along the way have

been moved to these spots by glaciers, remaining from the ancient ice sheets as they melted and retreated north. Striations on the rock surface can also be attributed to this period.

One of the nicest spots in all of New Jersey is about a half-hour hike along this ridgetop. Here, a large section of rock has split away from the base, leaving a deep crevice just to the left of the footpath. On the far side of the split is an attractive swamp. The separation of rock here possibly commenced as water seeped into cracks and then expanded with repeated freezings. Time and erosion have widened it to more dramatic dimensions. This is a good spot for a break.

Continuing ahead, pass a rather large boulder. After a while, cross a stream, then climb up through a rock notch. The ridge soon becomes less pronounced, with fewer rock outcrops, and rhododendron and mountain laurel reappearing. As the trail gently rises out of the woods, a symmetrical cedar tree dominates the skyline. In another 100 feet, three white paint blazes on the top of a small rock mark the end of the Bearfort Ridge Trail, about 2.5 miles (and about 2 hours) from the hike's start.

The view is extensive, including Surprise Lake, with only small traces of civilization visible. Off to the right in the distance is a section of the Monksville Reservoir. The hike now begins a loop that starts and ends on the yellow-blazed Ernest Walter Trail, named for a dedicated hiker and trailblazer.

The yellow blazes lead both right and left. Proceed left, following the loop in a clockwise direction. The trail steeply descends a rock face and continues along a narrow footpath. Because it crosses "against the grain" on the ridge, the route undulates pleasantly through

SURPRISE LAKE

the woods and rock outcrops, soon crossing Green Brook, the outlet stream of West Pond. This section of trail is particularly rugged, with many short but steep ups and downs. At the bottom of the second steep descent, you'll come to a T-intersection. A yellow arrow on a tree points right to a view. Turn right and follow a side trail for about 500 feet to a rock outcrop overlooking pristine West Pond. You'll want to spend a little time enjoying the view at this special spot.

When you're ready to continue, retrace your steps to the trail junction and continue ahead, heading west along the Ernest Walter Trail. You'll soon come to a third, very steep descent, at the base of which the trail crosses Green Brook, the outlet stream of West Pond. The trail

now proceeds through an attractive forest of hemlocks, pines, and deciduous trees. You'll pass a junction with an unofficial trail that goes off to the left, but you should continue to follow the yellow blazes of the Ernest Walter Trail.

About 0.5 mile from Green Brook, the trail crosses a small stream, the outlet of a wetland to the left. Just beyond, a rock outcrop to the left of the trail affords a view over the wetland. An unusual huge split boulder adds interest to this spot, which is another good place to take a break.

Soon, the trail traverses a long, narrow, smooth rock. A short distance beyond, it turns right and descends to end at a T-junction with the white-blazed Appalachian Trail (AT). See Hike #17, Appalachian Trail—Stairway to Heaven, for background information on this National Scenic Trail. Turn right onto the AT, which almost immediately climbs a steep ledge. You're now heading east, again crossing several sharp ridges. At a limited viewpoint to the east, the trail turns left and heads north.

A short distance beyond, you'll reach another limited viewpoint, with both east- and west-facing views from an open rock ledge. The AT now descends a long, sloped rock and reaches a junction with the blue-and-white-blazed State Line Trail (the junction is marked by paint blazes on a rock). Turn right and follow the blue blazes downhill off the ridge.

After about 15 or 20 minutes going generally downhill on the State Line Trail, you will encounter another junction. This spot is the other end of the U-shaped Ernest Walter Trail. Make a sharp right turn onto it and climb steeply up to a promontory overlooking Greenwood Lake.

Surprise Lake is now about 20 minutes away, but the journey may take longer because the views on this rise are outstanding and invite lingering. Much of the two-state area of Greenwood Lake is visible. The large island in the middle is Fox Island, and across the lake are the mountains of Sterling Forest State Park in New York and Long Pond Ironworks State Park in New Jersey. Area hikers were a major (arguably *the* major) supporting force in a successful campaign to bring these lands into the park systems of the two states.

Leave the ridge and turn right into the woods, passing a pile of shale ruins. Just before the shore of Surprise Lake, there are a few unmarked side trails, so keep a close watch on those yellow blazes. Your impressions of this graceful lake may be determined by how many people are there or the litter and debris they may have left. It sees heavy warm-weather use.

Here you have a choice. You can continue following the yellow Ernest Walter blazes for a half-mile climb to its end at the previously encountered junction with the Bearfort Ridge Trail. From there you would retrace your steps on the Bearfort Ridge Trail back to your car. This adds about a mile to the hike, but the trail looks surprisingly different when you're traveling in the opposite direction.

For the most direct return route (and to avoid retracing your steps), look for the orange-blazed Quail Trail. The orange and yellow trails split about 100 feet from the lake, the yellow-blazed Ernest Walter Trail turning sharply right and the orange-blazed Quail Trail going straight ahead.

The 2.5-mile-long Quail Trail is an old woods road that, at times, can be wet underfoot. However, it is mostly easy walking and passes by some lovely rock and cliff formations on both sides of the trail.

Just under 2 miles from the lake, the trail heads steeply downhill for a short stretch, then passes a distinct woods road heading sharply off to the left.

Two or three minutes farther along, you'll see the last orange blaze at the previously encountered junction with the Bearfort Ridge Trail. Continue ahead, now following the white blazes back to your car, just a few minutes away.

15

Pequannock Watershed

TOTAL DISTANCE: 8 miles (9.5 miles without car shuttle)

HIKING TIME: 6 hours

VERTICAL RISE: 400 feet

RATING: Moderately strenuous

MAPS: USGS Newfoundland; NY–NJTC North Jersey Trails #116; Pequannock Watershed trails map

TRAILHEAD GPS COORDINATES:
N 41° 04′ 30″ W 74° 26′ 46″

This outstanding hiking area is named for the Pequannock River. *Pequannock* is an Algonquin word said to mean "battlefield." The river is fed by the streams, lakes, and reservoirs of this mountainous and particularly scenic section of western Passaic County. Owned and managed by the city of Newark, this natural area just south of Wawayanda State Park supplies much of Newark's drinking water. Under the auspices of the New York–New Jersey Trail Conference, a network consisting of about 25 miles of hiking trails has been blazed in this largely uninhabited area, and the land is open for recreational use by permit only. At the time of this writing, the fee is $14 per year ($8 for seniors). For more information, or to obtain a hiking permit, contact the city of Newark, by mail at P.O. Box 319, Newfoundland, NJ 07435; or in person at their office, 223 Echo Lake Road, West Milford, NJ 07480; 973-697-1724.

This hike takes you on a grand tour of some of the watershed's more scenic and interesting features. Though it is long, the walking is not difficult, and much of it is along the shores of ponds and reservoirs. You will traverse some deep hemlock forests typical of this area, and there are a few overlooks, as well as the Bearfort Fire Tower, from which you can survey the area. Part of the hike follows the Bearfort Ridge, with its pink-to-purple sandstones and conglomerates. This ridge, composed of Paleozoic (Silurian and Devonian) sedimentary rock, occurs in the midst of the much older Precambrian Highlands formation. Apparently, Bearfort Mountain is the remains of the sand and silt deposits of a long, narrow inland sea or sound that penetrated the older Highlands. Notice the distinct change of bedrock as you hike from Bearfort

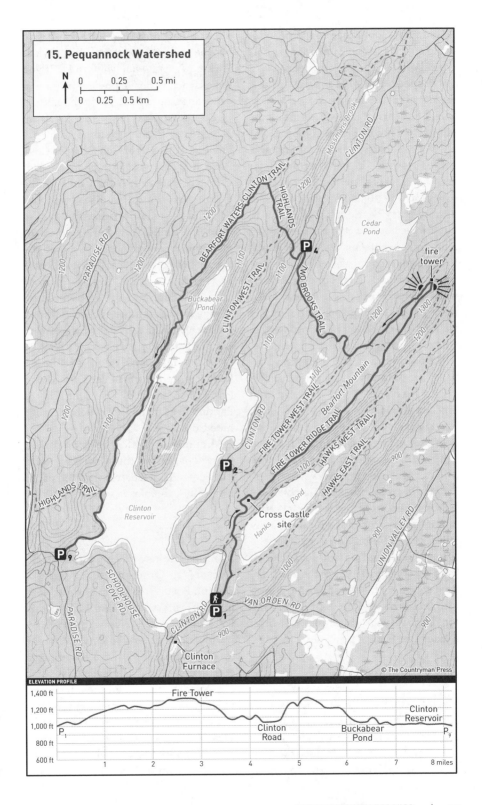

15. Pequannock Watershed

N

| 0 | 0.25 | 0.5 mi |
| 0 | 0.25 | 0.5 km |

Mossmans Brook

CLINTON RD

BEARFORT WATERS-CLINTON TRAIL

HIGHLANDS TRAIL

Cedar Pond

P₄

fire tower

TWO BROOKS TRAIL

CLINTON WEST TRAIL

Buckabear Pond

Bearfort Mountain

FIRE TOWER WEST TRAIL

FIRE TOWER RIDGE TRAIL

HAWKS WEST TRAIL

HAWKS EAST TRAIL

CLINTON RD

P₂

Hanks Pond

Cross Castle site

HIGHLANDS TRAIL

Clinton Reservoir

P₉

UNION VALLEY RD

SCHOOLHOUSE COVE RD

P₁

VAN ORDEN RD

CLINTON RD

PARADISE RD

Clinton Furnace

© The Countryman Press

ELEVATION PROFILE

Fire Tower

1,400 ft	
1,200 ft	
1,000 ft	Clinton Reservoir
800 ft	
600 ft	

P₁   Clinton Road   Buckabear Pond   P₉

1   2   3   4   5   6   7   8 miles

Mountain to Buckabear Pond, the latter being entirely in the Highlands with its typical gray Precambrian gneiss.

Of special interest on this hike is the site of the former Cross Castle (also known as Bearfort House), a large mountain estate built by Richard James Cross about 1907. Cross, a native of England, made a fortune in banking and later erected a fantastic but short-lived mansion. The 365-acre estate featured a three-story castle with views in all directions, hot and cold running water, numerous fireplaces, stables, carriage houses, guest cottages, and a boathouse on Hanks Pond. The foundations and walls of stone—which survived the dismantling of the mansion by the city of Newark when it acquired the property in 1919—were demolished in the late 1980s.

Also of interest is the Clinton Furnace, one of the very few furnaces surviving from the region's iron-making era. The furnace, located just off Clinton Road near its intersection with Schoolhouse Cove Road, is still in fairly good shape. Iron-smelting furnaces were always built near running water, necessary for the waterwheel-driven bellows. As you would expect, a substantial series of waterfalls can be found immediately adjacent to Clinton Furnace. Once the furnace was fired up and loaded with iron, it would burn for months at a time. Its location at the base of a sharp drop facilitated the loading of iron from the top of the furnace via a ramp known as a "charging bridge."

GETTING THERE

The hike can be done as a loop, or cars can be parked at each end and a shuttle arranged to avoid an additional 1.5 miles of road walking. The walk along the road is not at all unpleasant and will only add

about a half hour to your hike. If you choose to do the extra walking, park at Parking Area P9 and walk to P1. If you have two cars, leave one car at P9 and drive another to P1 to begin the hike.

To reach Parking Area P9 from NJ 23, take Clinton Road north for 1.2 miles and turn left on Schoolhouse Cove Road, a gravel road with good views of Clinton Reservoir. After 1 mile, make a right turn onto Paradise Road; you will find the small parking area on the right in 0.1 mile. After parking, walk or drive down Schoolhouse Cove Road the same way you came to Clinton Road. At this intersection, directly in front of you—though it may be obscured by foliage in the summer—are the Clinton Furnace and the falls described earlier. Turn left at the intersection and walk or drive 0.3 mile north on paved Clinton Road to the point where Van Orden Road (gravel) comes in on the right. This is Parking Area P1, and you will begin your hike from here.

A number of instances of vandalism to cars parked in these parking areas have been reported, so be certain not to leave any valuables in your car.

THE HIKE

The hike begins at a gate on the north side of Van Orden Road, just east of Clinton Road. Here, a triple-white blaze marks the start of the Hanks East Trail. Follow this trail, which heads north on a wide woods road. Soon, you'll come to a fork. Bear left onto a blue-blazed connector trail, which leads past some old foundations and crosses the outlet of Hanks Pond. After passing the start of the blue-and-white-blazed Hanks West Trail, the connector trail reaches a junction with the red-and-white-blazed Fire Tower Ridge Trail. Turn right and

VIEW FROM BEARFORT FIRE TOWER

follow the red-and-white blazes, which lead uphill on a grassy woods road to the site of the former Cross Castle.

After exploring the site, continue north on the Fire Tower Ridge Trail. Follow the red-and-white markers, passing the stone water-storage tower that supplied water to the castle. About three-quarters of a mile from the site of the castle, the woods road turns left and makes a steep but brief climb to a rock outcrop studded with cedar and white pine. Here, the woods road ends. The trail bears right and continues on a footpath along the ridge, following a series of interesting outcrops of conglomerate rock. White pine, mountain laurel, and an occasional cedar make this section of trail especially scenic. Continue following the red-and-white blazes over slabs of glaciated conglomerate bedrock, then downhill over a small stream and into

deeper woods. The blue-blazed Newark Connector Trail joins from the right, runs concurrently with the Fire Tower Ridge Trail for about 0.2 mile, then leaves to the left.

As you rise to the broad summit area of Bearfort Mountain, which contains oaks, laurels, and patches of grass, you'll see that the mountaintop is actually a series of parallel, narrow ridges separated by swamps and wet areas. Some of these ridges are well worth exploring. After less than an hour of walking from the Cross Castle site (and about 2.5 miles from the start of the hike), you'll come to a clearing, picnic tables, and the fire tower—a good place for a snack or lunch. Take the time to climb the five flights of steps to the top of the fire tower. You will be rewarded by views of the entire watershed.

When you're ready to continue, head

BEARFORT FIRE TOWER

half mile, when the blue-blazed Newark Connector Trail begins on the left, you should continue ahead on the joint Fire Tower West/Highlands Trail. But at the next junction, bear right, leaving the Fire Tower West Trail, and follow the Highlands Trail, along with the white-blazed Two Brooks Trail (which begins here), as they head downhill, off the mountain.

Soon you will come to a small clearing. Follow the Highlands/Two Brooks Trail through ferns and deep hemlocks and then out to a brook, which is crossed on rocks. If you look around, you may find beaver-gnawed trees in this area. After crossing the brook, the trail turns sharply to the right through tall and dense hemlocks. Continue over rocks and pine needles and then out to another brook with a log bridge. The trail now turns left and heads uphill. It then descends slightly through moss, pine, beech, maple, and especially hemlock, which gets thicker as the trail approaches Mossman's Brook. After a pleasant walk on hemlock needles through a primeval forest along the brook, the trail comes out to Clinton Road at P4. Here, the Two Brooks Trail ends, and you continue on the Highlands Trail.

Turn left onto Clinton Road and head south. In 300 feet, follow the teal-diamond blazes of the Highlands Trail as they turn right onto a woods road. The white-blazed Clinton West Trail begins here, and you will now be following both white and teal-diamond blazes. Another right turn comes up almost immediately as the trail briefly heads north. In a short distance, it swings left and heads steeply uphill. This climb is the longest of the hike. Notice that the rock in this area is different from that on which you have been walking. The rock here is Precambrian gneiss, a much older rock than

south from the tower. In about 50 feet, you'll notice the teal diamond blazes of the Highlands Trail to the right. Turn right (west) and follow this trail, which almost immediately turns left and heads south along the ridge, joined by the yellow-blazed Fire Tower West Trail. At the next fork, bear right to continue on the joint Highlands/Fire Tower West Trails.

You are now heading south through hemlock and laurel and will soon reach a viewpoint near a large glacial erratic. Cedar Pond, a natural glacial lake, is below to the north. Continuing, the trail traverses some beautiful woodland, with large puddingstone rock outcrops framed with white pine. In another the purple sedimentary sandstones and puddingstone conglomerates found on Bearfort Mountain.

When you reach the top of the rise, you will arrive at a junction. The white-blazed Clinton West Trail leaves to the left, but you should proceed straight ahead, continuing to follow the teal-diamond–blazed Highlands Trail. Soon, you'll come to another junction, where you turn left, now following both the Highlands Trail and the yellow-blazed Bearfort Waters–Clinton Trail.

The Bearfort Waters–Clinton Trail used to closely parallel the shore of Buckabear Pond. However, in recent years, beavers have enlarged the dam at the southern end of the pond, resulting in a rising water level and the flooding of sections of the trail along the shore. Volunteers have relocated a 1.5-mile section of the trail so that it now runs high above the pond, eliminating the flooding problem. As the trail approaches the southern end of the pond, it descends gradually until reaches the southern tip of the pond at the beaver dam.

Continue to head south on the yellow-blazed Bearfort Waters–Clinton Trail and the teal-diamond–blazed Highlands Trail, now following a wide woods road (formerly a horse trail) built by the Civilian Conservation Corps (CCC) in the 1930s. Soon you will see Clinton Reservoir, the largest body of water on this hike, on your left. The trail parallels the reservoir for about a mile, then bears right and heads away from the reservoir. Watch for a junction where the Bearfort Waters–Clinton Trail turns left, leaving the woods road and the Highlands Trail. Follow the yellow blazes, which head back toward the reservoir on a footpath.

The trail now hugs the shoreline with good views of water, islands, and hills, and again turns left and downhill where a rocky woods road comes in. In this vicinity, on the right and uphill, you will find a number of plaques set in boulders and rock outcrops commemorating the lives of hikers and trail builders of the past. Still following the shoreline, the trail passes a cove popular with Canada geese, which frequently forage there. Just a short walk ahead you will emerge from the woods at Parking Area P9, where you parked your car.

Note: Shorter explorations of this scenic but vast area are possible. Consider the following options: Park at P9 and walk along the shore of Clinton Reservoir for a mile or two and then turn back. Park at P1 and explore the shoreline of Hanks Pond. For a 4.5-mile loop hike, park at P2 and follow the yellow-blazed Fire Tower West Trail to the fire tower. To return, head south on the red-and-white Fire Tower Ridge Trail to the Cross Castle site, then turn right, following a blue-blazed connector trail that leads to the yellow trail. A left turn here will lead to your car.

16

Wawayanda State Park

TOTAL DISTANCE: 7.5 miles

HIKING TIME: 4 hours

VERTICAL RISE: 530 feet

RATING: Easy to moderate

MAPS: USGS Wawayanda; NY–NJTC North Jersey Trails #116; DEP Wawayanda State Park

TRAILHEAD GPS COORDINATES:
N 41° 11' 17" W 74° 25' 31"

Wawayanda State Park (885 Warwick Turnpike, Hewitt, NJ 07421; 973-853-4462; www.njparksandforests.org), which covers over 35,000 acres of forest and water, is located in Passaic and Sussex Counties, near the New Jersey–New York boundary. The park opened to the public in 1963. According to one source, the name *Wawayanda* is the phonetic rendition of a Lenape word meaning "water on the mountain." Another source claims it is a Munsee word meaning "winding, winding water."

Wawayanda offers a feeling of wilderness, and this hike is delightful in any season. In summer, you are protected from the heat of the sun by the leafy canopy of mature trees and can cool off in the lake after hiking; in fall, the same trees are a riot of color (although squirrels can bombard the unwary with acorns from above); in winter, these trails—gentle and wide—are admirably suited for cross-country skiing when the snow is deep enough. Because of the high elevation of the plateau, snow remains longer in Wawayanda State Park than in other areas. The terrain undulates and winds in a relaxed way, making for very pleasant walking. This hike uses the Double Pond (yellow), Cedar Swamp (blue), Banker (green), Old Coal (red), Lookout (white), Laurel Pond (yellow), and Wingdam (blue) Trails, as well as sections of Cherry Ridge Road. The hike makes a loop, meanders through areas of huge rhododendrons arching overhead, passes under tall hemlocks, and traverses the shores of several lakes.

GETTING THERE

You can reach Wawayanda State Park via Warwick Turnpike, approached from the north on NY 94 and from the south on Clinton Road. The park entrance is

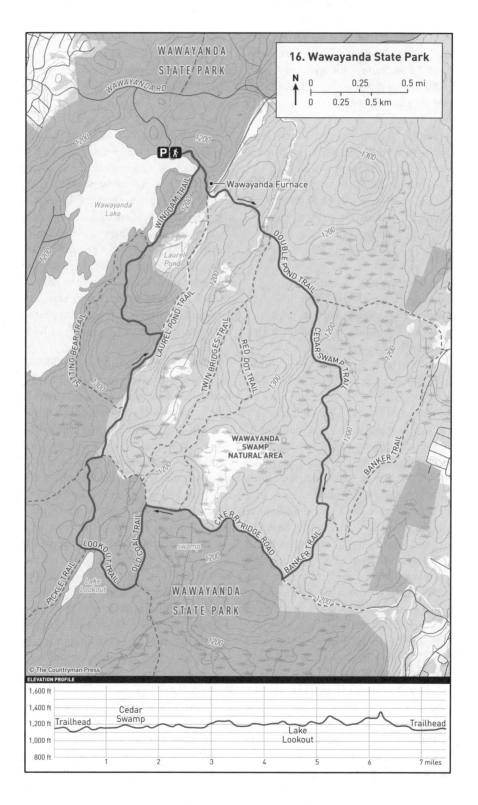

16. Wawayanda State Park

N
0   0.25   0.5 mi
0   0.25   0.5 km

WAWAYANDA
STATE PARK

WAWAYANDA RD

Wawayanda
Lake

Laurel
Pond

Wawayanda Furnace

WINGDAM TRAIL

LAUREL POND TRAIL

SITTING BEAR TRAIL

DOUBLE POND TRAIL

CEDAR SWAMP TRAIL

TWIN BRIDGES TRAIL

RED DOT TRAIL

WAWAYANDA
SWAMP
NATURAL AREA

BANKER TRAIL

CHERRY RIDGE ROAD

BANKER TRAIL

LOOKOUT TRAIL

OLD COAL TRAIL

PICKLE TRAIL

Lake
Lookout

swamp

WAWAYANDA
STATE PARK

© The Countryman Press

ELEVATION PROFILE

1,600 ft
1,400 ft
1,200 ft   Trailhead   Cedar
                          Swamp   Trailhead
1,000 ft   Lake
                                            Lookout
800 ft
          1   2   3   4   5   6   7 miles

on the west side of Warwick Turnpike, about 1.2 miles north of Upper Greenwood Lake. Follow the entrance road for about 2.5 miles to the boating-and-fishing parking area on Wawayanda Lake (there is an entrance fee from Memorial Day weekend to Labor Day). On the way, you may wish to stop at the park office to obtain the park map and other literature. During the summer months, it is advisable to arrive before 10 a.m. to be assured a parking space.

THE HIKE

With Wawayanda Lake on your right, leave the parking lot, walk left to a wide gravel road, and follow it alongside the lake. Wawayanda Lake was once two separate bodies of water called Double Pond. The narrow strip of land that divided the two ponds is still visible on the west side of Barker Island, now in the center of the lake. In winter, when the lake is frozen solid, it is pleasant to walk across to Barker Island and watch the people fishing through the ice. In 1862, the Thomas Iron Company built the stone dam at the northeastern end of the lake (as well as a wingdam), which raised the level of the lake 7.5 feet. On the lake, admire the many yellow pond lilies and white fragrant water lilies. The blue-blazed Wingdam Trail, your return route, leaves to the right within a few minutes, and very soon the remains of the old charcoal furnace come into view.

Pause here and imagine the busy scene of yesteryear, when Wawayanda was the center of the New Jersey iron industry. The stone charcoal blast furnace was built by Oliver Ames and his three sons, William, Oakes, and Oliver Jr. William was in charge. His initials W. L. A. and the date 1846 are still visible on a lintel in the main arch.

Iron ore from local mines was smelted here continuously from 1847 to 1857, when cheap coal became available in Pennsylvania, making it more economical to transport the ore for smelting to those hotter and more efficient furnaces. In an average day, the Wawayanda furnace produced 7 tons of iron, which was poured off twice daily, at noon and at midnight. Wawayanda iron was of such superior quality that it was used to manufacture railroad wheels. During the Civil War, the Ames factories also filled government orders for shovels and swords. Nothing remains of the small village that was established in the vicinity to house the workers. The furnace building is currently supported by metal framing and protected from vandals by fencing.

When you have absorbed enough history, walk toward the two portable toilets, and turn left in front of them, crossing a small wooden bridge across a stream and walking toward a sign marking the start of the yellow-blazed Double Pond Trail. The trail passes through group campsites, and for a short distance it is rocky and climbs slightly. The trail then descends to cross a wetland on a bridge, with a boardwalk along the right side. Just beyond, the Red Dot Trail begins to the right, but you should continue ahead on the Double Pond Trail, which goes through the Wawayanda Swamp Natural Area, a fascinating and ecologically significant tract. The vegetation changes to a dense mix of hemlock, mountain laurel, and rhododendron, with rhododendron soon becoming the dominant species.

About a mile from the furnace, you'll reach a junction with the blue-blazed Cedar Swamp Trail, which begins on the right. Turn right and follow the Cedar Swamp Trail—one of the highlights of

WETLAND ALONG THE DOUBLE POND TRAIL

Wawayanda State Park. Huge rhododendrons arch high overhead, and hemlocks soar above these shrubs. Look for a stand of inland Atlantic white cedar trees growing in this very wet environment, but be aware that parts of the trail may be quite wet, especially after heavy rains. At one point, you'll cross a 750-foot-long boardwalk. In about a half mile, watch on the left for an old rusted car in a clearing. A short distance beyond, follow the footpath as it makes a sharp left turn.

In about a mile and a half, the Cedar Swamp Trail ends at a junction with the green-blazed Banker Trail. Turn right and follow this old road for about 0.4 mile until it ends at Cherry Ridge Road, a wide dirt-and-gravel road. Turn right onto Cherry Ridge Road,

soon passing a locked gate. The road descends through beautiful rhododendron thickets to cross a stream, ascends to pass a pond on the left, then descends to cross another stream on a wooden bridge. Although you are walking along a dirt road, the trees form a canopy overhead, and the hiking is very pleasant.

After about a mile of hiking along the road, you'll notice a triple blaze on a tree on the left, which marks the start of the Red Dot Trail. Continue ahead on Cherry Ridge Road for another few minutes until you reach a T-intersection (ignore the woods road that leaves to the left about 200 feet beyond the intersection with the Red Dot Trail). At the T-intersection, turn left onto the red-blazed Old Coal Trail, another woods road. In about 0.4 mile, you'll arrive

WAWAYANDA FURNACE

trail bears right and begins to descend gradually through maples, with an understory of ferns. After turning left, the trail climbs gently, levels off, then descends a little to end at Cherry Ridge Road. Turn right onto Cherry Ridge Road, then (in about 500 feet) turn left onto the yellow-blazed Laurel Pond Trail, which follows a woods road. It descends gradually through rhododendron thickets, then levels off, passing the orange-blazed Sitting Bear Trail on the left. The Laurel Pond Trail now begins to climb gently, passing interesting rock outcrops on the left. In three-quarters of a mile, at the crest of the rise, you'll reach an intersection with the blue-blazed Wingdam Trail, which begins on the left. Take this trail, which climbs at first, but soon descends and then levels off. Continue ahead on the Wingdam Trail until you reach the wingdam over the outlet of Wawayanda Lake. The water comes over this dam in a wide, swift fall and rushes on its way to feed Laurel Pond, out of sight on the left. Wildflowers abound in this lush area at most times of the year. Benches have been placed here, and you might want to take a break at this scenic location.

Continue ahead on the Wingdam Trail through a mature hardwood forest and cross the main dam at the northeastern end of the lake. Walk through the barrier of large boulders, turn left, and retrace your steps back to the parking lot, perhaps taking the time to stop at the beach and swim in the cool waters of Wawayanda Lake.

at a Y-intersection. Bear right onto the white-blazed Lookout Trail and follow this pleasant grassy woods road, which soon reaches the outlet of Lake Lookout, with its beaver dam. The peaceful and seldom-visited lake is an attractive place to take a break. After crossing the dam, the green-blazed Pickle Trail begins on the left, but you should continue ahead, following the white blazes back into the woods.

The trail now narrows to a footpath and climbs to the top of a rise. Here, the

Appalachian Trail— Stairway to Heaven

TOTAL DISTANCE: 2.8 miles

HIKING TIME: 2.5 hours

VERTICAL RISE: 1,000 feet

RATING: Moderately strenuous

MAPS: USGS Wawayanda; NY–NJTC North Jersey Trails #116; NY/NJ Appalachian Trail Guide Map #3; DEP Appalachian Trail and Wawayanda State Park maps

TRAILHEAD GPS COORDINATES: N 41° 13′ 09″ W 74° 27′ 18″

The Appalachian Trail (AT) is our nation's first designated National Scenic Trail. It extends over 2,190 miles from Springer Mountain in Georgia to Mount Katahdin in Maine. The AT is a unique partnership among 14 states, the National Park Service, the United States Forest Service, and a network of hiking clubs coordinated by the Appalachian Trail Conservancy (P.O. Box 807, Harpers Ferry, WV 25425; 304-535-6331; www.appalachiantrail.org). Volunteers of the New York–New Jersey Trail Conference manage and maintain the 72 miles of the AT in New Jersey.

Entering from Pennsylvania at the Delaware Water Gap, the trail follows the crest of the Kittatinnies to High Point State Park, where it turns east along the New York–New Jersey border. After crossing Wawayanda State Park and passing through Abram S. Hewitt State Forest, the trail turns north into New York State just west of Greenwood Lake.

This hike follows an AT segment at the western edge of the 35,000-acre Wawayanda State Park built mostly by volunteers, with assistance from ATC trail crews, local Boy Scouts, New Jersey correctional inmates, and Wawayanda park personnel, who completed their huge 3-year cooperative effort in May 1991. You are about to see, appreciate, and enjoy the results of everyone's labors.

This relocation is a fine example of the concern trail builders now show for the environment. The old trail (about a half mile south) had changed little since it was first built in 1937. It shot straight up Wawayanda Mountain in just over a half mile. Without switchbacks, the climb was an exhausting boulder-hop and rock scramble up an ugly, erosion-scarred ditch. The new route, however,

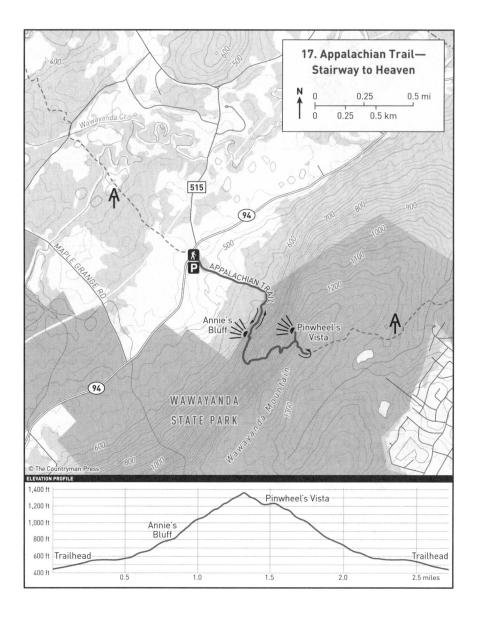

incorporates switchbacks and loops gracefully up the 900-foot elevation gain. Water bars protect the trail, and some 300 stone steps enable hikers to negotiate the steepest sections. Near the top of the climb is the impressive 60-step "Stairway to Heaven."

If you take this hike in the summer, many of the people you see along the trail carrying large packs are AT through-hikers, who are trying to complete the entire trail in one season. They are usually proceeding at a steady pace as they try to hike many miles, but more often than not they will stop for a short chat and tell you about their adventure.

Wawayanda is, according to one source, a Munsee word that translates to "winding, winding water," used by the Native Americans to refer to the creeks and meadows in the area. Another source asserts that Wawayanda is a phonetic translation of the Lenape term for "water on the mountain." In either case, the name was applied to the mountain before the Revolutionary War and given to the nearby lake in 1846.

GETTING THERE

You can access the trail from an AT parking area on NJ 94, about 2.4 miles north of Vernon (0.7 mile north of the Maple Grange Road junction) and 2 miles south of the New York–New Jersey border. The parking area is on the east side of the road just south of the Amity/Pine Island directional sign and the Heaven Hill Farm Stand. There is room for about eight cars.

THE HIKE

Your hike starts on the same side of the road as the parking area. Proceed up a small embankment on stone-and-log steps and continue on a wide footpath, passing a kiosk on the right. After crossing under power lines, the trail reenters the woods, but it soon emerges onto a successional field, with many young cedar trees. Looming ahead is the imposing Wawayanda Mountain, which you will soon climb. The trail is marked with the 2-inch-by-6-inch white paint blazes of the Appalachian Trail (where the trail crosses open fields, the blazes are on wooden posts).

VIEW FROM PINWHEEL'S VISTA

Soon, the trail crosses an old stone wall and re-enters the woods. It curves to the right and begins to run along the base of the mountain, weaving its way through an area of jumbled boulders that have tumbled down from the mountain. The trail then bears left and begins its 900-foot ascent of Wawayanda Mountain.

The climb basically follows two long switchbacks—first to the right, then to the left. Although, for the most part, the grade is moderate, the treadway is quite rocky, and you'll want to exercise caution with each step you take. After climbing about 250 vertical feet in 0.3 mile, you'll reach a rock outcrop on the right, with a steep drop. Known as Annie's Bluff, this spot affords a view of the Heaven Hill Farm below and Pochuck Mountain in the background. A short distance beyond, the trail switches back to the left.

You'll know that you're getting near the top when the trail turns left, runs along a ledge on the side of the mountain for a short distance, then turns right and steeply climbs several sets of rock steps (these steps—nicknamed "Stairway to Heaven"—were rehabilitated by the Trail Conference's West Jersey Trail Crew between 2016 and 2019). Not far beyond the top of the rock steps, you'll come to a huge cairn (probably larger than any other cairn you've ever seen). If you continue straight ahead, a blue-blazed trail leads to Pinwheel's Vista—the primary destination of the hike.

But first, you'll want to continue to the highest point on Wawayanda Mountain. Turn right at the cairn and continue uphill on a moderate grade. In about 5 minutes, you'll reach the top, marked by a mailbox attached to a tree on the right side of the trail. Inside the mailbox you should find a trail register, and you'll want to sign your name (as well as to read the comments of others who have reached this spot).

Now retrace your steps downhill to the cairn, turn right, and follow the short blue-blazed trail to a rock outcrop known as "Pinwheel's Vista." "Pinwheel" was the nickname of Paul DeCoste, who helped build this section of trail. Vernon Valley is directly below, with Pochuck Mountain in the background and the Kittatinnies beyond. On a clear day, you can also see the Shawangunks and Catskills in the distance to the north. You'll want to rest here and enjoy the views.

When you're ready to continue, return to the AT and resume your descent. Retrace your steps on the AT all the way back to the parking area where you left your car.

18

Pyramid Mountain

TOTAL DISTANCE: 3 miles

HIKING TIME: 2.5 hours

VERTICAL RISE: 500 feet

RATING: Easy to moderate

MAPS: USGS Boonton; NY–NJTC Jersey Highlands Trails (Central North Region) #125; Morris County Park Commission Pyramid Mountain Natural Historic Area map

TRAILHEAD GPS COORDINATES:
N 40° 56' 49" W 74° 23' 16.5"

At 934 feet in elevation, Pyramid Mountain is not the highest summit ridge in northern Morris County, but it has much to offer the hiker. It is crossed by foot trails that are steep and rugged in places, has several overlooks, and contains a mysterious glacial erratic that may be part of an ancient Native American calendar site. To the west and below the mountain ridge is Stony Brook and its wetland. Bear Rock, a gigantic granite monolith that towers over the brook and swamp, is found here. The land containing these wonders has been preserved, largely due to the work of an active grassroots committee, the Friends of Pyramid Mountain, together with the New Jersey Conservation Foundation, the Morris County Park Commission, the Mennen Corporation, and state agencies. Thanks to these organizations and many dedicated individuals, particularly Lucy Meyer, the next generation of New Jersey hikers will find this area as it is today—which is to say, not developed with private homes.

Pyramid Mountain Natural Historic Area is a hiker's paradise. Although the area is heavily used at times, hikers can choose from many trails. There are actually two trail systems: the Pyramid Mountain section, the focus of the hike described below, and the Turkey Mountain section on the east side of County Route 511. A longer loop hike around the Butler Reservoir is also possible (see NY–NJTC Jersey Highlands Trails Map #125).

This hike takes in the two most famous rock formations in the area, Bear Rock and Tripod Rock, as well as two vistas, Lucy's Overlook and the summit of Pyramid Mountain. It begins at the visitor center (973-334-3130), open daily from 9:00 a.m. to 4:30 p.m., which

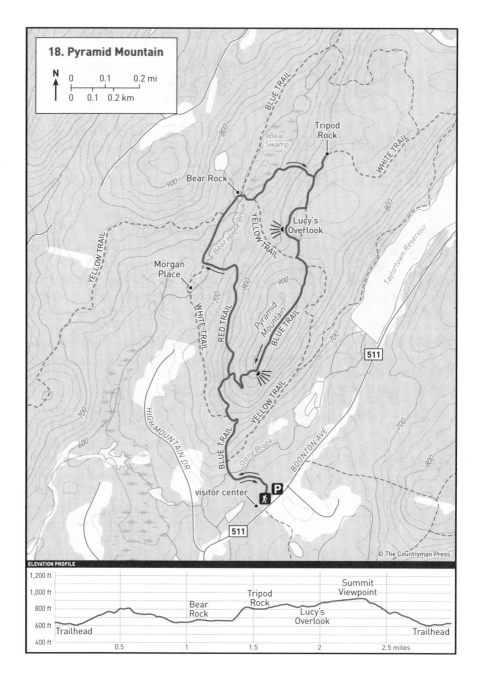

18. Pyramid Mountain

N

| 0 | 0.1 | 0.2 mi |

| 0 | 0.1 | 0.2 km |

BLUE TRAIL

Tripod
Rock

Bear
Swamp

WHITE TRAIL

Bear Rock

YELLOW TRAIL

Lucy's
Overlook

Bear House Brook

YELLOW TRAIL

900

Taylortown Reservoir

Morgan
Place

WHITE TRAIL

RED TRAIL

800

900

Pyramid
Mountain

BLUE TRAIL

700

700

511

700

HIGH MOUNTAIN DR

YELLOW TRAIL

600

BLUE TRAIL

Stony Brook

BOONTON AVE.

700

800

visitor center

P

511

© The Countryman Press

ELEVATION PROFILE

1,200 ft					Summit Viewpoint	
1,000 ft				Tripod Rock		
800 ft		Bear Rock			Lucy's Overlook	
600 ft	Trailhead					Trailhead
400 ft	0.5	1	1.5	2	2.5 miles	

contains displays and information about the area and its natural history.

How the name *Pyramid* came to be associated with the mountain is a fairly recent story. The first edition of the *New York Walk Book* (1923) directed hikers toward a "pyramidal shaped mountain." Indeed, the mountain has a triangular shape when viewed (without foliage) from near the present-day visitor center. Later editions of the book simply referred to it as "Pyramid Mountain," and the name stuck. In the 1990s, a conflict erupted over the proper name for the peak; some local residents contended that its official name should be High Mountain. The matter was handed over to the United States Geological Survey for a decision, and Pyramid Mountain became the official name.

GETTING THERE

If you are coming from the north, take I-287 South to Exit 47 (Montville/Lincoln Park) and turn left at the bottom of the ramp onto Main Road (US 202). In 0.7 mile, just before reaching a fire station, turn right onto Taylortown Road and continue for 1.8 miles to Boonton Avenue (County Route 511). Turn right and continue for 0.7 mile to the entrance to the Pyramid Mountain Natural Historic Area, on the left, opposite Mars Park.

If coming from the south, take I-287 North to Exit 44 (Main Street, Boonton) and bear right onto Lathrop Avenue. Turn right at the stop sign onto Main Street (County Route 511), proceed along Main Street for 0.3 mile, then turn right onto Boonton Avenue. Continue on Boonton Avenue, still designated County Route 511, for 3.3 miles to the parking area for the Pyramid Mountain Natural Historic Area, on the left (the parking area is opposite Mars Park, about 0.7 mile north of the intersection of Route 511 and Taylortown Road).

THE HIKE

From the southern end of the parking area, follow the access trail, which starts just north of a large bulletin board and immediately passes a memorial plaque for Stephen Klein Jr. In 150 feet, you'll reach a junction with the Blue Trail.

TRIPOD ROCK

Continue ahead on the Blue Trail, which soon crosses Stony Brook on a wooden footbridge. Just beyond, the Yellow Trail begins on the right, but you should continue ahead on the Blue Trail, which soon begins a short but steep climb to the shoulder of Pyramid Mountain. The climb continues under a high-voltage tower. A short distance ahead, a large cairn on the left marks the start of the White Trail, but you should bear right and continue to follow the blue blazes. When you reach the next junction (also marked by a large cairn), turn left and continue on the Red Trail.

The Red Trail heads through a rocky area, with many large boulders on the slope to the right, then makes a short, steep descent. The trail levels off, continues on a rocky footpath along the side of hill, then descends gradually and crosses footbridges over two branches of Bear House Brook to reach a junction with the White Trail. Turn right at this junction and follow the white blazes along an old road, with Bear House Brook on the right.

In a quarter mile, the Yellow Trail joins from the left, and a short distance beyond, you'll reach the massive Bear Rock. Standing alone in the woods at the edge of a large swamp, Bear Rock has been used as a boundary marker for at least 200 years. Even today, it marks the borders of Kinnelon and Montville boroughs. Although it is difficult and even dangerous to scale, there are some very old surveying markers found near its highest points. Bear Rock is one of the largest glacial erratics in New Jersey,

BEAR ROCK

made up of a type of light-colored granite called alaskite. Alaskite does not occur at Pyramid Mountain and was probably transported by the glacier from outcrops southeast of Greenwood Lake. After the encasing glacial ice melted, Bear Rock split along a fracture, and the top third of the boulder toppled over. This fragment, now lying on its side, can be visually refitted, with a little imagination, back onto the side of the main boulder. The original boulder weighed approximately 600 tons; the main piece today weighs about 450 tons. About 500 feet to the northwest is a waterfall that cascades over bare rock during the spring and after heavy rains.

From Bear Rock, turn right, now following white, blue, and yellow blazes, cross a wooden footbridge over the brook, and continue on a footpath lined with many dwarf ginseng plants, pepperbush, and spicebush. Soon you'll come to a fork, where the Yellow Trail leaves to the right. Bear left, following the sign for "Tripod Rock," and continue along a level footpath, parallel to the stream, marked with blue and white blazes. Soon you'll begin a steep, rocky climb up to the ridge of Pyramid Mountain on a trail lined with mountain laurel. You'll gain only about 150 feet in elevation, but this is the steepest climb of the hike. Just beyond the crest of the ridge, the trail arrives at a T-junction. Turn left here, following the white blazes, and in about 500 feet you'll reach Tripod Rock.

Perhaps the most massive perched boulder of its kind in the entire Northeast, Tripod Rock is the focal point of what may be an ancient calendar site. The sheer size and bizarre appearance of it—a 160-ton boulder standing on three medicine-ball-sized rocks—staggers the imagination. If it is simply a chance product of the last Ice Age, as most geologists believe, then it is unique. Others suggest that it was modified by humans. Nearby are two smaller stones partially perched on exposed bedrock. An observer seated on a lip protruding from a piece of bedrock 4 feet high will see, through the gap between these two stones, the summer solstice sunset. The alignment constitutes a simple solar observatory. Whether or not it was used by the early inhabitants of the area is an open question.

From Tripod Rock, retrace your steps to the junction and continue heading south along the ridge, now following the Blue Trail. Soon, you'll notice a blue-and-white-blazed side trail on the right. Follow this trail, which leads in a short distance to Lucy's Overlook, named for Lucy Meyer, who led the long crusade to save this beautiful area from development. The overlook offers views to the south and west over Stony Brook Mountain from rock outcrops. Continue ahead on the blue-and-white-blazed side trail until it ends at the Blue Trail, then turn right (south), now once again following blue blazes. Soon, the Yellow Trail joins from the right and, in a short distance, leaves to the left.

The Blue Trail gradually climbs to the highest elevation on the Pyramid Mountain ridge (934 feet). Here, you should bear left and head to an east-facing overlook from open rocks, with the New York City skyline visible on the horizon on a clear day.

After taking in the view, return to the Blue Trail and follow it as it gradually descends the southwest face of the mountain on switchbacks. Continue ahead past the junctions with the Red, White, and Yellow Trails, and follow the blue blazes back to the parking area where the hike began.

19

Mount Hope Historical Park

TOTAL DISTANCE: 2.7 miles

HIKING TIME: 2 hours

VERTICAL RISE: 350 feet

RATING: Easy

MAPS: USGS Dover; Morris County Park Commission Mount Hope Historical Park map

TRAILHEAD GPS COORDINATES:
N 40° 55' 17" W 74° 33' 11"

Most of the hikes in this book lead you through forests to natural areas such as ponds, lakes, mountaintops, rock formations, interesting botanical areas, and the ocean itself. On this hike you tour a natural area of a different sort—a human-modified area. What this area looked like 100 years ago is hard to imagine, but whatever was going on there left a powerful imprint. There is nothing quite like the landscape you will traverse on this hike. Some may find it disturbing, while others may find it utterly fascinating. Yet there is a wildness to the park that stands in sharp contrast with its obvious human disturbance.

Iron mining in the Dover area of New Jersey has a long history, and towns like Mine Hill and Mount Hope were built around this economic activity. The oldest mines in the region date back to 1710. The Dickerson Mine in Mine Hill is the oldest iron mine in the United States. The Mount Hope Mine, just to the north of this hike, was the largest iron ore producer in New Jersey, with 6 million tons having been produced since it was first opened. Mount Hope Historical Park itself is a historic site that preserves the remains of one of the more active mining and processing sites in the region. It is composed of three distinct groups of mines: the Allen Mine, the Richard Mine, and the Teabo Mine. Three veins of high-grade magnetite iron ore that ran the length of the park were mined here over the course of about 150 years. Approximately 5.7 million tons of ore were removed from these mines. During the early 20th century, the mines were consolidated into one holding, but in 1959 operations ceased and the property was abandoned. This very recent ending of mining in the park will give you much to think about—especially with regard to nature's power to heal itself.

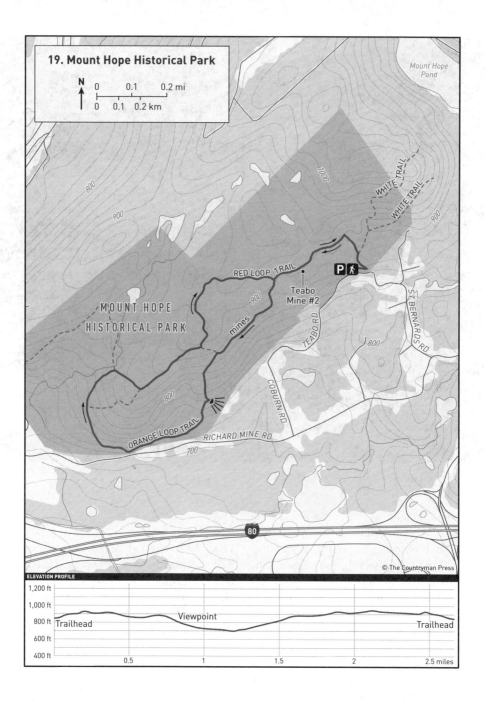

The Mount Hope Historical Park mines are located in the New Jersey Highlands province, a belt of mostly Precambrian (roughly 500 million to 1 billion years old) gneisses that have limited deposits of iron and zinc ore. Veins of iron ore vary from a few inches to over 50 feet in thickness and can be a mile or more wide. These belts follow the fold patterns of the gneiss and trend,

IRON BARS AND ROCK WALLS FROM FORMER MINING ACTIVITY

as do the Highlands, in a northeast-to-southwest direction. Mining operations would follow a vein as far as was possible as it dipped into the ground. The landscapes at Mount Hope Historical Park are the remnants of collapsed mine shafts that look like huge craters today.

The hike described below is not particularly strenuous, but some special factors should be taken into consideration. First, the mine pits present something of a hazard. Tailings from the mines are not always stable, and hiking with small children will require that you keep them safe. Much of the hike is quite rocky, and sturdy boots are recommended.

GETTING THERE

From I-80, take Exit 35 (eastbound) or Exit 35A (westbound) and proceed north on Mount Hope Avenue, passing the Fox Hills condos. In 0.5 mile, turn left onto Richard Mine Road. Signs will direct you through winding roads in a residential area—drive carefully. Follow Richard Mine Road for 0.7 mile and turn right onto Coburn Road. The park entrance is 0.7 mile ahead on the left. The parking area for Mount Hope Historical Park is located just below the power lines that mark the southern boundary of the park.

THE HIKE

The trailhead is at the east end of the parking area near a kiosk. A historic plaque for Richard Mine and a picnic table can be found here, too. Follow an unmarked trail up a switchback to a trail junction under the power lines. It is here that the trail system of the park actually begins. To the right is the White Trail, which leads to the northernmost mines. For this hike, we turn left onto the Red Loop Trail and enter the woods.

The trail proceeds through a second-growth forest and soon turns left at a junction. By now you will notice that the surroundings are not like most Highlands woods. All around you are piles of rocks, pits, and small rock walls—signs of human activity that has shaped the landscape. After making this left turn, the trail becomes rockier, and soon you will begin to notice that the pits on your left are getting progressively deeper.

After crossing a seasonal stream, the mine pits of Teabo Mine #2 will be on your left. Just beyond, you'll come to a junction. Bear left and continue following the red-blazed trail around a huge pit (a veritable crater) on your left and then past a series of pits on your right. At the next junction, continue straight ahead, leaving the Red Loop Trail (which goes off to the right) and begin following the Orange Loop Trail, which heads downhill. Just before the trail crosses under the power lines, look for unmarked paths that lead up to an overlook just beyond the power lines. The vista includes the Rockaway Town Square Mall, with I-80 in the foreground. You will also find two old, rusted water tanks and the remains of a small reservoir.

Return to the main trail and continue following the Orange Loop Trail as it crosses the power line cut, turns right, then immediately turns left into the woods again. Now following a cinder path, the trail parallels the power line cut, passes under it again, and swings very close to paved Richard Mine Road, which it follows for a short distance before it swings to the right. Next, watch for another junction—keep right here on a gravel road that begins to climb. At the next junction, which faces a vernal pond and lies in a wet area, turn right. After another climb the trail enters a dry oak forest and begins to level off. Just past a mine pit on your left, you will arrive at another junction with the Red Loop Trail. Turn left here.

The trail now climbs to the highest point in the hike and then swings gradually around to the east. The land is very dry here, and there are no mines. Just after passing two small boulders on your left, you will reach the junction you came to earlier, where the Red Loop Trail splits. At this junction, make a left. Walk past the pits, keep right at the junction, and reach the power lines. From here, follow the path downhill to the parking area, where the hike began.

20

Mahlon Dickerson Reservation

TOTAL DISTANCE: 4.9 miles	

HIKING TIME: 3 hours

VERTICAL RISE: 400 feet

RATING: Easy to moderate

MAPS: USGS Franklin; NY–NJTC Jersey Highlands Trails (Central North Region) #126; Morris County Park Commission Mahlon Dickerson Reservation map

TRAILHEAD GPS COORDINATES:
N 41° 00' 45" W 74° 33' 52"

The Morris County Park Commission (300 Mendham Road, Morris Township, NJ 07960; 973-326-7600, www.morris parks.net), steward of this 3,500-acre reservation, believes that only 10 percent of its parkland should be developed for intensive recreation (picnic sites, ball fields, and playgrounds), while most of it should be left in its natural state. As a result, hikers in Morris County have a number of excellent nearby parks to enjoy. Mahlon Dickerson Reservation, the largest county park, contains tent sites, several Adirondack-type shelters, and trailer camping areas. There is also a ball field, an extensive network of multiuse trails, a picnic area, and Saffin Pond.

The reservation was named for one of Morris County's great achievers, Mahlon Dickerson (1770–1853). Dickerson, who lived near Dover, lived a model life of political service. He never married but was successful in nearly everything he tried. He mastered several languages and attained distinction as a botanist. He owned and operated the Succasunna iron mines, some of the largest in the county. He was a general in the military, served in the state legislature, and was governor of New Jersey for a short period. He served as a United States senator between 1817 and 1833 and, during the presidencies of Andrew Jackson and Martin Van Buren, served as secretary of the navy. He was said to have been popular with everyone and very consistent in his political faith.

Many of the marked hiking trails in the reservation are old logging roads and fire lanes. Some are covered with gravel. These woods roads are well suited for cross-country skiing, and because the average elevation in the park is 1,200 feet, snow remains on the ground longer than in many other

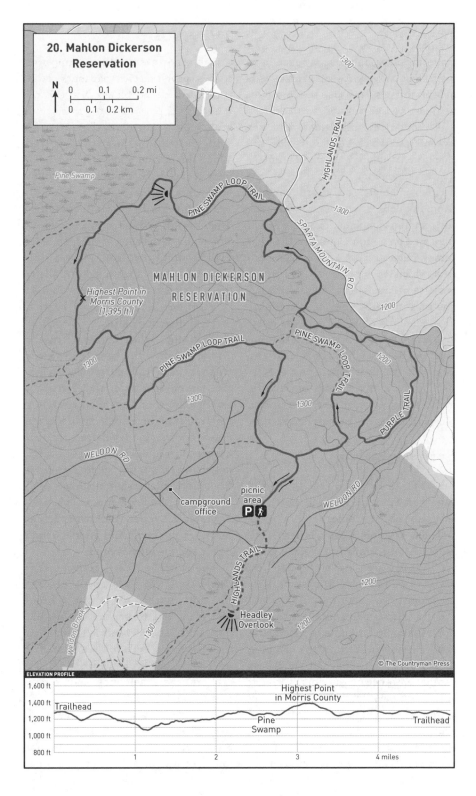

20. Mahlon Dickerson
Reservation

N

0   0.1   0.2 mi

0   0.1   0.2 km

Pine Swamp

PINE SWAMP LOOP TRAIL

HIGHLANDS TRAIL

1300

1300

SPARTA MOUNTAIN RD

MAHLON DICKERSON
RESERVATION

1200

Highest Point in
Morris County
(1,395 ft.)

1300

PINE SWAMP LOOP TRAIL

PINE SWAMP LOOP TRAIL

1200

1200

PURPLE TRAIL

1300

1300

WELDON RD

WELDON RD

picnic
area

campground
office

P

HIGHLANDS TRAIL

1200

Weldon Brook

1300

Headley
Overlook

1200

1200

© The Countryman Press

ELEVATION PROFILE

1,600 ft

Highest Point
in Morris County

1,400 ft Trailhead

1,200 ft

Pine
Swamp

Trailhead

1,000 ft

800 ft

1   2   3   4 miles

areas in northern New Jersey. Many of the marked trails are open to horses and mountain bikes, and you may encounter them along the way. A section of the 150-mile Highlands Trail (see the Introduction) also passes through the park.

Although this hike does not offer sweeping views of the countryside, the change in woodland environments more than makes up for it. Along the route are deciduous forests, rocky scrub growth, damp hemlock groves, laurel thickets, and remote swampland. The reservation is located on a high plateau in the New Jersey Highlands Province. The bedrock, which is very close to the surface because of glaciation, is Precambrian gneiss, a granitic rock that contains large amounts of iron. There are a few long-abandoned iron mines in the reservation. Because the park is large and located in the most remote part of Morris County, many species of wildlife, including red-tailed hawks, deer, and an occasional bear, make their homes here.

GETTING THERE

Take I-80 to Exit 34B (NJ 15 North/Jefferson/Sparta). Proceed north on NJ 15 for about 5 miles, and take the exit for Weldon Road (Milton/Oak Ridge). After 1.2 miles on Weldon Road, you'll pass a sign indicating that you have entered Mahlon Dickerson Reservation. In another 1.5 miles, you'll pass the entrance to Saffin Pond on the right. Continue for 1 mile beyond Saffin Pond, passing an entrance to a camping area on the left. Just beyond, you'll pass another entrance on the right. Turn left at the next park entrance—this one, an entrance to a picnic area on the left—and continue ahead to the parking area. (The entrance to the picnic area is 4 miles along Weldon Road from Route 15.)

THE HIKE

From the north end of the parking area, follow a paved service road marked with the teal-diamond blazes of the Highlands Trail, passing through a picnic area. Soon, a sign marks the start of the white-blazed Pine Swamp Loop Trail. When the paving ends, proceed ahead on a gravel road, continuing to follow both white and teal blazes.

In 0.2 mile, you'll reach a T-intersection with a sign and a kiosk, which marks the start of the loop of the Pine Swamp Loop Trail. Make a right turn at this junction; walk downhill and cross a small brook. At the next junction, bear left, continuing to follow the white and teal-diamond blazes.

At the top of the climb, you'll reach a Y-intersection with a bench and a kiosk. On the right, a triple purple blaze marks the start of the Purple Trail. Turn right, leaving the road, and follow the Purple Trail into the woods on a footpath. After traversing a level area, the trail descends gradually and curves to the left, joining a woods road that comes in from the right. In a short distance, you'll reach a limited viewpoint (partially obscured by vegetation) over the Jefferson High School and Middle School below and the hills beyond.

The Purple Trail continues to descend. At the base of the descent, the trail reaches a cascading brook and turns left to parallel it, heading upstream. The trail bears left, away from the brook, descends to the brook in an area where the brook widens into several branches, then once again climbs away from the brook.

The Purple Trail ends at a wide woods road—the route of the white-blazed Pine Swamp Loop Trail. Turn right and follow the trail downhill to cross a brook

PINE SWAMP

(the same brook that the Purple Trail parallels) on a wooden footbridge. The trail now climbs gently and bears left at a fork, continuing through dense thickets of mountain laurel. Soon, it bears right and continues on a footpath, which approaches Sparta Mountain Road.

At the next intersection, with Sparta Mountain Road just to the right, the Highlands Trail turns right, but you should turn left to continue on the white-blazed Pine Swamp Loop Trail. The trail climbs a little, levels off, and gradually descends.

Soon, you'll observe hemlock and mountain laurel along the trail. You're now entering the Pine Swamp, after which the trail is named. Just ahead, you'll notice a short unmarked side trail on the left. Follow this trail to a rock ledge overlooking the Pine Swamp below. This rocky spot is a pleasant place to stop for a rest or to have a snack or lunch. Below you is not a typical swamp of grasses and water, but a pine swamp with tall spruce, hemlock, rhododendron, and laurel.

Continue along on the trail, which now heads downhill to the level of the swamp, and get a closer look at this fascinating area. About 0.2 mile ahead, the trail—a dry woods road—comes closest to the swamp itself. Off to your right you can see how wet the area is and how huge boulders protrude from the ground, providing drier areas in their cracks for plants incapable of growing in water or very wet soil.

You are now in one of the most remote areas of the reservation. On your right, the swamp extends for about half a mile into Sussex County. It is virtually inaccessible, and no paths cross it. You get a feeling of wilderness here, broken only by the calls of birds or an occasional aircraft. In fact, some years ago, a small private plane crashed in the swamp one May. It wasn't until that November that the wreckage and the bodies were found.

The trail, which follows a high area

LARGE BOULDERS ALONG THE PINE SWAMP LOOP TRAIL

between two parts of the swamp, continues under tall hemlocks, crosses a small brook, and then begins a climb, leaving the swamp for good. You'll pass a junction with an orange-blazed trail on the right. Continue climbing gradually on the white-blazed trail to the flat, rounded summit of an unnamed hill that, at 1,395 feet, is the highest point in Morris County. The trail passes just to the northeast of the height of land, but unfortunately there are no views except through the trees during winter. Just beyond, at a curve to the left, a black-dot-on-blue-blazed trail begins on the right, but you should bear left to follow the white-blazed Pine Swamp Loop Trail.

The Pine Swamp Loop Trail continues to descend. In half a mile, after a slight climb, you'll reach a junction. Turn left here, then left again in another 75 feet (where a blue-blazed trail on the right leads to the trailer area). Along the next section of the trail, there are a number of interesting large boulders on both sides.

In another half mile, three pink blazes mark the start of the Pink Trail, which proceeds ahead on the woods road, but you should turn right onto a footpath, continuing to follow the white blazes. When the footpath ends, the trail turns right onto a woods road, then in 100 feet turns left onto another road (following the sign to the "picnic area"). At the next T-intersection, you turn left again and soon reach the start of the loop of the Pine Swamp Loop Trail (marked by a sign). Turn right (again following the sign to the "picnic area"), and follow the road back to the parking area where the hike began.

If you still have energy and would like to take in a vista, the Headley Overlook is only a short distance away. Follow the teal-diamond blazes of the Highlands Trail as they leave the parking area behind the kiosk, cross Weldon Road and continue to the overlook. The rocky overlook offers a view to the south and west that includes an arm of Lake Hopatcong.

Jenny Jump State Forest

TOTAL DISTANCE: 5 miles

HIKING TIME: 3.5 hours

VERTICAL RISE: 950 feet

RATING: Moderate

MAPS: USGS Blairstown; DEP Jenny Jump State Forest map

TRAILHEAD GPS COORDINATES: N 40° 54' 42" W 74° 55' 17"

Jenny Jump State Forest was named for a young colonial girl. As the tale goes, Jenny was out picking berries with her father. Some hostile Native Americans came across the pair, and her father yelled out for her to jump from the cliff—if only to save her chastity. Although Jenny was successful at keeping herself pure, the result was her death . . . or so the tale goes.

In addition to about 12 miles of hiking trails, this state forest has a number of campsites that may be rented by the public. There are also eight shelters (which are actually enclosed cabins) for rent. Each shelter has four bunks and a wood-burning stove, with restrooms located nearby. For more information, contact Jenny Jump State Forest, P.O. Box 150, Hope, NJ 07844; 908-459-4366; www.njparksandforests.org.

GETTING THERE

To reach Jenny Jump from Exit 12 of I-80, turn left at the bottom of the ramp (turn right if coming from the west) onto County Route 521 and drive 1.1 miles into the village of Hope. At the blinking light, bear left onto County Route 519 (Johnsonburg Road). In another mile, turn right onto Shiloh Road (this and other intersections are marked with small Jenny Jump State Forest directional signs). In 1.1 miles, turn right onto State Park Road and proceed to the park entrance, 1 mile away on the left. After entering the park, stop at the park office for a free map, then drive uphill and park in a small parking area opposite a restroom building.

THE HIKE

You'll begin your hike on the red-blazed Swamp Trail, which is co-aligned with

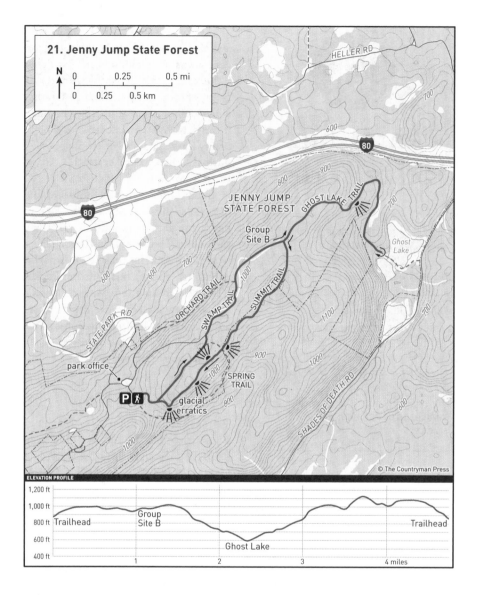

21. Jenny Jump State Forest

ELEVATION PROFILE

the yellow-blazed Summit Trail for the first few minutes. A sign at the end of the parking area marks the start of these trails, which head uphill on a woods road and bear right. After passing Campsite #9, the trails bear left. Soon afterward, you'll reach a junction, marked by a signpost, where the two trails split. Bear left to continue on the red-blazed Swamp Trail. (The yellow-blazed Summit Trail will be your return route.)

The wide Swamp Trail climbs gently through a grove of fir trees and then through a forest of deciduous trees. The gorge off to the right contains some small, wet areas that probably gave the trail its name; however, the going is generally dry and easy. Soon, the trail begins to descend, and its end is marked by a triple blaze just before reaching Campsite #18. Continue ahead, passing a sign for the Swamp Trail, a sign for Campsite #18, and then a sign for the Summit and Spring Trails. A short distance beyond the signs, you'll reach a paved road opposite a restroom building.

Turn right and follow the paved road past several more campsites. Just beyond another restroom building, note the large glacial erratic on the left side of the road—as well as the small tree growing right out of the rock. Continue ahead on the road, passing a sign for the white-blazed Orchard Trail, which leaves to the left. Just before Group Site B, there is a sign on the right for the Ghost Lake and Summit Trails. Turn right, following the co-aligned turquoise-blazed Ghost Lake Trail and yellow-blazed Summit Trail, which climb gently on a woods road, then bear left and descend.

At a signpost, the yellow-blazed Summit Trail leaves to the right. Unless you want to significantly shorten the hike (and forgo a 500-foot, up-and-down elevation change), stay on the turquoise-blazed Ghost Lake Trail, which continues straight ahead. It narrows to a footpath and climbs a little, passing some rock outcrops on the right, then continues over undulating terrain.

At a high point, marked by a glacial erratic on the left, the trail begins a steady descent. At first, the descent, for the most part, is gradual, but after a short ascent, the trail begins a rather steep, rocky descent. At the base of the steep descent, the trail turns left onto a woods road, which it will follow the rest of the way to the lake. A short distance beyond, a branch road to the right leads to the foundations of a former cabin, with east-facing views over Allamuchy Mountain State Park and the Pequest River Valley. (One version of the legend contends that this is the actual site from which Jenny jumped.)

ERRATIC SANDSTONE ALONG THE SUMMIT TRAIL

GHOST LAKE

As the trail continues to descend on the woods road, it approaches I-80, which may be heard and seen (in leaf-off season) ahead through the trees. The trail now bends sharply right and begins to head south, away from the noisy highway. It passes several huge, moss-covered rock outcrops on the left, then swings left and parallels a stream, below on the right, in an area covered with ferns. The Ghost Lake Trail ends just before the grass-covered causeway across Ghost Lake, about 45 minutes to 1 hour from Group Site B.

There is some debate about how Ghost Lake acquired its name. One story involves a massacre between two warring Native American tribes, and the other references a mucky, pre-lake swamp where mosquitoes bred, spreading sickness and death. The local road leading to the lake is named Shades of Death Road—the subject of a page or two of the Weird New Jersey Web site (www.weirdnj.com/stories/shades-of-death-road).

After spending some time at the lake (which, despite its name, is actually very attractive), retrace your steps, following the Ghost Lake Trail back to the signpost at the junction of the Ghost Lake and Summit Trails, and turn left onto the yellow-blazed Summit Trail. (If you start seeing both blue and yellow blazes, you've gone too far, and you need to return to the junction.) You'll follow the yellow blazes of the Summit Trail for the rest of the hike.

The Summit Trail climbs steadily to the ridge of Jenny Jump Mountain. When it reaches the top, it begins to descend, following along the crest of the ridge. After a relatively level section where the trail runs a little below the crest, it continues along the ridge, following gently undulating terrain.

About two-thirds of a mile from the junction, the Summit Trail begins a steady climb. At the top, you'll pass a yellow-tipped concrete post on the right marked "NJ 78." This may be a forest boundary marker (the park map shows the Summit Trail crossing outside the forest boundary for a short distance). Here, a side trail on the left leads to an east-facing viewpoint from a rock outcrop (the view is partially blocked by vegetation). A short distance beyond this point, you'll reach a junction with the blue-blazed Spring Trail. Continue ahead on the yellow-blazed Summit Trail. You're now entering a more heavily used area of the park and will likely encounter a greater number of hikers.

In another 300 feet, you'll reach a west-facing viewpoint over the Delaware Water Gap from a rock outcrop to the right of the trail. A bench has been placed at the viewpoint. In another 5 minutes, you'll come to two large glacial erratics, one on each side of the trail. The one on the right is formed of sandstone, while the one on the left is composed of granite gneiss. The bedrock in the area is granite gneiss, not sandstone, so the erratic on the right must have been transported a considerable distance. About 100 feet beyond, a side trail leads left to a panoramic, unobstructed southeast-facing viewpoint.

The yellow trail now widens into a woods road and begins to descend. In another 5 minutes, it turns right and begins to descend even more steeply. Just beyond this turn, a side trail on the left leads 100 feet to a panoramic viewpoint from a rock outcrop amid cedars. The Pinnacle is directly ahead, farmlands are below to the left, and the Kittatinnies are visible to the right (if there are no leaves on the trees). Notice, too, the rock surface underfoot. The striations were made by the glaciers during the Ice Age.

After enjoying the view, return to the main trail and turn left, continuing to descend. Soon, the red-blazed Swamp Trail joins from the right. The co-aligned trails pass Campsite #9 and end at the parking area where the hike began.

22

Point Mountain

TOTAL DISTANCE: 2.8 miles	
HIKING TIME: 2.5 hours	
VERTICAL RISE: 535 feet	
RATING: Moderate	
MAPS: USGS Washington; Hunterdon County Division of Parks and Recreation Point Mountain Trail Map and Guide	
TRAILHEAD GPS COORDINATES: N 40° 45′ 59″ W 74° 54′ 39″	

As you drive along NJ 57 south of Hackettstown, you will notice that you are in a very fertile valley, nestled between two long mountain ranges. On your left is the distinctive Musconetcong mountain range, the remains of an ancient thrust fault in the Precambrian rock of the New Jersey Highlands. This thrust fault pushed older resistant rock on top of younger and softer rock, resulting in a ridge and an accompanying valley through which the Musconetcong River flows. The highest point on the ridge is Musconetcong Mountain in Bloomsbury, reaching an elevation of 955 feet. The vertical relief from river valley to the nearby summit ridge is substantial—from 400 to 500 feet. Point Mountain, named for its sharp profile when seen from the south, is an outstanding feature of the Musconetcong mountain range and attains an elevation of 935 feet.

The 1,140-acre Point Mountain Reservation is managed by the Hunterdon County Division of Parks and Recreation (P.O. Box 2900, Flemington, NJ 08822; 908-782-1158; www.co.hunterdon.nj.us/depts/parks/parks.htm). Located in the northernmost portion of the county, this mostly undeveloped area (no facilities other than parking) is open for fishing, hiking, horseback riding, cross-country skiing, and mountain biking. There are two main access points to the trail system on Point Mountain. One is located on Penwell Road, where you pass a series of fields before entering the forested mountain ridge. The Penwell Mill, named for a descendant of the Penn family in Pennsylvania, as well as an 1830 farmhouse and barn (now a private residence), are located near the Penwell Road trailhead. The other access point, the one used for this hike, is on Point Mountain Road, just below the summit of Point Mountain.

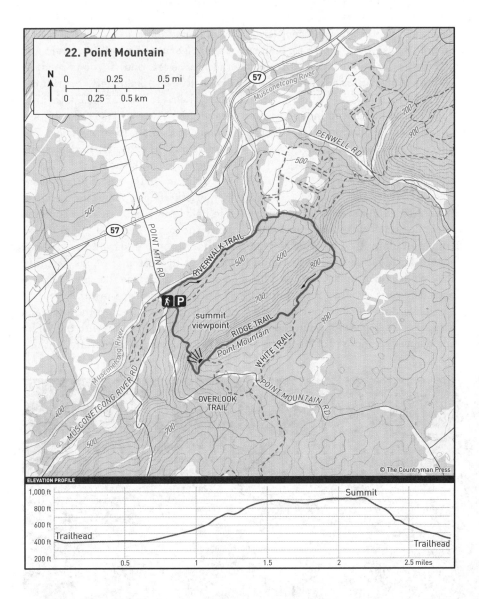

22. Point Mountain

N

| 0 | 0.25 | 0.5 mi |
| 0 | 0.25 | 0.5 km |

ELEVATION PROFILE

The hike described below first leads alongside the Musconetcong River and past open fields. It then climbs the ridge of Point Mountain to arrive at the spectacular viewpoint near the summit.

A short but steep descent from this viewpoint brings you back to your car. Those with less time to spare may wish to walk directly from the parking area to the viewpoint—a short but very steep hike.

GETTING THERE

From Exit 26 on I-80 (Budd Lake/Hackettstown), proceed west on US 46 for 7.4 miles to Hackettstown. Turn left onto NJ 182 and follow it for 1 mile, then turn right onto NJ 57, following signs to Washington and Phillipsburg. Follow NJ 57 for 6.5 miles and turn left onto Point Mountain Road. The parking area is 0.5 mile ahead on the left, just past the bridge over the Musconetcong River. From I-78, take NJ 31 North for 8 miles and turn right onto County Route 632 (Asbury–Anderson Road). Drive 4 miles to NJ 57, follow NJ 57 to Point Mountain Road, turn right, and continue across the bridge over the Musconetcong River to the parking area on the left.

THE HIKE

From the parking area (trail maps may be available at a kiosk), walk back down Point Mountain Road toward the Musconetcong River. Just before reaching the bridge, turn right onto the blue-blazed Riverwalk Trail and follow it alongside the river in a northeasterly direction. You'll pass rock outcrops and boulder fields composed of Precambrian

Highlands gneiss on your right. At a small clearing, the trail jogs right and then turns left onto a woods road. At the next fork, keep left, continuing along the river. Not far ahead, the trail leaves the river, crosses a tributary stream, and climbs to an open field. The trail follows the edge of the woods along the right side of the field.

At the end of the field, the trail turns left, briefly follows the eastern edge of the field, and soon reaches a junction with the orange-blazed Ridge Trail. Turn right onto it, passing an owl box on a tree in a patch of woods. The trail continues alongside the south edge of the field as it rises up the hill. At the end of the field, the trail enters the forest and soon reaches a junction with the White Trail, which begins on the left. Continue

MUSCONETCONG RIVER

VIEW FROM POINT MOUNTAIN

ahead on the orange-blazed Ridge Trail, which begins a steady climb up the ridge of Point Mountain on a woods road.

After crossing a stream, the trail turns right, leaving the road, and continues on a footpath. It climbs a bit farther and soon reaches the crest of Point Mountain. In another quarter mile, the trail turns sharply left and descends to an old stone wall. It turns right and parallels the wall, soon reaching a junction with another branch of the White Trail, which begins on the left. Continue on the orange-blazed Ridge Trail, which now turns right, climbs a little to regain the ridge, and heads southwest along the ridge.

As the trail climbs ever higher, views over the Musconetcong Valley begin to appear to your right. The trail becomes increasingly rugged as it works its way past boulders and rock outcrops. Huge boulders jut out from the ridgetop, and you may need to use your hands in places. After descending to a junction

with the yellow-blazed Overlook Trail, the Ridge Trail climbs to reach a panoramic viewpoint over the Musconetcong River valley from a rock outcrop just to the right of the trail at the summit of Point Mountain.

After taking in the view, continue ahead on the orange-blazed Ridge Trail, which heads steeply downhill on a rocky footpath. Be aware that poison ivy may be found here, especially during the first part of the descent. With a private home visible ahead, the trail curves to the right and continues to descend. Trail builders have made a few stone steps in places that offer some relief from the steady downhill walking—and you will thank them for their efforts. After the descent becomes more moderate, the trail reaches a junction. Here, the Ridge Trail ends at a junction with the blue-blazed Riverwalk Trail. Continue straight ahead (do not turn right) and follow the blue blazes down to the parking area where you left your car.

23

Schooley's Mountain County Park

TOTAL DISTANCE: 2.3 miles

HIKING TIME: 2 hours

VERTICAL RISE: 500 feet

RATING: Easy to moderate

MAPS: Morris County Park Commission Schooley's Mountain County Park map (available online at www.morrisparks.net)

TRAILHEAD GPS COORDINATES: N 40° 48' 08" W 74° 47' 00"

Schooley's Mountain County Park is a relatively small park of only 823 acres, but it has much to offer outdoors enthusiasts. The hiking trails are mostly easy, except along the first part of this hike, where the footing on the Falling Waters Trail is quite rocky. However, the gorge and falls made by the Electric Brook are well worth the trip. Electric Brook takes its name from the old electric generating plant once installed here, which used the brook for power. There is only one viewpoint, but the shade trees make for a very pleasant outing on a hot summer day. Benches have been placed at various locations along the trails.

The park is administered by the Morris County Park Commission (300 Mendham Road, Morris Township, NJ 07960; 973-326-7600; www.morrisparks .net). Restrooms, a picnic shelter, a playground, and a lodge are located near the main parking area (the lodge may be rented for functions such as weddings and parties). Paddleboats and rowboats may be rented for use on Lake George (fishing is permitted, but swimming is not allowed).

The park is named for the Schooley family, who owned much land in this locality in the 1700s. Originally a large part of the park was used for a Morristown YMCA camp called Camp Washington, but it was purchased by the Morris County Park Commission in October 1968 and opened to the public in May 1974.

GET THERE

Take I-80 to Exit 27A, proceed south on US 206 for 4.4 miles, and turn right onto Flanders-Bartley Road (County Route 612). In 1 mile, bear right just before a railroad crossing to continue on Bartley Road. Proceed another 2.5 miles and

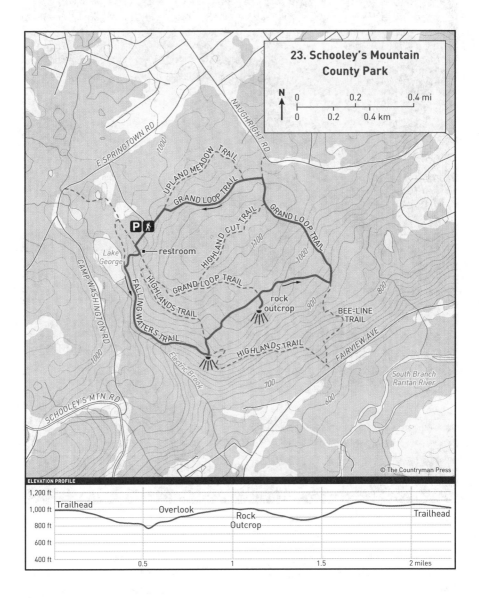

23. Schooley's Mountain County Park

ELEVATION PROFILE

turn right onto Naughright Road. In 2.2 miles, turn left onto East Springtown Road. Follow East Springtown Road for 0.5 mile to the park entrance, on the left. Parking is available at the end of the park entrance road.

THE HIKE

From the kiosk at the end of the parking area, cross a grassy strip and turn left onto a paved service road, with a restroom building ahead on your left. To the right of the building, you'll notice a trail junction. Do not take the Grand Loop Trail straight ahead; rather, head downhill on a gravel road toward Lake George, bearing right at the fork (the path on the left leads to an overlook above the lake). Turn left at the base of the short descent and follow along the lake. Just past the dam at the south end of the lake,

WATERFALL IN ELECTRIC BROOK

you'll notice a triple-blue blaze on a tree that marks the start of the Falling Waters Trail.

The Falling Waters Trail descends steadily along the pools and cascades of Electric Brook. The path is rocky, and care needs to be taken, particularly after rain, when the footpath may be slippery. Be sure to stop and look around to admire the unspoiled scenery. Two attractive waterfalls are reached within 0.3 mile; this is a good spot for a break.

A short distance beyond, at a private property sign, the Falling Waters Trail turns left, leaving the brook, and begins a steady climb. At the top of the climb, a huge jumble of large boulders remaining from a rock quarry is on your right. Here, a triple-blue blaze marks the end of the Falling Waters Trail. Turn right and follow the joint Patriots' Path (white blazes) and Highlands Trail (teal-diamond blazes) for only about 50 feet. At the point where the trail makes a sharp left turn, continue ahead to a rock outcrop with a south-facing overlook. Rest awhile and enjoy the view over a serene, beautiful valley, then

LAKE GEORGE

retrace your steps to the junction with the Falling Waters Trail. Proceed ahead another 50 feet, but when the Patriots' Path/Highlands Trail turns left, continue ahead on a wide gravel road with pink blazes.

Soon, you'll reach a junction (marked by a sign) with the yellow-blazed Grand Loop Trail. Just before this junction, a short unmarked trail on the right leads to an interesting rock outcrop. This is a worthwhile detour (there are limited views through the trees from the outcrop during leaf-off season).

After taking a short break here, return to the junction. To the left, the Grand Loop Trail leads directly back to the parking lot, but you should turn right, following the arrow that points to the Bee-Line Trail. The Grand Loop Trail descends on a narrower footpath to another junction, where the Bee-Line Trail heads right toward Fairview Avenue and the Columbia Trail. You,

however, should turn left to continue along the yellow-blazed Grand Loop Trail. The trail now heads steadily uphill until the height of land is reached. Here, you will find a cairn, a signpost, and a triple-red blaze marking the start of the Highland Cut, which heads southwest across the mountain.

Do not take the Highland Cut, but continue ahead on the Grand Loop Trail, which now descends gently. Be alert for a sharp left turn, where the trail leaves the wide woods road it has been following and continues on a narrower path through ferns. Stay on the yellow-blazed Grand Loop Trail when the orange-blazed Upland Meadow Trail goes off to the right. After walking through an attractive forest, you'll reach the end of the Grand Loop Trail (there is a triple-yellow blaze here facing the other direction). Turn left, passing a bench and a signpost, and you'll emerge at the parking lot where the hike began.

Black River Trails

TOTAL DISTANCE: 6.6 miles

HIKING TIME: 4 hours

VERTICAL RISE: 800 feet

RATING: Moderate to strenuous

MAPS: USGS Chester; Morris County Park Commission Black River Trails (available online at www.morrisparks.net)

TRAILHEAD GPS COORDINATES: N 40° 46' 43" W 74° 43' 13"

This linear hike, which runs from north to south in Chester Township, requires a short car shuttle. If you don't have two cars, a one-car option is provided toward the end of this hike description. This walk has much to recommend it. In addition to the hike itself, there are interesting historical features to visit at both ends, if time permits. The terrain used by the hike is varied. After following an old railroad grade, the trail parallels the Black River as the water rushes through its rocky gorge, then climbs through cool and dense deciduous and pine forests, to finish with a meander through several meadows.

Cooper Mill, at the northern end, is a gristmill dating from 1826. Both the visitor center and the mill are closed during the winter, and opening times vary from April through October. The Bamboo Brook Outdoor Education Center is at the southern end of the hike, and the Willowwood Arboretum is also close by. The hike uses the Black River, the Conifer Pass, and the Bamboo Brook Trails, and crosses two paved roads—Pottersville Road and Longview Road. The Patriots' Path is co-aligned with these trails, and occasionally you will notice its distinctive path-and-tree logo.

GETTING THERE

Drive both cars to the Bamboo Brook Outdoor Education Center parking lot. Head south on I-287 to Exit 22 (Bedminster/ Pluckemin) and continue north on US 206 for 4 miles to Pottersville Road (County Route 512). Turn left and continue on Pottersville Road for 0.5 mile, then turn right onto Lisk Hill Road.

Continue for 0.1 mile to a T-junction, turn right onto Union Grove Road, and proceed for 0.3 mile to a Y-junction, where you turn left onto Longview Road.

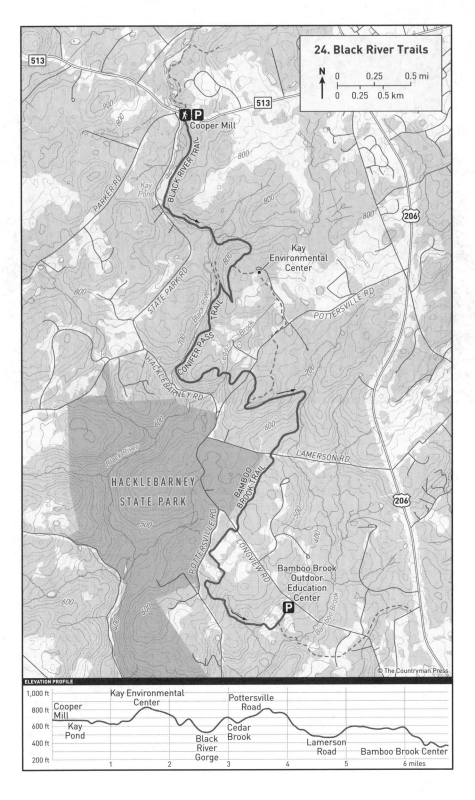

24. Black River Trails

N

| 0 | 0.25 | 0.5 mi |
| 0 | 0.25 | 0.5 km |

513

513

206

Cooper Mill

BLACK RIVER TRAIL

Kay Pond

STATE PARK RD

900

800

800

800

800

800

Kay Environmental Center

POTTERSVILLE RD

CONIFER PASS TRAIL

Black River

Cedar Brook

700

700

HACKLEBARNEY RD

600

600

600

Black River

HACKLEBARNEY STATE PARK

500

BAMBOO BROOK TRAIL

LAMERSON RD

206

500

POTTERSVILLE RD

LONGVIEW RD

400

Bamboo Brook Outdoor Education Center

P

Bamboo Brook

600

800

© The Countryman Press

ELEVATION PROFILE

1,000 ft		Kay Environmental Center			Pottersville Road			
800 ft	Cooper Mill							
600 ft	Kay Pond			Cedar Brook				
400 ft			Black River Gorge			Lamerson Road	Bamboo Brook Center	
200 ft		1	2	3	4	5	6 miles	

KAY POND

Proceed for about 1 mile until you reach the parking lot for the Bamboo Brook Outdoor Education Center, on the left.

Leave one car at the Bamboo Brook parking lot, and drive north to the Cooper Mill and visitor center. Turn left out of the parking lot onto Longview Road and continue for 0.8 mile to a T-junction with Pottersville Road. Turn right onto Pottersville Road, and in 0.7 mile turn left onto the unsigned Hacklebarney Road. Infrequent brown signs for Cooper Mill will confirm your route. Continue on this narrow, partly gravel road for 0.7 mile and turn right onto State Park Road. Proceed for another 2 miles, passing the old Kay Pond ice house, and turn right onto County Route 513.

Almost immediately, turn right into the parking lot for the Cooper Mill and visitor center.

If you drive back to the Cooper Mill at the end of your hike, a right turn onto County Route 513 leads to US 206, where a left turn (north) accesses I-80, and a right turn (south) takes you to I-287.

THE HIKE

Walk to the northwest corner of the parking lot toward the Cooper Mill County Park sign, and continue to the kiosk in the direction of the mill. When the demand for local grains declined in 1913, this last operating mill in Chester was closed. Descend the small flight of wooden stairs by the side of the mill and begin the hike on the Black River Trail, marked with blue paint blazes. The Black River (aka the Lamington River) is now on your right, but the trail soon leaves its banks. The area is lush, with some large trees, and the dirt footpath, which crosses several small plank bridges, is crisscrossed by tree roots.

About 0.3 mile from the start, the trail turns left onto the abandoned route of the Hacklebarney Branch of the Central Railroad of New Jersey, built in 1873 to transport ore from the Hacklebarney Mine and abandoned in 1900. The now wider trail soon passes through a cut with piles of rocks to the side and blasting grooves in the rock wall.

After about 20 minutes, lily pad–covered Kay Pond can be seen on the right. Great blue herons and other wildlife can often be seen around the pond, which is man-made. The pond takes its name from Alfred and Elizabeth Kay, who moved from Pittsburgh in 1924 and built their summer home, called Hidden River Farm, nearby. During the 1930s, Mrs. Kay grew herbs that she sold by mail, and she also opened a local tearoom called the Herb Farm. The Kays donated much of their property to the Morris County Park Commission, and in 1994 Hidden River Farm was dedicated as the Elizabeth D. Kay Environmental Center. The building is now an office for The Nature Conservancy. A few steps to the right of the trail, the dam makes a pleasant place to take a quick break. One of the remaining ice houses still stands on the other side of the dam.

A short distance beyond, the trail passes the old Hacklebarney Mine on the left. This mine was closed in 1896 and is now protected by fencing. Hacklebarney was Chester's oldest and most productive iron mine. At first limited to surface mining, Hacklebarney was developed into an underground mine after large iron deposits were found. This mine recorded more accidents than any other in Chester.

Almost immediately, the trail crosses a tributary on a substantial bridge with a handrail and, on the right, approaches a barricaded paved road. The blue blazes indicate that the trail turns left. Soon, the railroad grade ends and the trail continues on a slightly rougher footpath parallel to the river.

About 1.2 miles from the start, the trail bears left and begins to head uphill. Here, to the right of the trail, a short herd path leads to abandoned concrete abutments in the river.

The trail bears left at the next fork and soon begins to parallel a tributary stream. The trail now curves right and continues to climb, passing a stone wall on the right and continuing through former fields, now overgrown with dense vegetation.

Soon, the trail reaches a junction in a clearing, marked by a signpost. Turn right and begin to follow the red-blazed Conifer Pass Trail, which follows switchbacks on sidehills on its way down to the Black River. The river, with its waterfalls, can be glimpsed through the trees on the right, but when the trail begins to descend more steeply, the river becomes more visible as it tumbles through its deep and narrow gorge. The trail parallels the Black River for a short distance before climbing on switchbacks away from this wild and scenic spot. Take care to follow the red trail blazes, given that the trail is sometimes a little indistinct here, and notice the indications of some test mining.

After descending to cross Cedar Brook, the trail begins to climb, passing through a stand of evergreens to reach paved Pottersville Road. The trail

BLACK RIVER GORGE

crosses the road and continues to climb. After leveling off, the trail bears left and reaches a wooden signpost that marks the end of the Conifer Pass Trail. (One-car option: Turn left at the signpost to reach the Kay Environmental Center in 2.2 miles and the Cooper Mill in 3.6 miles.)

Our hike continues by turning right and following the Bamboo Brook Trail. After about 10 minutes of walking downhill, the trail reaches the brook itself and turns left to parallel it. On the left is an old stone wall that the trail crosses several times before reaching Lamerson Road.

Cross the road and continue ahead on a woods road. In this section, there are several intersecting woods roads, so be sure to follow the blue blazes. After several turns, the trail becomes more open and receives more sunshine. In about a half mile, the trail reaches an old rock wall and turns right. Follow the wall for about 50 feet, then turn right and continue to Longview Road.

Cross Longview Road and follow the Bamboo Brook Trail, which heads through the woods and then emerges onto an open field. Here, the trail turns right and continues along the side of the field. After turning left and following another side of the field, the trail heads to a second field, which it skirts on the left. It then reenters the woods.

After passing through a pine plantation, the trail descends and begins to parallel a tributary of Bamboo Brook, to the left. Soon, the trail crosses the stream and climbs to skirt a field. It reenters the woods and then skirts a second field. Finally, the trail emerges onto yet another field, with the Bamboo Brook parking lot visible down to the right. Walk around the sides of this last field and head down to your car.

Merrill Creek Reservoir

TOTAL DISTANCE: 6.7 miles

HIKING TIME: 4 hours

VERTICAL RISE: 400 feet

RATING: Easy

MAPS: USGS Bloomsbury; Merrill Creek Reservoir trail map

TRAILHEAD GPS COORDINATES:
N 40° 44' 25" W 75° 05' 33"

Merrill Creek Reservoir, located in Harmony Township, Warren County, was built to augment the supply of water from the Delaware River when its water levels were low. The present reservoir replaced a smaller one built in 1903 by Ingersoll-Rand to supply water to its plant in nearby Phillipsburg. Ground was broken for the new reservoir in September 1985 and, because of the workers' long hours—sometimes as many as 20 a day—the reservoir was completed in April 1988. Seven electric utility companies combined efforts on this project.

The 650-acre reservoir is stocked with a variety of game fish. It has a maximum depth of 225 feet and more than 5 miles of shoreline. The reservoir stores 16 billion gallons of water for release to the Delaware River during low-water periods to augment the river water used by its generating stations. A 3-mile pipeline, 57 inches in diameter and about 6 feet below ground, links the reservoir to the Delaware. Water is pumped up the mountain from the river by three 8,000-horsepower pumps and returned through the same pipeline when needed. The inlet/outlet tower controls water flow. Ports are provided along the tower to permit water to be released from whatever depth in the reservoir best matches the river's temperature.

A 290-acre wildlife preserve juts into the reservoir, and a total of 2,000 acres of open space surround it. Nesting bald eagles have been observed at Merrill Creek Reservoir since 1997. In June 2011, two eagle chicks born at the reservoir were fitted with satellite transmitters that allowed scientists to monitor the birds' travels for over 5 years as they moved away from their nest and established their own territories. This was the first instance of a long-term eagle telemetry research project being

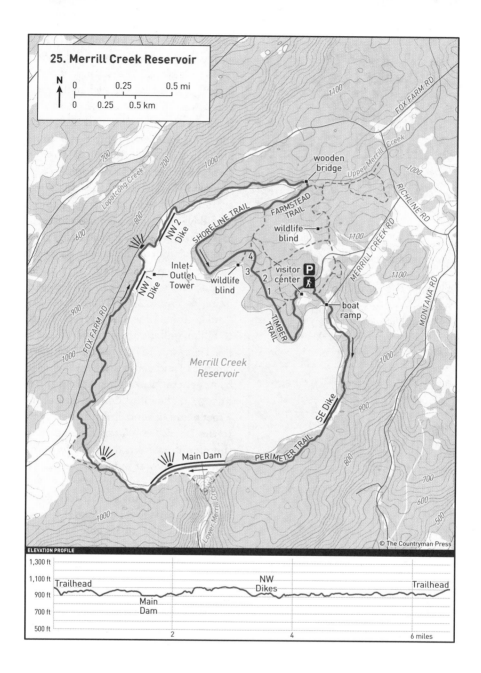

25. Merrill Creek Reservoir

N
0   0.25   0.5 mi
0   0.25 0.5 km

wooden bridge

FOX FARM RD

1100

Upper Merrill Creek

RICHLINE RD

SHORELINE TRAIL

FARMSTEAD TRAIL

wildlife blind

NW 2 Dike

NW 1 Dike

MERRILL CREEK RD

1100

1100

MONTANA RD

Inlet-Outlet Tower

wildlife blind

4
3
2
1

visitor center

P

boat ramp

Lopatcong Creek

FOX FARM RD

700

700

1000

800

600

900

1000

TIMBER TRAIL

Merrill Creek Reservoir

1000

SE Dike

900

Main Dam

PERIMETER TRAIL

800

700

600

500

Lower Merrill Creek

1000

© The Countryman Press

ELEVATION PROFILE

1,300 ft

1,100 ft

900 ft   Trailhead

700 ft

500 ft

Main Dam

NW Dikes

Trailhead

2   4   6 miles

---

conducted in New Jersey. The visitor center contains an exhibit that uses a unique method to illustrate in sand the tracks left by wild animals. A large collection of native birds is displayed in a glass case, and more stuffed birds are suspended from the ceiling of a large classroom. Alongside the visitor center is a small garden whose plants were chosen to attract butterflies, bees, hummingbirds, and beneficial insects. The visitor center is open daily (except on certain holidays), and the hiking trails are open daily from dawn to dusk. For more information, contact Merrill Creek Reservoir, 34 Merrill Creek Road, Washington, NJ 07882; 908-454-1213; www .merrillcreek.com.

This hike is easy walking, largely on flat, wide trails, but with a few rocky sections. The trails used are the Perimeter Trail (black), which circles the reservoir, as well as parts of the Farmstead (yellow), Timber (red), and Shoreline (blue) trails. The trails are for hiking only and are blazed with metal markers with the MCR logo, as well as with some paint blazes. The Perimeter Trail, which you will follow for most of the hike, has markers that give the distance each half-mile.

GETTING THERE

From I-78 take Exit 4 (Warren Glen/ Stewartsville). Turn right at the bottom of the exit ramp and continue for 1.8 miles to a blinking stoplight in Stewartsville. Turn right onto County Route 638 (Washington Street, then New Village Road) and continue 2.3 miles to NJ 57 (along the way, you will see a sign that instructs you to turn left to reach NJ 57; ignore this sign and continue straight ahead). Turn right onto NJ 57, then immediately turn left onto Montana Road. In 2 miles, bear left at a fork onto Richline Road, and in another 0.3 mile, turn left onto Merrill Creek Road. Bear right at the next fork and continue to the main parking lot for the Merrill Creek Reservoir. Park here and walk to the visitor center, where you can obtain a trail map and view the interesting exhibits (if the visitor center is closed, a trail map may be obtained from a kiosk in the parking lot).

THE HIKE

With your back to the front door of the visitor center (the reservoir is to your right), proceed ahead (away from the visitor center) and bear right when you reach a paved road. Just ahead, on your right, you'll notice a black MCR blaze, marking the start of the Perimeter Trail, which will be your route for the first 5 miles of the hike. Turn right, downhill, and enter the woods. Soon, you'll reach a junction. Bear right and continue to descend on the black-blazed trail to the boat ramp and boaters' parking area. Continue straight ahead across the parking area (keeping the boat ramp and the reservoir on your right), but before you reach the second parking area, bear right and proceed uphill along a wide gravel road. Go around a gate and cross a beautiful meadow. Bluebirds, a common sight at Merrill Creek Reservoir, like to nest in the open, and nesting boxes have been erected in many locations (including this area). Two of the dams crossed by the Perimeter Trail are visible. After a gentle upgrade, followed by a slightly steeper downgrade, you'll cross the first dam of the reservoir (shown on the map as "SE Dike"). At the end of the dam, the trail heads slightly uphill and continues through the woods.

After a short descent, you'll reach the main dam of the reservoir, which provides excellent views of the reservoir, as well as a south-facing vista over the hills of Warren County. On the left, you'll pass the end of a wooden instrument-access staircase, which is closed to the public. A pipe under the rocks is used to release water from the reservoir into Lower Merrill Creek.

When you reach the west end of the half-mile-long main dam, turn sharply right onto a footpath (do not follow the paved road uphill), immediately passing the 2-mile marker, and continue through the woods. The pleasant footpath you are following should provide a welcome contrast with the gravel road that you traversed to reach this point.

After passing a viewpoint over the reservoir on the right, you'll continue through a former red pine forest that was devastated by Hurricane Sandy in October 2012. The hurricane toppled most of the trees in this area, and although the area has begun to regenerate, only a few scrawny red pines remain. Bear right at the next junction to continue on the black-blazed Perimeter Trail. Soon, the trail climbs slightly until it reaches a bench, with a limited view of the reservoir.

Just beyond, you'll come to an intersection. Turn right to continue on the Perimeter Trail, but bear left at the following intersection. The trail to the right leads down to an observation point along the shore of the reservoir (an optional side trip, but you've already been afforded many panoramic views of the reservoir from the Perimeter Trail). Continue ahead, gently downhill, passing through another area devastated by Hurricane Sandy but now starting to regenerate. You're now heading parallel to Fox Farm Road (on your left), and you'll be able to hear the sounds of traffic on the road, which is occasionally visible through the trees.

After passing the 3.5-mile marker, you'll reach a third crushed-rock dam (shown on the map as "NW 1 Dike"). Cross the dam, with the Inlet-Outlet Tower, which controls the flow of water between the Delaware River and the reservoir, on your right. Go around the gate at the end of the dam and cross a paved road. Here there is a portable toilet screened by a wooden fence and a kiosk.

Just ahead, turn left, go around another gate, and continue on a gravel road that soon bears right. To the left, the view across the valley (when there are no leaves on the trees) includes two gaps (the more northerly one is the Delaware Water Gap). Through the tunnel under this valley, the water makes its way back and forth between the reservoir and the Delaware River.

After bearing right and then left again, you'll reach the southern end of another crushed-rock dam (shown on the map as "NW 2 Dike"). Cross the dam and, when you reach the northern end, turn sharply right and follow a footpath that parallels the shore of an arm of the reservoir. You will notice many dead and submerged trees in this arm of the reservoir. Also look for tulip trees with their long straight trunks, as well as a spruce fir stand. This section of the trail is rather rocky and has many exposed tree roots, but it is quiet and secluded.

After closely following the arm of the reservoir for about a mile, the trail turns right and crosses a wooden footbridge over Upper Merrill Creek. You now have walked over 5 miles. Just beyond the bridge, you'll come to a T-junction. Here, the yellow-blazed Farmstead Trail comes in from the left. Turn right, leaving the Perimeter Trail, and begin to follow the yellow blazes along a wide woods road, climbing gently. At the next intersection, you should turn right onto the blue-blazed Shoreline Trail. The Shoreline Trail follows a rocky footpath along an arm of the reservoir, with the route of the Perimeter Trail, which you followed earlier in the hike, across the water. Many dead trees, killed when the reservoir was filled with water, can be seen at the edge of the reservoir.

As you approach the end of a peninsula that juts out into the reservoir,

MERRILL CREEK RESERVOIR

the last dam you crossed (NW 2 Dike) comes into view. Before reaching the tip of the peninsula, the trail bears left and heads gradually uphill on a grassy road. Just past the crest of the rise, a side trail leads right to an open area, with views of the Inlet/Outlet Tower across the reservoir. You can often see geese and other waterfowl from here. Just beyond, a wooden bench provides an enjoyable resting place, and the tall post with the nesting platform attracts ospreys.

Now proceed downhill until, almost at the water's edge, the blue markers direct you left onto a wide woods road. Soon, a side trail to the right leads 500 feet to a wildlife observation blind on the water's edge, crossing two boardwalks over wet areas along the way.

From this point, the visitor center is approximately 1 mile away.

At the next intersection, you'll notice the ruins of a lime kiln on the right (#4 on the park map). Lime kilns were built on high ground where timber was plentiful and where the elevation caused an updraft, rather than close to the source of the raw materials needed for making lime. The kilns resembled huge stone fireplaces and sometimes served more than one farmstead. A wagon path was built to the top of the kiln. The kiln was loaded with alternating layers of fuel—usually wood—and limestone chunks. When the fire was lit, temperatures frequently reached 2,000 degrees Fahrenheit, sometimes breaking up the stone with an explosive bang. The burnt lime

STONE RUINS OF THE SPRING HOUSE

filtered down and was used on the fields as a fertilizer.

Bear right at this intersection, now following both blue and yellow blazes. The yellow blazes leave to the left at the next intersection, with the Cathers-Shafer Farm site (#3 on the park map) on the right. Continue straight ahead, now following just blue blazes. Soon, you'll notice the stone ruins of the Spring House (#2 on the park map) on the left. A little farther down the trail, after crossing a wet area on puncheons, the ruins of the Cathers House (#1 on the park map) are on the left (surrounded by a wooden fence).

At the next intersection, you can return to the visitor center by turning left, following both blue and red blazes. But if you want to take in the final loop, continue ahead, now following the red-blazed Timber Trail. The fence on the left is a deer exclosure, designed to prevent deer from nibbling on the vegetation. You'll soon reach the shore of the reservoir. The red-blazed trail continues along the reservoir for a short distance, then heads inland. When you reach the top of a rise, the blue trail joins in, and the visitor center can be seen directly ahead.

26

Dismal Harmony Natural Area

TOTAL DISTANCE: 2.6 miles	
HIKING TIME: 2 hours	
VERTICAL RISE: 380 feet	
RATING: Easy to moderate	
MAPS: Available online at www .hikemendham.org.	
TRAILHEAD GPS COORDINATES: N 40°47'45.1"W 74°33'36.4"	

If there ever were a park with an inappropriate name, this is it. The name "dismal" conjures up notions of a place that is dingy, gloomy, and dreary. But this preserve is just the opposite. It features some of the most delightful hiking in Morris County, with trails paralleling a cascading brook and climbing to an unusually shaped boulder. On a recent visit, the author encountered a local resident who mentioned that, for years, he never visited the preserve because he expected it to be a gloomy, depressing place. Once he checked it out, though, he was amazed by its beauty, and now he regularly hikes there. This wild and scenic preserve is not to be missed!

GETTING THERE

Take I-287 South to Exit 36 (County Route 510/Morris Avenue). Continue ahead past the first traffic light, proceed past the Morristown railroad station, then turn right onto Morris Street. At the next intersection, bear left, then turn right onto East Park Place, passing the Morristown Green on the left. Turn left at the following intersection onto North Park Place, then turn right onto Washington Street. (In each case, follow signs for County Route 510 West.) In 4 miles, after passing a pedestrian crossing with a blinking light, turn right onto Tingley Road. In 0.7 mile, turn left onto East Main Street and proceed for 0.2 mile to the parking area for Dismal Harmony Natural Area, on the right.

THE HIKE

From the parking area, follow the white-blazed Patriots' Path as it heads north on a footpath parallel to the cascading Dismal Brook. After crossing two wooden bridges over tributary streams, the trail

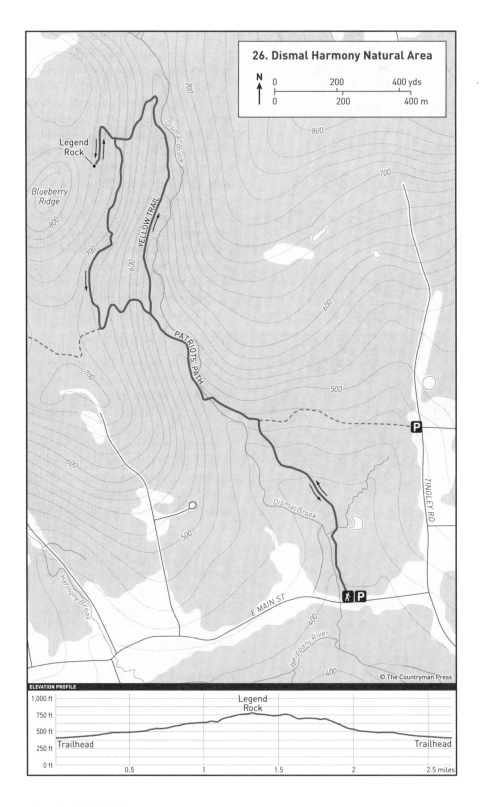

26. Dismal Harmony Natural Area

N

| 0 | 200 | 400 yds |
| 0 | 200 | 400 m |

Legend Rock

Blueberry Ridge

DISMAL BROOK

YELLOW TRAIL

PATRIOTS' PATH

700

800

800

800

700

700

600

600

600

500

500

500

500

400

400

Dismal Brook

Harmony Brook

E MAIN ST

Whippany River

TINGLEY RD

© The Countryman Press

ELEVATION PROFILE

1,000 ft

750 ft

500 ft

250 ft

0 ft

Legend Rock

Trailhead

Trailhead

0.5　1　1.5　2　2.5 miles

moves away from the brook, climbing gradually on a woods road. At 0.4 mile, it reaches a T-intersection and turns left onto a gravel road; to the right, the road leads 0.3 mile to a small parking area at the intersection of Tingley Road and Washington Valley Road. Once again, the Patriots' Path closely parallels the brook, now below on the left.

The trail bears left at 0.5 mile and crosses a wooden bridge over Dismal Brook. It immediately turns right onto a woods road and continues to parallel the brook, now on the right. Just ahead, the trail bears left onto a footpath to avoid a wet section of the road, which it soon rejoins.

At 0.6 mile, the woods road followed by the Patriots' Path bears left and heads uphill, continuing to run parallel to the brook. Then, in another 500 feet, a junction marked by a huge cairn is reached. Here, the Patriots' Path bears left, but you should continue ahead on a yellow-blazed trail, which begins here. The trail continues north, parallel to the brook, climbing gradually. Several unmarked side trails lead down to beautiful cascades in the brook.

At 1 mile, follow the yellow-blazed trail as it turns sharply left, away from the brook, and begins to climb more steeply. After a short, relatively level section, you'll reach a T-intersection, where the yellow blazes lead both ways. Turn right, then bear left a short distance ahead, continuing to follow the yellow blazes leading to a huge boulder known as Legend Rock. (The story goes that, in the 1700s, Scottish people who

DISMAL BROOK

FOOTBRIDGE OVER DISMAL BROOK

settled the area hid from the Native Americans by crawling into cracks in this boulder.) Although there is a sheer face on the east side of the rock, the rock can easily be climbed from the west side.

After exploring this interesting feature, retrace your steps to the second junction (where the trail came up from the brook) and bear right, now heading south. The next 0.4 mile on the yellow-blazed trail is relatively level, with one short stretch where the trail descends on switchbacks.

At 1.7 miles, you'll reach another junction, also marked by a cairn. Turn left here, and follow the white-blazed Patriots' Path as it descends rather steeply on switchbacks. At the base of the descent, at 1.9 miles, you'll return to the junction near the brook marked by a huge cairn. Turn right and continue along the white-blazed Patriots' Path, now retracing your steps to the parking area on East Main Street where the hike began.

Jockey Hollow

TOTAL DISTANCE: 5.3 miles	

HIKING TIME: 3 hours (allow additional time for a visit to the Wick House)

VERTICAL RISE: 670 feet

RATING: Easy to moderate

MAPS: USGS Mendham; NPS Jockey Hollow Area trail map

TRAILHEAD GPS COORDINATES:
N 40° 45' 43" W 74° 32' 33"

At just under 1,000 acres, Jockey Hollow is the largest section of the Morristown National Historical Park (Morristown, NJ 07960; 973-543-4030; www.nps.gov/morr), about 3 miles south of the city of Morristown. The site, a unit of the National Park Service, is open year-round during daylight hours. The visitor center and Wick House are generally open from 10 a.m. to 4 p.m. Wednesday to Sunday (they are closed on Thanksgiving, Christmas, and New Year's Day).

The visitor center offers a small book and souvenir shop, an orientation film, and a reconstructed soldier hut. Trail maps are available for purchase at a nominal cost (or you can download a map from the park's website before you arrive).

You should allow time, before or after the hike, to visit the Wick House, just behind the visitor center. Henry Wick built his house around 1750 and made his living from farming and from his large woodlot. While better off than most, the family was by no means wealthy. During the winter encampment of 1779–80, the farm served as both the Wicks' home and as the headquarters of Major General Arthur St. Clair. The main building has been restored, and there is usually a ranger in attendance in period dress to explain the fascinating history.

The hike is suitable for cross-country skiing (conditions permitting) as well as hiking. There are signposts at almost every trail junction, which each include a trail map and corresponding location number. These location numbers are indicated in the text (usually within parentheses).

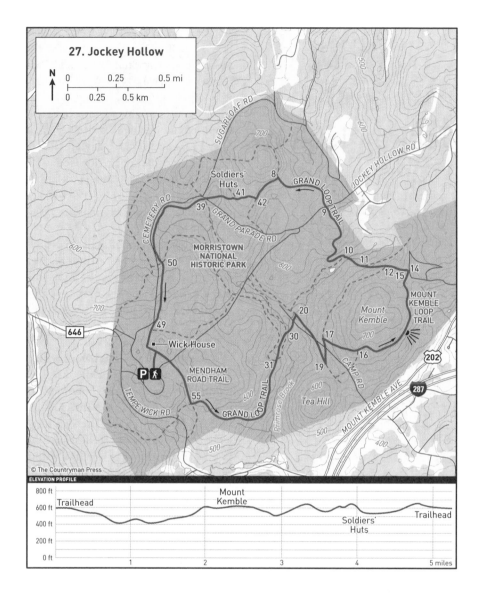

27. Jockey Hollow

ELEVATION PROFILE

GETTING THERE

Take I-287 to Exit 30B. Turn right at the traffic light onto US 202 north and follow it for 1.8 miles to Tempe Wick Road. Turn left onto Tempe Wick Road and continue for 1.3 miles to the park entrance, on the right. Drive uphill to the parking area behind the visitor center.

THE HIKE

After stopping at the visitor center, leave by the rear door and continue along a paved path for about 250 feet. When the paved path curves left (just before an interpretive sign for the Wick Farm), you should turn right, leaving the paved path, and continue along a grassy road (shown on the park map as Mendham Road).

SOLDIER HUTS

You parallel a split-rail fence on the left, with the Wick Farm orchard beyond. After crossing a paved park road, you'll pass an interpretive sign for Hand's Brigade. Continue straight ahead on the grass-covered woods road, descending slightly.

After about 5 minutes, you will reach a junction, marked by signpost 55. Turn left and proceed into the woods on the joint Patriots' Path/Grand Loop Trail, marked with the distinct Patriots' Path logo blaze (a tree with a path underneath on a white background) as well as white paint blazes for the Grand Loop Trail. This multiuse trail (no bikes are allowed in the park, but horses can use the trails) is a partially completed linear park, running generally alongside the Whippany River from Mendham to East Hanover.

The trail follows a wide woods road, and the walking is easy. Take time to note the surrounding forest. The huge tulip trees are not typical of New Jersey. Since the National Park Service began managing the area in the 1930s (and probably for some time before that), there has been only inconsequential cutting of timber. The result is an unusually mature forest with a lush understory. Unfortunately the lushness is mostly the invasive Japanese barberry, a big problem in this area. For 15 to 20 minutes, the route ambles through this forest, passing many huge trees felled by Hurricane Sandy in October 2012.

After descending steadily, the trail begins to run along the side of a hill, and it becomes narrower. The trail climbs a little and descends to reach Junction 31, where it meets the red-blazed Primrose Brook Trail, a loop trail that you will cross again in a short distance. Continue ahead, crossing two streams flowing under wide wooden bridges, the first one with a railing and the second without. Just beyond the second bridge is signpost 30 and the second crossing of the Primrose Brook Trail. Continue ahead on the joint Patriots' Path/Grand Loop Trail, which bears left.

At the next signpost (20), the Patriots' Path/Grand Loop Trail turns left, but you should turn right onto a blue-blazed trail, which heads uphill. In about 10 minutes, you'll come to the next

WICK HOUSE

signpost (19). Ahead is a National Park Service (NPS) ranger residence, but your route turns sharply left toward the Mount Kemble Loop. A few minutes later you reach another signpost (17). Going straight ahead would shorten the hike a little by eliminating the loop, but, unless you're tired, make a right as the trail, still marked with blue blazes, now starts to circle Mount Kemble. Soon, you'll see a yellow house through the woods on the right—the same NPS ranger residence you already saw. The sounds you now hear are from I-287—the eastern boundary of the park is close by.

When you reach the next signpost (16), continue ahead on the blue-blazed trail. Just ahead, off the trail on the right, is a fenced-in exclosure. This and four others in the park were erected in the late 1980s to keep the deer out of these small areas and to study the effect their browsing has on the local vegetation.

You will shortly reach an opening in the woods with a view to the east. If you are lucky enough to have a clear day, you might be able to see the tips of the skyscrapers of Manhattan. The rest of New York City is hidden from view by the Watchung Mountains. This area was the camping grounds of Stark's Brigade—New Hampshire frontiersmen who fought at Bunker Hill, Trenton, and Princeton. Take a few moments to read the signs. This is a good spot for a break or lunch. The Watchung Mountains are the reason George Washington chose this tract for his winter encampment. Some 30 miles from New York City, and Howe's British troops, they provided a fine natural defense. Lookouts posted on ridgetops could easily spot enemy troop movements toward Morristown or across the plains toward the "capital" of Philadelphia.

In another 5 minutes, you'll reach a metal gate and signpost (15). A woods road leads left to a grassy area, but you should continue ahead on the blue-blazed trail, passing a private home on the right. In another minute, you'll reach signpost 14. Here, you should turn left, continuing to follow the blue blazes. You pass another metal gate and proceed slightly downhill.

When you reach the next signpost (12), which is where you would rejoin the hike if you had shortened it, take the right fork and continue to follow the blue blazes, heading slightly downhill. Bear left at signpost 11 and soon cross a small stream running through a culvert. Just beyond the culvert, you reach signpost 10. Here, the blue-blazed trail branches off to the left, but you should bear right and begin to follow the white-blazed Grand Loop Trail, which winds uphill. The trail runs close to the northeastern boundary of the park, where you can see more private residences to your right.

Cross paved Jockey Hollow Road (9), with metal gates on both sides. After descending gently, the trail begins to climb—first gradually, then more steeply. This section is the only one on which most novice skiers may have to walk.

The climb is short, and soon you reach signpost 8 at a T-intersection. The white-blazed Grand Loop Trail turns right, but you should turn left onto an unmarked trail. This trail follows undulating terrain for about 5 minutes until it reaches signpost 42. Here, you turn right on the yellow-blazed Soldier Hut Trail, which heads over the hill, toward the soldiers' huts. Bear left at signpost 41, and soon you'll reach the huts.

The NPS has reconstructed five huts as typical examples of those built by Continental troops. The one you come to first was for officers; the ones with 12 beds were for the troops.

Some 200 huts lined this hillside during the winter of 1779–80, while perhaps as many as a thousand stood in all

of Jockey Hollow. Washington ordered all of them to be constructed alike, in neat lines, with officers' huts in the rear. The majority were finished by Christmas, those for the officers in January and February.

Proceed down and across the open field. At the base of the descent, there are several interpretive signs which explain the conditions the soldiers endured during the harsh winter they spent here. Cross the road and proceed ahead through a grassy field with some mature cedar trees. After passing a boulder with a plaque commemorating the war dead buried here, you'll come to signpost 39 at the edge of the woods. Continue ahead along the yellow-blazed Soldier Hut Trail, which heads gently uphill, roughly paralleling Cemetery Road.

After about 10 minutes, observe a narrower path parallel to you on the left. Look down. The stone structure with the slate top is a springhouse. The trail circles above it and soon reaches signpost 50. Turn right, following the sign for the Wick House, and proceed uphill on a yellow-blazed gravel path, passing by a number of tall trees. After descending and going through an area with much barberry and many fallen trees, the trail ends on a paved road at signpost 49, just below the Wick House barn. Turn left and follow the paved road past the barn to the Wick House. If you didn't visit the house at the start of the hike, now is a good time to do so. Follow the paved path from the Wick House back to the visitor center and your car.

You may wish to combine the hike with a visit to Washington's Headquarters and Fort Nonsense in Morristown, also part of the Morristown National Historical Park. You also might want to visit the nearby Scherman Hoffman Wildlife Sanctuary (see Hike #28).

28

Scherman Hoffman Wildlife Sanctuary

TOTAL DISTANCE: 1.5 miles

HIKING TIME: 1 hour

VERTICAL RISE: 300 feet

RATING: Easy

MAPS: USGS Mendham/Bernardsville; Scherman Hoffman Wildlife Sanctuary park map

TRAILHEAD GPS COORDINATES: N 40° 44' 29" W 74° 33' 12.5"

The sanctuary is named for Mr. and Mrs. Harry Scherman, who donated the first 125 acres of land to the New Jersey Audubon Society in 1965, and for G. F. Hoffman, who donated adjacent parcels in 1973 and 1975 and bequeathed his home and the adjacent grounds to the society upon his death in 1981. The two-story Hoffman house, built in 1929, is now the center of sanctuary operations, housing offices, a museum, a bookstore, and rooms for programs. No dogs are permitted in the sanctuary, which covers almost 300 acres of open space and supports more than 60 species of nesting birds.

The hike begins near the New Jersey Audubon Society facility in Bernardsville (11 Hardscrabble Road, P.O. Box 693, Bernardsville, NJ 07924; 908-766-5787; www.njaudubon.org). The Morristown National Historical Park at Jockey Hollow and the Cross Estate property are adjacent. The Hoffman Building, which houses the visitor center, should not be missed. It includes a well-stocked book and gift store, as well as an observation window overlooking a bird-feeding area. Stop here to obtain the park map. The Hoffman Building is closed on Mondays, although the parking lot is open daily until 5:00 p.m.

GETTING THERE

Take I-287 to Exit 30B and bear right at the end of the ramp onto North Maple Avenue. At the traffic light by the Olde Mill Inn, go straight across US 202 onto Childs Road; in a short distance, bear right at the fork onto Hardscrabble Road. Proceed on Hardscrabble Road for 0.9 mile to the entrance to the New Jersey Audubon Society's Scherman Hoffman Sanctuary, on the right. Continue up the driveway to the Hoffman Building.

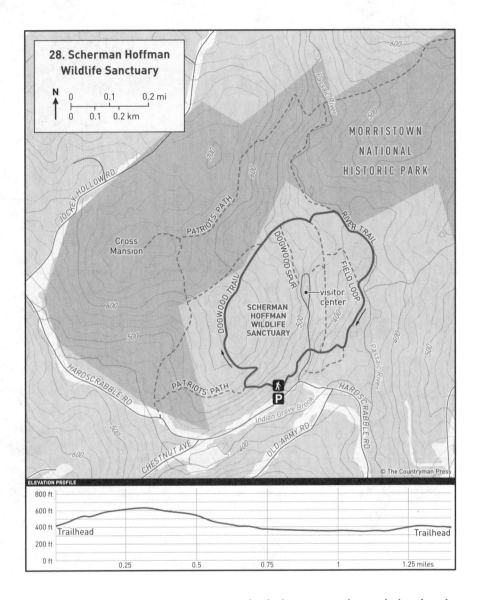

28. Scherman Hoffman
Wildlife Sanctuary

THE HIKE

To begin the hike, leave the Hoffman Building and drive back down the entrance road. Turn right onto Hardscrabble Road and take the first right into the Scherman parking lot (51 Hardscrabble Road). Walk to the kiosk at the eastern end of the parking area. Just beyond the kiosk, the footpath splits, and the Dogwood Trail is signed for both directions. The trail ahead is the one on which you will return at the end of the hike, but for now turn left and head uphill. The trail is marked by New Jersey Audubon logo blazes and Patriots' Path logo blazes (a tree with a path underneath on a white background); you will also find some faded red paint blazes along the trail. The trail climbs on switchbacks, steeply in places. In 0.2 mile, you'll reach a junction, marked

RIVER TRAIL ALONG THE PASSAIC RIVER

by a signpost. Here, the Patriots' Path leaves to the left, but you should bear right to stay on the Dogwood Trail, which continues to ascend. The invasive, nonnative species of barberry has a real hold on these woods. Seeds of these plants are spread by birds and animals, and the bushes are difficult to eradicate.

As the trail approaches the crest of the rise, the grade moderates. There are some interesting boulders to the right of the trail at the very top. The trail now begins to descend, soon passing a tree wedged at a 45-degree angle between two trunks of another tree. Interestingly, both trees are still alive, and the tree on the angle now has a trunk that is growing straight up!

A short distance beyond, an unmarked connecting trail from the

you should continue ahead on the main Dogwood Trail. Just beyond, you'll pass several huge fallen trees below on the left. These trees were blown down by Hurricane Sandy in 2012.

At the next junction, bear left, following the sign for the River Trail. Follow this yellow-blazed trail (also marked with New Jersey Audubon Society logo markers) down to the Passaic River. Here, the river is an uncontaminated brook funneled between two hills, tumbling over rocks toward the Great Swamp and to Paterson and Newark beyond. Those familiar with the Passaic River farther downstream, where it is polluted and runs through industrial areas, will be surprised to find it in such pristine condition here.

The trail continues along the river for about 0.25 mile, passing several huge trees along the way—including a tulip tree that is four feet in diameter. This is the most beautiful part of the hike, and it's a good spot to take a short break.

After crossing a footbridge over a tributary stream, the River Trail ends at a junction with the green-blazed Field Loop. Turn left onto the Field Loop, which follows a wide woods road along the river, then bears right, away from the river. The trail crosses several wet areas on raised boardwalks and soon reaches an intersection with a signpost. Turn right, following the sign for the Field Loop, which begins to ascend.

Soon, you'll emerge onto a paved road. Follow the road uphill, cross the entrance road to the sanctuary, and reenter the woods, now following the red-blazed Dogwood Trail. Continue along the Dogwood Trail for about 750 feet, until you reach the parking area on Hardscrabble Road where the hike began.

Cross Estate comes in from the left. You should bear right, continuing along the Dogwood Trail, which now descends a little more steeply. Just beyond, watch carefully as the Dogwood Trail bears left onto a narrower footpath, diverging from the wider path it has been following. Soon, you'll reach a sign that indicates that the Dogwood Spur to the Hoffman Center goes off to the right, but

III.

PIEDMONT

Palisades

TOTAL DISTANCE: 5.5 miles

HIKING TIME: 4 hours

VERTICAL RISE: 600 feet

RATING: Moderate

MAPS: USGS Central Park (NY/NJ); NY–NJTC Hudson Palisades Trails #108 & #109; Palisades Interstate Park Commission map

TRAILHEAD GPS COORDINATES: N 40° 57′ 11″ W 73° 55′ 14″

The Palisades Interstate Park Commission was established in 1900, mainly to curb the opening of quarries that supplied traprock for the concrete used in building roads and skyscrapers. Initially, the commission acquired the land along the face of the Palisades, and it subsequently also acquired land on top of the cliffs. Today, the New Jersey Section of the Palisades Interstate Park includes 2,472 acres. The average width of the parkland between the Hudson River and the clifftop is less than 0.2 mile. Apart from the talus at their bases, the cliffs are well wooded, with a variety of trees and shrubs, some of them remaining from former estate gardens. The highest elevation along the Palisades cliffs in this hike is 520 feet.

The Long Path runs along the top of the Palisades, and the Shore Trail runs along the Hudson River, following the base of the Palisades. These trails are linked by several connecting trails. This hike uses the Closter Dock Trail (orange) to descend to the Shore Trail (white), ascends on the Forest View Trail (blue/white), and returns using a section of the Long Path (aqua).

Enjoyment of the Shore Trail is enhanced by the sound of lapping water, and both the Shore Trail and the Long Path offer many superb views of the river and the Westchester County communities on the opposite shore. Hikers should beware of the ubiquitous poison ivy, especially on the Shore Trail.

GETTING THERE

The hike begins at the Administration Building of the New Jersey Section of the Palisades Interstate Park (Alpine, NJ 07620; 201-768-1360; www.njpalisades.org). Access is from Exit 2 of the Palisades Interstate Parkway,

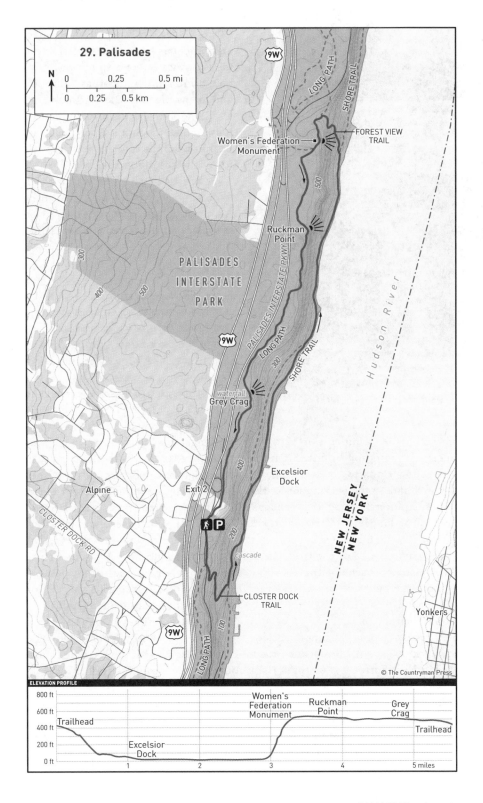

29. Palisades

N

0   0.25   0.5 mi
0   0.25   0.5 km

9W

LONG PATH

SHORE TRAIL

Women's Federation
Monument

FOREST VIEW
TRAIL

500

Ruckman
Point

PALISADES
INTERSTATE
PARK

300

400

500

PALISADES INTERSTATE PKWY

9W

LONG PATH

300

SHORE TRAIL

Hudson River

waterfall
Grey Crag

400

Excelsior
Dock

Alpine

Exit 2

200

CLOSTER DOCK RD

cascade

NEW JERSEY
NEW YORK

CLOSTER DOCK
TRAIL

Yonkers

9W

LONG PATH

100

© The Countryman Press

ELEVATION PROFILE

800 ft
600 ft
400 ft   Trailhead
200 ft
0 ft

Excelsior
Dock

Women's
Federation
Monument

Ruckman
Point

Grey
Crag

Trailhead

1   2   3   4   5 miles

THE WOMEN'S FEDERATION MONUMENT

Closter Dock Trail, which heads east and proceeds through a tunnel under the Palisades Interstate Parkway. After going through the underpass, turn left and follow the joint Closter Dock Trail and Long Path north for 0.2 mile to a tunnel under the Alpine Approach Road. At the end of the tunnel, turn right and follow the description below.

Before starting the hike, you may wish to obtain a copy of the park map at the Administration Building (the map is also available online at www.njpalisades.org).

THE HIKE

From the wooden sign that reads NEW JERSEY HEADQUARTERS, PALISADES INTERSTATE PARK COMMISSION (at the southern end of the parking lot), proceed ahead (south) on the Alpine Approach Road. After a very short roadwalk, you'll notice a path diverging to the left. Bear left and follow this path, marked by the aqua blazes of the Long Path. After passing a seasonal stream on the left, you'll come to a stone tunnel. Here, the Long Path turns right and goes through the tunnel, but you should continue straight ahead, now following the orange-blazed Closter Dock Trail, which descends on switchbacks, along a stone-lined road. The descent is about 350 feet over the course of 0.5 mile. At the base of the descent, the Closter Dock Trail ends at a junction with the white-blazed Shore Trail.

If time permits, you might want to take the opportunity, before continuing on the hike, to visit the Kearney House, just 0.1 mile down the trail to the right from this junction. Part of the house probably dates to the 1760s, and it was formerly known as Cornwallis's Headquarters. The house is usually open from May through October between noon and 5 p.m., but check at the Administration

approximately 7 miles north of the George Washington Bridge. From the exit, follow signs to POLICE HEADQUARTERS and park in the parking lot for the Administration Building (on weekdays, the main parking lot is restricted to park employees, and hikers should park in a gravel parking area on the west side of the Alpine Approach Road).

The hike can also be accessed by public transportation. Take the Rockland Coaches (Coach USA) #9 or #9A bus from the George Washington Bridge Bus Terminal at 179th Street and Broadway in New York City (or the #9T or #9AT bus from the Port Authority Bus Terminal at 42nd Street and Eighth Avenue in New York City) to Closter Dock Road and US 9W in Alpine, NJ. Walk north along US 9W for about 500 feet and turn right onto the orange-blazed

Building for current hours if you wish to visit the house.

If you don't visit the Kearney House, turn left at the junction and head north on the Shore Trail, which follows a wide, level path. Soon, you'll notice stone steps climbing the hillside on the left. These steps lead to a stone bunker that was once used by the park to store dynamite. A short distance beyond, you'll pass a waterfall, with a circular stone wall, on the left. Then, a little farther along the Shore Trail, a side trail on the right leads downhill to Cape Flyaway—a small, rocky beach with views of Yonkers, directly across the river.

About a half mile north of the Closter Dock Trail, you'll come to a fork in the trail. Here, a stone marker indicates that the path to the left is known as the Upper Trail. You should bear right and continue to follow the white-blazed Shore Trail, which descends to the river on a stone-lined road. As you approach the river, you'll pass cascades on the left and a stone jetty on the right. This jetty is all that remains of the former Excelsior Dock.

The trail continues along the river on a rocky path, with panoramic views across the river. You can see both Amtrak and Metro-North trains traveling along the east bank of the river. In half a mile, you'll pass another cascade on the left and then a stone jetty on the right. This is the site of Twombly's Landing, believed to have been a Native American campsite because of the layers of oyster shells found here. A short distance beyond, you'll pass on the left the northern end of the Upper Trail and continue ahead on a level dirt path, soon passing some old stone picnic tables on the left.

A little farther north on the trail, you'll reach the first unobstructed views of the Palisades cliffs. Above, you can see

Ruckman Point, and it is interesting to note that in a little while you will be looking down at the river from this point on the cliffs. A short distance beyond, you get a good view of Indian Head, farther north along the river, and you can see the Tappan Zee Bridge in the distance.

After passing through an area with many tangled vines, you'll reach a junction with the blue/white-blazed Forest View Trail, marked by a sign and a triple blaze. The Shore Trail continues ahead to the Giant Stairs, a difficult rock scramble, but you should turn left onto the Forest View Trail, which begins a steady climb on switchbacks and rock steps. You'll be climbing about 400 vertical feet in only 0.35 mile.

At the top of a long flight of rock steps, you'll come to a trail junction. Directly ahead, the trail crosses a stream on a wooden footbridge, but you should turn left to continue on the blue-and-white-blazed Forest View Trail, which is now joined by the aqua-blazed Long Path.

After climbing another 100 vertical feet, you'll reach a stone "castle," known as the Women's Federation Monument. This "castle" was built by the New Jersey Federation of Women's Clubs in 1929 to commemorate their efforts in the late 19th century to protect the Palisades from quarrying. This spot offers a panoramic view over the Hudson River, and you'll want to stop here and take a break.

When you're ready to continue, proceed ahead on the joint Forest View Trail/Long Path. In a short distance, the Forest View Trail turns right onto a woods road leading to a footbridge over the Parkway, but you should cross the woods road and continue ahead. In about 500 feet, follow the aqua-blazed Long Path as it turns left onto another woods road. Soon, you'll pass through an area where many trees were felled

VIEW FROM RUCKMAN POINT

by Hurricane Sandy in October 2012. A short distance beyond, the road curves to the left and crosses a concrete bridge over a stream. Just ahead is a concrete-block wall at the cliff edge. To its right is Ruckman Point, a rock outcrop with carved graffiti, some of which is more than a century old! This outcrop, which stands 520 feet above the river, offers panoramic views up and down the Hudson, with a particularly dramatic section of the cliffs visible just to the north. In the river, just beyond these cliffs, you may notice some pilings jutting out of the water. These are the remains of the former Forest View marina, abandoned after World War II.

The Long Path now heads south, parallel to the cliffs. At one point, it bears right, crosses a stream on rocks, then turns left and runs closer to the Parkway. In the next mile, you'll follow a stretch of puncheon over a wet area and cross two wooden bridges over streams.

Just beyond the second bridge, look for a short trail on the left that heads toward the cliff edge. The trail leads to a viewpoint over a seasonal waterfall pouring through a cleft in the cliff, with panoramic views of the Hudson River below. Be sure to take care when you approach the cliff edge; there is no protective fencing at this location. In the spring, drifts of snowdrops bloom here.

Only a short distance farther down the main trail, watch for another footpath to the left, leading over a bridge to a secluded lookout called Gray Crag. Here, a section of rock has separated from the cliff. The bridge has no railings, so use caution if you choose to cross it.

A short distance beyond, you'll cross another stream on a wide wooden bridge. Soon, the trail approaches the ramps of Exit 2 of the Parkway, and it finally emerges onto the parking lot by the Administration Building, where you left your car.

Rockleigh Woods Sanctuary and Lamont Reserve

TOTAL DISTANCE: 2.2 miles

HIKING TIME: 1.5 hours

VERTICAL RISE: 400 feet

RATING: Easy to moderate

MAPS: Maps: USGS Central Park (NY/NJ); NY–NJTC Hudson Palisades Trails #109; NY–NJTC Rockleigh Woods/Lamont Reserve trail map

TRAILHEAD GPS COORDINATES: N 41° 00' 14.5" W 73° 55' 32.5"

The land traversed by this hike, on the western slope of the Palisades, was formerly owned by the Lamont family, who donated it to the Boy Scouts of America, Greater New York Councils. For many years, it was part of the Boy Scouts' Alpine Scout Camp. In 1975, the Borough of Rockleigh (one of the smallest municipalities in New Jersey, with a population of only about 500) purchased more than 81 acres of the Lamont tract from the Boy Scouts and established the Rockleigh Woods Sanctuary.

Then, in the early 1990s, the Scouts decided to put the remainder of the Lamont tract—which was not extensively used as part of the camp—up for sale. The most likely use was going to be residential development. Residents of the boroughs of Rockleigh and Alpine, in which the tract was located, did not wish to see houses built on the slope of Palisades overlooking their communities. Working with Bergen County and the Green Acres program of the State of New Jersey, they raised the necessary funds to acquire the 134-acre Lamont Reserve and preserve it as open space.

Soon after the Lamont tract was acquired in 1996, a network of trails was established on the property and on the adjacent Rockleigh Woods Sanctuary. The trails, however, were not maintained and became difficult to follow. In 2005, the New York–New Jersey Trail Conference assumed maintenance of the trail system in the area, and the trails have been improved and expanded by dedicated volunteers under the leadership of the late Jakob Franke, who resided in nearby Northvale.

This delightful hike loops around the reserve and sanctuary, climbing a scenic ravine along Roaring Brook, with attractive cascades when the water is high, and passing several features of

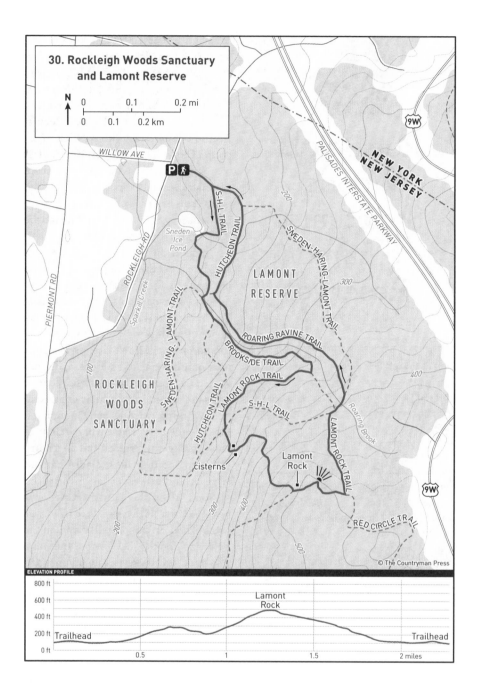

30. Rockleigh Woods Sanctuary
and Lamont Reserve

historical interest. The trailhead is at the rear of Rockleigh Borough Hall, where parking is available. For more information, contact the Borough of Rockleigh, 26 Rockleigh Road, Rockleigh, NJ 07647, 201-768-4217; www.rockleighnj.org. A free trail map (without contours) is available online at www.nynjtc.org.

GETTING THERE

Take the Palisades Interstate Parkway to Exit 4. Turn left at the bottom of the ramp onto US 9W (if coming from the north, turn right onto US 9W) and proceed for 1.1 miles, entering New York. At the next traffic light, turn left onto Oak Tree Road and, in 0.2 mile, turn left onto Closter Road. In 0.5 mile, after crossing under the Parkway, you reenter New Jersey, and the road becomes Rockleigh Road. Continue for another 0.2 mile to the Rockleigh Municipal Building (26 Rockleigh Road) and turn left into the driveway. Park behind the building.

THE HIKE

From the parking area, follow a handicapped-accessible path to a playground, where a triple blue blaze on a tree to the right marks the start of the Hutcheon Trail. Follow this blue-blazed trail past a Green Acres sign into the woods.

In a short distance, you'll notice a triple yellow blaze on a tree to the right. Turn right and follow the yellow-blazed Sneden-Haring-Lamont Trail, which heads south, closely paralleling the sanctuary boundary. Continue to follow this trail as it turns right and crosses a brook on a culvert. To the right is the Sneden Ice Pond. In the 19th century, ice was cut from this pond in the winter and sold locally to those who had their own ice houses. When snow covered the ground, the ice was transported in horse-drawn wooden sleds. Just beyond, the trail turns left at a signpost and crosses the inlet stream of the pond.

As the trail approaches the wide Roaring Brook, the blue-blazed Hutcheon Trail joins from the left, and both trails cross the brook on rocks. On the other side, turn left and follow the blue blazes, which parallel the brook. Soon,

LAMONT ROCK

OLD STONE CISTERN ALONG THE LAMONT ROCK TRAIL.

you'll notice a triple-orange blaze, marking the start of the Brookside Trail, on a tree to the left.

Turn left and follow this trail—the newest trail in the sanctuary, blazed by volunteers in 2013—which continues to parallel the scenic Roaring Brook.

In a quarter mile, the Brookside Trail ends at a junction with the white-blazed Lamont Rock Trail. Turn right onto this trail, which descends briefly, then bears left, crosses an old, eroded woods road, and passes an area with many trees toppled by Hurricane Sandy in October 2012. The Lamont Rock Trail briefly joins the yellow-blazed Sneden-Haring-Lamont Trail, but when the two trails diverge, turn left and continue to follow the white blazes.

The Lamont Rock Trail now climbs steadily, soon passing two old stone cisterns, part of a system that once supplied water to homes in the area. It continues to climb to Lamont Rock (a huge boulder), on the left. Note the rectangular depression on one side of the boulder, where a plaque was once affixed. Just beyond, the white trail turns left and is joined by the Red Circle Trail that leads into Boy Scout Camp Alpine. Follow the joint white and red trails as they climb on a footpath to the highest point in the preserve (440 feet). The view from this spot is largely obscured by foliage, but you can catch a glimpse of the Hudson River through the trees when they're bare.

The joint trails now turn right and begin to descend. Soon, the Red Circle Trail leaves to the right, but you should turn left and continue along the white-blazed Lamont Rock Trail. In about 0.2 mile, the yellow-blazed Sneden-Haring-Lamont Trail joins from the left, and the Lamont Rock Trail ends just beyond.

Bear right and follow the yellow trail along a wide woods road, crossing Roaring Brook on rocks. A short distance beyond, turn left onto the red-blazed Roaring Brook Trail and follow it as it descends along the north side of the brook. You followed the other side of this brook on the way up. At the base of the descent, the Roaring Brook Trail ends at a junction with the blue-blazed Hutcheon Trail. Turn right onto the blue-blazed trail, which descends gradually, crossing an old stone bridge over a brook, and follow it back to the parking area where the hike began.

31

High Mountain

TOTAL DISTANCE: 4 miles

HIKING TIME: 2.5 hours

VERTICAL RISE: 400 feet

RATING: Moderate

MAPS: USGS Paterson; NY–NJTC Jersey Highlands Trails (Central North Region) Map #125; Wayne Township High Mountain Trails Map

TRAILHEAD GPS COORDINATES:
N 40° 57' 07" W 74° 12' 01"

This loop hike traverses the 1,154-acre High Mountain Park Preserve. In August 1993, Wayne Township, the State of New Jersey, and The Nature Conservancy acquired the lands that now comprise this preserve from Urban Farms, Inc., a subsidiary of McBride Enterprises of Franklin Lakes, New Jersey. The three owners manage the preserve jointly. It is situated along the Preakness Range, a northern continuation of the Second Watchung Ridge. The hike climbs to the summit of High Mountain, the highest mountain on the East Coast south of Maine with a view of the ocean, which offers a spectacular view of the New York City skyline.

A free trail map is available online at www.waynetownship.com/maps/mountainpark.pdf.

GETTING THERE

Take NJ 208 west to the second Goffle Road exit (toward Hawthorne/Paterson) and turn right at the end of the ramp. At the next light, just beyond the intersection with Goffle Hill Road, turn right onto North Watchung Drive. At a stop sign at the top of the hill, turn sharply right onto Rea Avenue, which becomes North Haledon Avenue and then Linda Vista Avenue. At a T-intersection with Terrace Avenue, turn right, then bear left to continue on Linda Vista Avenue, which leads into William Paterson University (Entry 6). At the next stop sign, turn right and continue for 0.4 mile to a small parking area on the right, with a sign reading HIGH MOUNTAIN PARK.

THE HIKE

From the kiosk near the entrance to the parking lot, follow a gravel path across an open area that heads northeast,

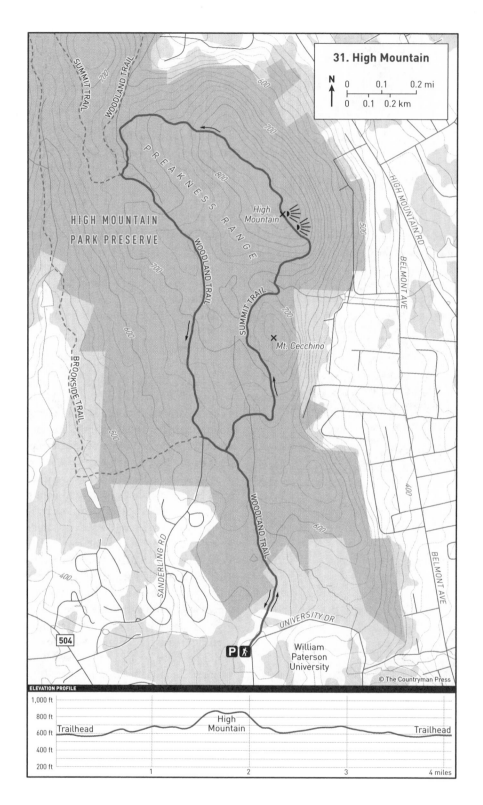

31. High Mountain

N

| 0 | 0.1 | 0.2 mi |
| 0 | 0.1 | 0.2 km |

SUMMIT TRAIL

WOODLAND TRAIL

P R E A K N E S S   R A N G E

700

600

700

800

HIGH MOUNTAIN
PARK PRESERVE

High
Mountain

WOODLAND TRAIL

SUMMIT TRAIL

700

BROOKSIDE TRAIL

600

500

700

× Mt. Cecchino

HIGH MOUNTAIN RD

BELMONT AVE

500

400

WOODLAND TRAIL

SANDERLING RD

400

600

BELMONT AVE

504

P

UNIVERSITY DR

William
Paterson
University

© The Countryman Press

ELEVATION PROFILE

1,000 ft				
800 ft		High		
600 ft	Trailhead	Mountain		Trailhead
400 ft				
200 ft				
	1	2	3	4 miles

EAST-FACING VIEW FROM THE SUMMIT OF HIGH MOUNTAIN

parallel to University Drive. A double-red blaze at the edge of the woods marks the start of the red-blazed Woodland Trail, which you should follow into the woods. After passing a huge boulder on the left, the Woodland Trail turns left onto a footpath. It soon reaches a T-intersection, where it again turns left, this time onto an eroded woods road.

In another half mile, you'll reach a high point on the trail where a triple-yellow blaze on a small rock marks the start of the yellow-blazed Summit Trail. Turn right onto this trail, which descends to cross a small stream in a wet area. It then curves north, passing just west of the low ridge known as Mt. Cecchino. Three-quarters of a mile along the yellow trail, you'll cross a small stream. From here, the trail begins a steady climb to the summit of High Mountain. Near the top, the trail bears left, bypassing an eroded section of the road, but it soon rejoins the road.

Just before arriving at the summit, you'll reach a panoramic east-facing viewpoint. On the horizon, beyond the suburban sprawl of northeastern New Jersey, you can see the New York City skyline, the Verrazano-Narrows Bridge and even a corner of the Atlantic Ocean. Continue up to the summit, which resembles a grassy southern bald, with a few large exposures of the basaltic bedrock. From the summit, both the New York City skyline to the east and the ridge of the Watchung Mountains to the south are visible.

Head northwest across the broad summit, following the yellow blazes on rocks, and continue downhill on the Summit Trail. Take care to follow the yellow blazes, because several paths and woods roads lead down the mountain. The Summit Trail crosses a secondary summit, levels off, and then descends steeply on an eroded woods road.

CLIMBING HIGH MOUNTAIN ON THE SUMMIT TRAIL

Near the base of the descent, be alert for a sharp left turn where the yellow blazes leave the woods road and enter the woods on a footpath. This section of the trail is a refreshing change from the worn woods roads you have been following. Continue along the Summit Trail, which descends to a stream, parallels it, and then crosses it. About 250 feet beyond the stream crossing, you'll reach a woods road.

The Summit Trail turns right here, but you should turn left onto the road, marked with the red blazes of the Woodland Trail. Head south on this trail, passing through an area which is often wet. After a woods road branches off to the left, the trail becomes drier.

Further down the road, the trail passes several clusters of cedar trees, and it descends over slabs of exposed basalt. After you hike about a mile on the Woodland Trail, the white-blazed Brookside Trail begins on the right, but you should continue following the red-blazed Woodland Trail. Then, in another 500 feet, you'll reach the junction with the yellow-blazed Summit Trail you encountered earlier in the hike. Proceed ahead on the red-blazed trail (now retracing your steps) and follow it back to the parking lot where the hike began.

32

South Mountain Reservation

TOTAL DISTANCE: 9.3 miles (short hike is approximately 5 miles)

HIKING TIME: 6 hours (short hike is approximately 4 hours)

VERTICAL RISE: 750 feet

RATING: Moderate

MAPS: USGS Caldwell/Roselle; Essex County Park Commission South Mountain Reservation map

TRAILHEAD GPS COORDINATES: N 40° 43′ 39″ W 74° 18′ 14″

South Mountain Reservation has much to offer in the midst of a built-up area. The 2,048-acre tract contains a substantial river, many streams and cascades, a 25-foot waterfall, and 19 miles of trails through gentle woodland. At least for the first part of the hike, the trails are mostly free from traffic noise. The first and second of the three Watchung ridges form the eastern and western boundaries of the reservation. The name *Watchung* is a legacy from the Lenape Native Americans, who thought of the ridges as the "high hills." The Watchung ridges are intrusions (or extrusions) of lava similar to those in the Palisades. As these layers rose from west to east and were glaciated, the top layer of the Watchungs cooled more quickly than the lower layers that formed the Palisades. Because the layers in South Mountain Reservation cooled more quickly, the hexagonal columns that formed are considerably smaller than those in the Palisades. These ridges were heavily lumbered before the Revolutionary War to supply firewood for New York City and again in the late 19th century to provide wood for the nearby paper mills. A number of very large trees remain in the reservation, some of them twisted into deformed shapes.

This figure-eight hike follows the yellow-blazed Lenape Trail, the orange-blazed Turtle Back Trail, and the white-blazed Rahway Trail. The Lenape Trail honors the state's original inhabitants and preeminent foot travelers; the Turtle Back Trail was named for the rocks in the reservation that show erosion markings similar to the markings on a turtle's back; and the Rahway Trail takes its name from the river it parallels. Turtle-back rocks were formed when the volcanic basalt rock characteristic of the Watchungs, known as "traprock,"

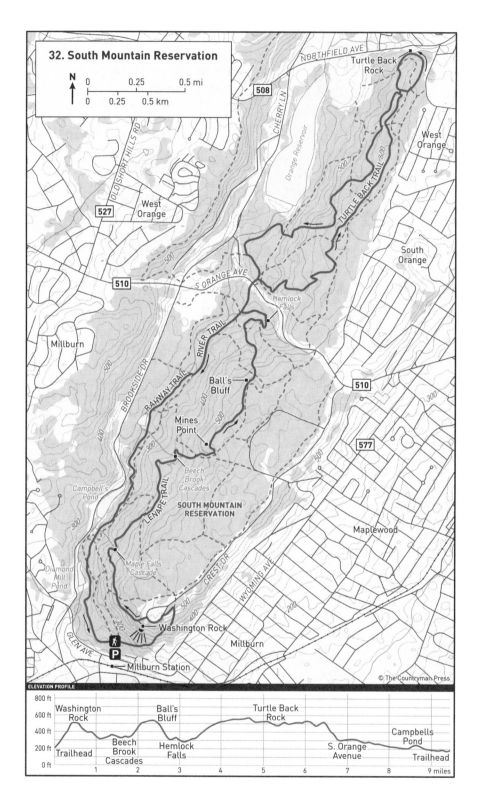

32. South Mountain Reservation

N

| 0 | 0.25 | | 0.5 mi |
| 0 | 0.25 | 0.5 km | |

NORTHFIELD AVE

Turtle Back Rock

508

CHERRY LN

Orange Reservoir

West Orange

OLD SHORT HILLS RD

West Orange

527

500

510

S ORANGE AVE

Hemlock Falls

South Orange

TURTLE BACK TRAIL

600

500

Millburn

BROOKSIDE DR

RIVER TRAIL

RAHWAY TRAIL

Ball's Bluff

Mines Point

Beech Brook Cascades

510

577

500

300

LENAPE TRAIL

500

400

300

Campbell's Pond

300

SOUTH MOUNTAIN RESERVATION

Maplewood

Diamond Mill Pond

Maple Falls Cascade

CREST DR

WYOMING AVE

500

400

200

Washington Rock

GLEN AVE

P

Millburn Station

Millburn

© The Countryman Press

ELEVATION PROFILE

800 ft									
600 ft	Washington Rock		Ball's Bluff		Turtle Back Rock				
400 ft									Campbells Pond
200 ft		Beech Brook Cascades	Hemlock Falls				S. Orange Avenue		Trailhead
0 ft	Trailhead								
	1	2	3	4	5	6	7	8	9 miles

fractured into small hexagonal blocks. The cracks filled with minerals, and, when erosion wore away the traprock faster than the minerals, the result was a patterned rock similar to the markings on the back of a turtle. There are several examples of this type of rock throughout South Mountain Reservation; one at the northeastern corner of the park, along the route of this hike, is actually called Turtle Back Rock. It is believed that the word *traprock* is derived from the Scandinavian word, *trappa*, meaning "stair step." When the traprock layers erode, the resulting rock formation often resembles steps.

The Essex County Park Commission was established in 1895, and one of its first projects was the acquisition of property for South Mountain Reservation. Drawing on the ideas of famed landscape architect Frederick Law Olmsted, and in consultation with his firm, the Commission created 23 parks and three reservations within the county. Olmsted also designed New York City's Central Park. Although the concept of South Mountain Reservation was Olmsted's, many of the features of the reservation, such as bridges, trails, and steps, were built by the Civilian Conservation Corps in 1934.

The distance covered in this hike is over 9 miles, although a shorter 5-mile option, which leaves out the northern loop, is also possible. Except at the very start, there are no long climbs, so the hike is useful for developing a good walking pace and increasing hiking stamina. The woods and rhododendron groves make the trail an excellent spring hike, although the area near the Rahway River is sometimes wet. The groves of rhododendron, wild azalea, and mountain laurel were planted, together with white pine and hemlock, when the land

was acquired by the Essex County Park Commission at the beginning of the 20th century in an effort to eradicate the damage done previously by logging and paper mills.

GETTING THERE

Driving from the east, take I-78 to Exit 50B (Maplewood, Millburn) and continue north on Vaux Hall Road for 0.7 mile. Turn left onto Millburn Avenue, and in 0.5 mile, bear right onto Essex Street, where a one-way traffic system begins. Just past the Millburn railroad station, turn right onto Lackawanna Place. Turn right at the next intersection (Glen Avenue) and make an immediate left turn into the Locust Grove parking area.

Approaching on I-78 from the west, you will need to make a U-turn at Exit 54.

The trailhead is readily accessible by public transportation, given that the Millburn station on the Morristown Line of NJ Transit is directly opposite the Locust Grove parking area. From the western end of the platform at the Millburn station, walk down the stairway to Lackawanna Place, turn right, and cross Glen Avenue to enter the park at the Locust Grove parking area.

THE HIKE

From the kiosk at the northeast corner of the parking area, follow the yellow-blazed Lenape Trail, which bears right onto a gravel road leading to a picnic area. The trail continues through the picnic area, where there is a fenced-in spring on the left. Past the rain shelter and picnic tables, the trail begins climbing the First Watchung Mountain on a wide, rocky path. It bears right at a

HEMLOCK FALLS

ahead, the trail descends to cross the road and reach a boulder with a plaque, known as Washington Rock.

Dedicated in 1992, the plaque describes the events of 1780, which George Washington watched from this point. It details the efforts of the British to destroy the American supply base at Morristown, the burning of Connecticut Farms (now called Union), and other military events. The plaque notes that, after the British efforts failed, they were forced to retire and "quit New Jersey soil forever." History tells us that, at the time of the Revolution, nearly all the trees in New Jersey suitable for shipbuilding and housing had been chopped down, providing enough visibility to observe the movements of the British in the valley. A sentry was posted at Washington Rock, and as soon as he became aware of troop movements in the valley below, a bonfire was lit to alert the soldiers at Jockey Hollow. Another stone marker commemorates Paul R. Jackson, a friend of the park.

Continue along the yellow-blazed Lenape Trail, which descends to an observation platform with stone pillars. The view from here is to the southwest, with Millburn and the NJ Transit railroad tracks visible below (partially obscured by the trees), and I-78 and the Watchung Reservation—the continuation of the Watchung range beyond the Millburn-Springfield gap—ahead in the distance.

When you're ready to continue, turn left and follow the Lenape Trail, which descends on a footpath. Several unmarked side trails go off to the left, but continue ahead on the yellow-blazed Lenape Trail. Soon, you'll notice a fenced overlook on the left. An abandoned quarry is directly below, with Millburn and the Watchung range in

fork, then turns right at a T-intersection (marked by a chain-link fence) onto a woods road, continuing to climb. As you climb, you will pass below a large concrete structure, part of the old waterworks system used to supply East Orange with water.

At the top of the rise, follow the yellow blazes as they turn left, leaving the road, and continue on a footpath to the paved Crest Drive (closed to vehicular traffic). The Lenape Trail crosses the road, reenters the woods, and begins parallel the road. It reaches a limited viewpoint (marked by two benches) from which the New York City skyline may be seen to the left on a clear day if there are no leaves on the trees, with the towers of the Verrazano-Narrows Bridge visible in the distance to the right. Just

the distance. A short distance beyond, the Lenape Trail crosses a bridle path designated the Sunset Trail on the park map. After a short descent, it crosses a small stream, with the Maple Falls Cascade—where the stream plunges down a 25-foot sluiceway of exposed basalt—to the left, downstream. This is a good spot for a short break.

After climbing away from the brook, the trail follows a relatively level footpath, crossing another bridle path (this one named the Pingry Trail). It turns sharply right at Lilliput Knob (an example of a turtle-back rock) and reaches Beech Brook Cascades—where two brooks converge—about 1.8 miles from the start. Beyond the cascade, the trail begins a gradual climb, paralleling a brook in a shallow ravine to the right. After bearing left and crossing a bridle path called the Overlook Trail, the trail climbs to reach Mines Point, named for exploratory pits dug by copper prospectors around 1800. Here, the trail bears right and heads north, first climbing gently through a relatively open area, and passing a deer enclosure on the left, then descending to reach Ball's Bluff, where old stone pillars are remnants of a picnic shelter built in 1908.

The Lenape Trail continues to descend, crossing a bridle path (the Ball's Bluff Trail) on the way. Toward the base of the descent, it begins to parallel a stream flowing through a ravine to the right.

After crossing the stream on rocks, the trail cross a road improved with large stone steps, then bears right and passes through an area with many rhododendron bushes. It turns left at a T-intersection, descends along a switchback, and then turns sharply left. Just beyond, it reaches the base of Hemlock Falls, a scenic waterfall, and crosses a footbridge over the stream. A red-on-white-blazed trail climbs stone steps to the top of the waterfall, and benches afford an opportunity to rest and enjoy the beautiful setting. You are now about 3 miles into the hike, and the falls are a wonderful place to take a break.

When you're ready, cross a stone footbridge over the stream. The Lenape Trail heads west, following a wide path along the stream and passing Hobble Falls on the right. Soon, it reaches a T-intersection with a bridle path, marked by signpost for the Rahway Trail. (If you wish to shorten your hike to approximately 5 miles, turn left on the bridle path and pick up the description below.)

The River Trail, the bridle path to the left, will be the route for your return journey, and the white-blazed Rahway Trail is straight ahead. Turn right, following the yellow blazes of the Lenape Trail uphill on a wide woods road to the top of the rise, then turn left at an enormous deformed oak tree, just before a metal gate and a small parking lot on South Orange Avenue.

Soon, the trail crosses over South Orange Avenue on a footbridge. Just beyond, you'll reach a junction, where the yellow-blazed Lenape Trail turns left. Turn right, leaving the Lenape Trail, and follow the orange-blazed Turtle Back Trail, which curves right, then left, and passes a huge tree. After crossing a bridle path at a culvert, you'll reach a signpost for the Turtle Back Trail. Follow the orange blazes uphill, and at a double blaze, continue along the Turtle Back Trail as it turns left onto a footpath and climbs on switchbacks. The trail follows along the side of a hill, overlooking the valley below, then winds around more switchbacks and begins to parallel a ravine, below on the right.

After climbing yet another switch-

TURTLE BACK ROCK

back, you'll reach a four-way junction, where an orange/white-blazed trail begins on the left. You should turn right to continue on the orange-blazed Turtle Back Trail. A short distance beyond, the orange trail approaches a bridle path (the Longwood Trail) but turns left and continues on a footpath. Follow the trail, which now heads north, roughly parallel to the bridle path.

The orange-blazed trail proceeds along a relatively level footpath, passing many trees felled by Hurricane Sandy in October 2012. After crossing three more bridle paths in the next mile, the trail reaches a T-intersection. Here, the orange blazes turn left. You'll be returning on the orange-blazed trail, but you'll first want to see the interesting Turtle Back Rock. To reach this feature, turn right onto an orange-and-white-blazed trail. Just ahead, follow the orange-and-white blazes as they turn left onto

a bridle path, but when the bridle path curves left, continue straight on a footpath.

The orange-and-white-blazed trail soon curves to the left and begins to run above the busy Northfield Avenue. After a turn to the right, you'll reach the Turtle Back Rock, named for the patterns on the surface of the rock. An interpretive sign explains how this unusual rock was formed. The best examples of the turtle-back patterns can be seen on the back of the large rock, as well on smaller adjacent rocks.

Continue ahead, crossing another bridle path (the North Trail), and you'll soon reach a four-way junction. The orange-and-white-blazed trail turns left here, but you should continue straight ahead, now once again following the orange-blazed Turtle Back Trail. Over the next mile, the trail crosses two bridle paths and begins to descend. You may be able to glimpse the southern end of the Orange Reservoir through the trees when they are bare.

Be alert for a sharp right turn where the orange-blazed trail descends to cross another bridle path (the Reservoir Trail), then bears left and continues to descend on a woods road. Before reaching a stream, the orange-blazed trail turns left onto a footpath and continues parallel to the stream. After climbing a little and passing a cascade in the stream, the trail proceeds through a pine grove. It soon reaches a junction with the yellow-blazed Lenape Trail, where you should turn left and proceed uphill on a wide path, now following both yellow and orange blazes. After passing through a pine grove, you'll reach the junction where you began the loop on the Turtle Back Trail. Turn right, rejoining the yellow-blazed Lenape Trail, and recross the footbridge over South Orange Avenue. Turn right at the familiar distorted old tree on your left and walk down to the signpost. (If you have shortened the hike, pick up the description at this point.)

Head south, straight ahead, on the bridle path (the River Trail) and in about a half mile, turn right toward a bridge over the Rahway River. Just before the bridge, look for white blazes on a tree to the left. Turn left and head south on the white-blazed Rahway Trail, which you will follow to the end of the hike. As of this writing, sections of the trail are poorly blazed, but you should be able to follow its route between the bridle path and the river. After passing two low concrete dams in the river, the Rahway Trail detours up to the River Trail to make use of the bridges over streams, crosses another woods road, and enters a prolific rhododendron grove. A short distance beyond, Campbell's Pond comes into view.

Near the southern end of the pond, the trail passes close to an old building that once served as a steam-driven pumping station. The large boilers housed in this building formerly provided steam for pumping water to a reservoir on the hills, using water from Campbell's Pond. Campbell's Pond is very shallow, probably not more than a foot in depth. Traffic noise from Brookside Drive is encountered along this section of the trail.

South of Campbell's Pond, the Rahway Trail crosses Maple Brook on a stone-faced bridge, then crosses two branches of the bridle path. A short distance beyond, the trail turns left onto the bridle path, follows it for 200 feet, then turns right onto a footpath. About 0.2 mile beyond the next pond (Diamond Mill Pond), the Rahway Trail turns left, away from the river. It now passes through an area where tiny "fairy houses" built of natural materials are tucked into tree hollows and roots. Soon, the library and the parking lot for Millburn Station become visible on the right. Just beyond, you arrive at the Locust Grove parking area and your car.

33

Watchung Reservation

TOTAL DISTANCE: 6.5 miles

HIKING TIME: 4 hours

VERTICAL RISE: 500 feet

RATING: Moderate

MAPS: USGS Chatham/Roselle; Union County Department of Parks and Recreation park map

TRAILHEAD GPS COORDINATES: N 40° 40' 59" W 74° 22' 27"

Watchung Reservation is a 2,000-acre patch of wooded land straddling the first and second Watchung ridges in central New Jersey. Although it sits in the middle of suburbia, the reservation is large enough for a good workout and also contains a number of interesting features, most of which you will see on this hike.

The name *Watchung* comes from the Lenape word for "high hills," *Wachunk*. Along with South Mountain Reservation and Eagle Rock Reservation to the north, Watchung Reservation has preserved as wilderness a portion of the long mountain that overlooks the flat plains leading toward New York City and the Atlantic Ocean. General George Washington used the long Watchung ridge as a natural fortification against the British during the Revolutionary War. He planted a number of lookouts along the ridge and kept his troops safely to the west, in Loantaka and Jockey Hollow. At the end of the previous Ice Age, the Watchung ridge formed the eastern rim of the basin that contained glacial Lake Passaic, a 30-by-10-mile lake, of which the Great Swamp is but a remnant.

Watchung Reservation is laced with wide lanes and horse trails. Several shorter marked trails are found in the vicinity of the Trailside Museum. The longest trail is the white-blazed Sierra Trail. It is 10 miles long, has many ups and downs, and passes just about every interesting feature the reservation has to offer. It is not a simple path, but one that links many trails in the reservation, making it necessary to watch for double blazes that signal turns. You will use a large portion of this trail for your hike.

Unfortunately, I-78 runs along the northern boundary of the reservation, and the noise from this busy highway's traffic can be heard for part of the hike. During the late 1970s and early 1980s,

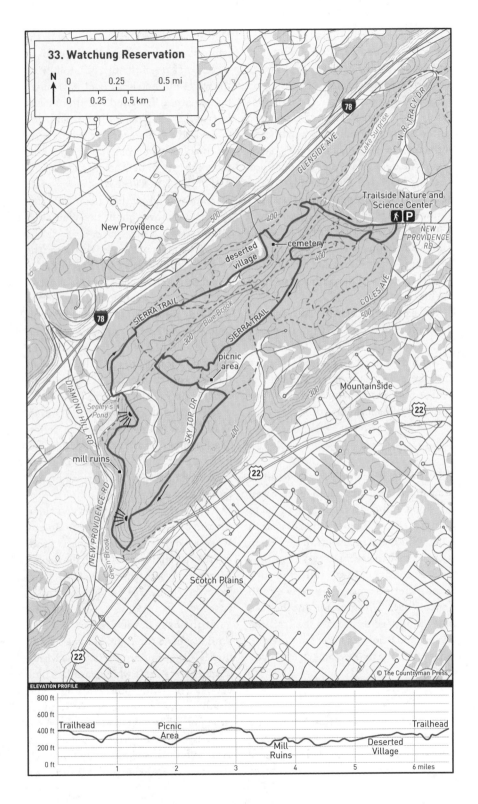

33. Watchung Reservation

N

| 0 | 0.25 | 0.5 mi |
| 0 | 0.25 | 0.5 km |

78

GLENSIDE AVE

Lake Surprise

W. R. TRACY DR

New Providence

Trailside Nature and Science Center

NEW PROVIDENCE RD

deserted village

cemetery

78

SIERRA TRAIL

Blue Brook

SIERRA TRAIL

COLES AVE

picnic area

DIAMOND HILL RD

SKY TOP DR

Seeley's Pond

Mountainside

22

mill ruins

(NEW PROVIDENCE RD)

Green Brook

22

Scotch Plains

© The Countryman Press

ELEVATION PROFILE

800 ft						
600 ft						
400 ft	Trailhead	Picnic Area				Trailhead
200 ft			Mill Ruins	Deserted Village	
0 ft	1	2	3	4	5	6 miles

many conservation-minded people tried to prevent the construction of this major interstate highway, which planners wanted to route through the northern section of the reservation. The issue was finally settled by replacing the land used for the highway, totaling about 70 acres, with land from an adjacent rock quarry. When the deal was struck, $3.6 million was appropriated for the upkeep and development of the reservation. The highway was built low in the ground and is flanked by walls that muffle the sound somewhat. In one place, a cut-and-cover structure—a 220-foot-wide bridge with soil and plants—allows animals to cross the highway safely.

An excellent map of the reservation, published by the Union County Department of Parks and Recreation, is available at the Trailside Nature and Science Center or online at ucnj.org/wp-content/uploads/2019/03/Watchung-Reservation.pdf.

GETTING THERE

Take US 22 West to Summit Road in Mountainside. Turn right onto Summit Road and continue for 1.2 miles to Summit Lane. Turn left onto Summit Lane. When you reach a traffic circle in 0.7 mile, take the second exit to continue on Summit Lane. In 0.5 mile, the road turns right and becomes New Providence Road. Continue for another 0.2 mile to the parking area for the Trailside Nature and Science Center (on the right, where the road makes a sharp left turn).

THE HIKE

After visiting the Trailside Nature and Science Center, return to the entrance to the parking area and turn right, proceeding west (downhill) on the extension of New Providence Road, marked with the white blazes of the Sierra Trail. Opposite a DO NOT ENTER sign, turn left, following the white-blazed Sierra Trail, now joined by the Green Trail and the pink-blazed History Trail. The trails descend log steps and cross a wooden bridge over a brook. As you cross the bridge, note the exposure of bedrock in the streambed on the left. These rocks are basalt, or traprock, which has been quarried extensively throughout the Watchung Mountains.

The trail continues through the woods and, after crossing a wet area on puncheons and wooden bridges over two more streams, reaches a T-intersection with the Yellow Trail. Turn right, now following both white and yellow blazes, and descend to reach the same brook that you crossed previously. Turn left (do not cross the wooden bridge over the brook), joining the Orange Trail. Soon, you'll reach a junction where the Orange Trail leaves to the right and the Yellow Trail begins. Continue ahead, now following both white and yellow blazes, but at the next junction, turn right, and follow only white blazes.

The Sierra Trail now takes you along the rim of a glen, quite beautiful in any season. On the left, the brook is eroding the red shales overlaying the basalt. Along the way, the Blue Trail joins from the right, and the path begins to descend.

At the base of the descent, the Blue Trail leaves to the right, but you should turn left, continuing to follow the white-blazed Sierra Trail, which parallels Blue Brook. The trail soon bears left and climbs away from the brook. It turns left again at the next intersection, where it briefly joins the pink-blazed History Trail, then turns right at the following junction (here, the pink-blazed trail

DESERTED VILLAGE OF FELTSVILLE

leaves to the left). In another quarter mile, the trail crosses a small brook and bears left, uphill.

After passing several houses on the left, the trail crosses a dirt road. Just beyond, it crosses a stream and soon begins a long, gradual descent.

At the base of the descent, about 2 miles from the start, follow the white-blazed Sierra Trail as it turns left onto a dirt road. The trail follows the dirt road for a short distance and then turns left, leaving the road and continuing on a footpath. It ascends through a pine forest, planted by the Civilian Conservation Corps in the 1930s. Unfortunately, most of the pines have died, and the area is now dominated by deciduous trees. Soon, you'll reach an open grassy area,

with a picnic pavilion ahead. Bear right here and follow a gravel service road out to the paved Sky Top Drive. The trail crosses the road and reenters the woods. It climbs some more to reach a T-intersection, where it turns right onto a woods road that runs parallel to Sky Top Drive (the paved road may soon be seen to the right). After climbing gradually, the trail begins to descend. As the trail bends to the left, a short path to the right leads to an overlook above a quarry, with I-78 visible in the distance.

After descending more steeply, the trail turns sharply right onto a footpath and descends to the Green Brook. It runs along the brook, with New Providence Road on the other side. Green Brook is a stocked trout stream and attracts many

WILLCOCKS AND BADGLEY CEMETERY

anglers. As the trail heads north along the bank of the brook, it traverses several rocky sections. Other sections of the trail are quite smooth, covered with fine gravel. The trail, the brook, and the road all pass together through a gap in the long wall of the Watchungs.

In about a third of a mile, you will reach the site of an old mill, with many brick and concrete ruins still visible. The mill used the water power from the brook to make paper; later it held a 10,000-gallon still operated by bootleggers, whose product is said to have been world-renowned. Here, on the right, are cliffs formed of basalt rock. After passing the ruins of the dam used to divert water to the mill, the trail bears right and climbs steeply to a viewpoint from a rock outcrop. It then heads east

and soon reaches a T-intersection with a woods road. Here, it turns left and descends to Sky Top Drive. You've now hiked about 4.5 miles.

The Sierra Trail turns left and crosses Blue Brook on the highway bridge, with Seeley's Pond to the left. This point is at the edge of the reservation, and suburbia is just across the street. After crossing the bridge, the trail immediately turns right, traverses a grassy area, and reenters the woods. You will notice wild roses along this section of the trail, as well as poison ivy. The trail continues through some fairly dense vegetation, then crosses several small brooks on a long wooden boardwalk

Just beyond the long boardwalk, the pink-blazed History Trail joins from the right, and both trails climb wooden steps, passing a historical marker for the Drake Farm. The trail now passes through another area of dense vegetation, then reenters the woods and begins to climb. After descending to cross a stream, the trail proceeds ahead to reach a T-intersection. Here, the Sierra Trail turns left, while the History Trail turns right.

With a hemlock grove visible directly ahead, the Sierra Trail turns left onto a gravel road. A short distance beyond, you'll emerge onto a paved road, with a large building facing you. You have now entered the Deserted Village of Feltsville. From 1845 to 1860, David Felt, a New York City businessman, owned and operated a paper mill on Blue Brook. Feltsville was a factory town then, but when the mill closed, it became Glenside Park, a Victorian retreat with lawn tennis and pure water. Some say there are a salt brook and a magnesium spring in the vicinity, which may explain why the area was developed into a mini-resort between 1882 and 1916. In 1991, a New Jersey Historic Trust grant was awarded for the preservation of Feltsville as a unique resource.

The Sierra Trail follows the paved road through the village for 0.4 mile, passing a number of deteriorated cottages. Markers along the way relate the history of the area. After the road curves left and passes the church/store building and an adjacent residence, the Sierra Trail turns right on a bridle path. In 200 feet, it turns right again onto another dirt road and soon passes a small cemetery, which contains the graves of the Willcocks and Badgley families, who first settled the area about 1736. William Willcox, a judge and advocate of the Revolutionary War, died in 1800. Joseph Badgley was a private in the First New Jersey Regiment and died in 1785. John Willcocks, Sr., a member of the Light Horse Company of the New Jersey militia, died on November 22, 1776.

The road bears left, just beyond the cemetery, and soon narrows to a footpath that meanders through the woods. About a third of a mile from the cemetery, the white-blazed trail turns right and descends on a dirt road. In 400 feet, the white blazes bear left, leaving the road, but you should continue ahead on the dirt road, now unblazed, and cross a bridge over Blue Brook. Just beyond, bear right, then continue ahead on a wide path as the Blue Trail joins from the right. The trail parallels a tributary stream and continues uphill on wide wooden steps. Soon, the blue blazes are replaced by orange blazes. After a few more minutes, you will reach a paved road. Bear right here and walk uphill. The parking area will be on your left.

34

Sourland Mountain Preserve

TOTAL DISTANCE: 4.7 miles

HIKING TIME: 3 hours

VERTICAL RISE: 500 feet

RATING: Easy to moderate

MAPS: USGS Rocky Hill; Somerset County Park Commission Sourland Mountain Preserve trail map

TRAILHEAD GPS COORDINATES:
N 40° 28' 27" W 74° 41' 38.5"

Sourland Mountain is really a 10-by-4-mile sheet of Triassic traprock, similar to the Palisades, Watchungs, and Cushetunk Mountain (see Introduction). Here a portion of a buried igneous intrusion was tilted, with its eastern edge leaning up; then it was uplifted. Erosion left the harder igneous rock exposed, and it now overlooks the surrounding plain. The highest elevation on the mountain is 586 feet. Contrast this with the 120-foot elevation of the eastern plain, and you have one of the steepest gradients in central New Jersey. It is on this eastern edge that the hiking trails are located. The western portion of the mountain slopes off into the plain more gradually.

Two factors have allowed Sourland Mountain to remain mostly undeveloped. The first is the fact that the land has never been of much agricultural or commercial worth—something that seems to be reflected in the name. The name *Sourland* may have stemmed from the German term *sauerland*, meaning "land that is not sweet." The soil is rocky and acidic, and there is little groundwater. The name may also refer to the reddish-brown ("sorrel-land") color of the soil found on the plains beneath the mountain. In some old records, the name is given as *Sowerland*.

The second factor that explains why Sourland Mountain has not been developed is that it is far from any major thoroughfare. It has served as a retreat for many, including Charles Lindbergh, whose child was kidnapped from there in 1932. The broad, flat top of the mountain is quite rocky, is mostly wooded, and includes about 400 acres of old growth.

Many historic buildings still stand along the several quiet country roads that cross over it. But developmental pressure in New Jersey is relentless, and many people have become concerned.

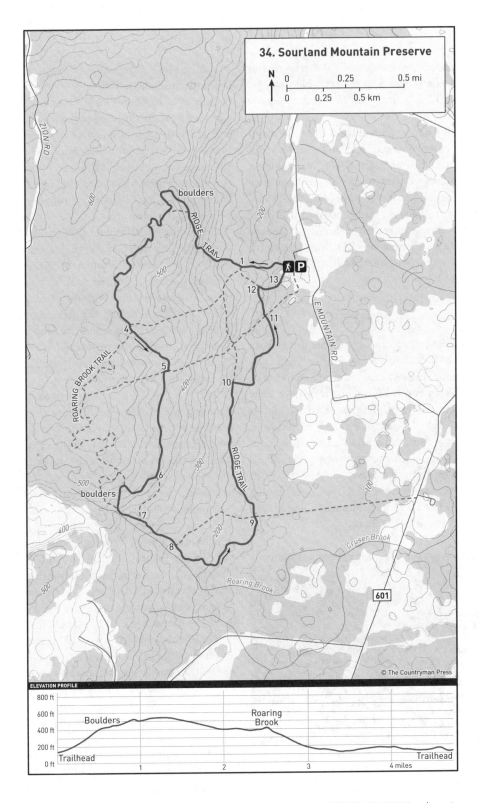

34. Sourland Mountain Preserve

N

| 0 | | 0.25 | | 0.5 mi |
| 0 | | 0.25 | 0.5 km | |

ZION RD

600

boulders

RIDGE TRAIL

200

500

1

13

12

11

4

ROARING BROOK TRAIL

5

400

10

E. MOUNTAIN RD

300

RIDGE TRAIL

500

boulders

100

6

7

9

8

200

400

Cruser Brook

500

Roaring Brook

601

© The Countryman Press

ELEVATION PROFILE

800 ft
600 ft
400 ft
200 ft
0 ft

Boulders

Roaring Brook

Trailhead

Trailhead

1   2   3   4 miles

One such voice is the Sourland Planning Council, which has pushed for preservation of the area since 1986. The matter is complicated by the fact that portions of the mountain fall in Mercer, Hunterdon, and Somerset Counties. To date, only Somerset and Hunterdon Counties have preserved sections of the mountain. The section of the mountain in Mercer County has not yet been protected. The 4,000-acre Sourland Mountain Preserve, the location of this hike, is administered by the Somerset County Park Commission (P.O. Box 5327, North Branch, NJ 08876; 908-722-1200; www .somersetcountyparks.org).

GETTING THERE

Take I-287 to Exit 17 and continue south on US 206 for about 7.6 miles. Turn right onto Amwell Road (County Route 514), being careful not to turn right at New Amwell Road, and proceed for 2.8 miles to East Mountain Road. Turn left onto East Mountain Road and follow it for 1.9 miles to the entrance to Sourland Mountain Preserve, on the right. If you are using a GPS device, enter this address: 425 East Mountain Road, Hillsborough, NJ 08844.

TREE GROWING OUT OF A HORIZONTAL CRACK IN A BOULDER

THE HIKE

From the kiosk at the edge of the parking area (trail maps of the preserve are usually available here), head west across a grassy field. At the edge of the woods, you will notice a wooden post with three blazes: white triangle, white circle, and white square. This marks the start of the three loop trails in the preserve, which head uphill into the woods, paralleling a brook to the left.

Follow the joint trails for about 5 minutes until you reach post #1 (all intersections are marked with white-on-green reflective numbers on wooden posts). Here the white-triangle and white-circle trails turn left, crossing the stream on a footbridge, but you should continue ahead on the white square–blazed Ridge Trail, which proceeds steadily uphill through a heavily wooded area.

After about 15 minutes of steady climbing, the trail levels off. Soon, after another short climb, you'll come to an area of huge boulders. This is the most interesting part of the hike, so take your time to enjoy the unusual boulders. At one point, the trail goes through a narrow passage between two huge boulders. Toward the end of the boulder field, you'll notice a large tree that has grown out of a horizontal crack in a boulder. The trail continues through a forest that features many tall, straight tulip trees. In some cases, several tulip tree trunks grow out of the same set of roots.

Finally, after about an hour of hiking, you'll reach post #4. To the left, a connector trail (marked by "C" blazes) leads back toward the parking area, but you should bear right to continue along the white-square-blazed trail. At the next junction, bear left, as the red circle-blazed Roaring Brook Trail begins on the right. Proceed ahead on the white

THE TRAIL PASSES BETWEEN THESE TWO HUGE BOULDERS

square–blazed trail, which descends, crosses a bridge over a stream, and reaches the right-of-way of the Texas Eastern Gas Transmission Corporation pipeline at post #5. The trail jogs to the right along the right-of-way, then turns left and reenters the woods. Continue following the white square–blazed trail, which crosses several wet areas on a series of boardwalks.

When you reach post #6, at a break in a fence, bear right to continue along the white square–blazed trail (a connector trail, marked by "C" blazes, begins on the left). The white square–blazed trail now begins to descend. Bear left at a junction with another connector trail and continue down to Roaring Brook, passing some more large boulders on the way.

In about 5 minutes, you'll go through a gap in another chain-link fence. Just beyond, you'll notice post #8. A connector trail goes off to the left, but you should bear right to continue on the white square–blazed Ridge Trail. Soon, the trail bears left and heads away from Roaring Brook.

In another 15 minutes, you'll cross a boardwalk over a stream and pass an old stone-and-concrete wall (possibly built as a dam) on your left. Just beyond, you'll reach a four-way intersection marked by post #9, where you should continue straight ahead.

The next stretch of trail is nearly level, with one long boardwalk as well as many short stretches of boardwalk. In another 20 minutes or so, you'll reach post #10. Here, you should turn right and follow both white-square and white-triangle blazes, soon crossing another section of boardwalk.

A short distance beyond, at post #11, you'll again cross the Texas Eastern gas pipeline. Continue straight ahead, and you'll soon reach post #12. Turn right and begin to follow three co-aligned trails, blazed with white triangles, white circles, and white squares. Soon, you'll emerge onto a grassy area and descend toward a small pond. Bear left around the pond, pass post #13, and you'll reach the parking area where you left your car.

35

D & R Canal– Washington Crossing to Scudder's Falls

TOTAL DISTANCE: 6.3 miles

HIKING TIME: 3 hours

VERTICAL RISE: 100 feet

RATING: Easy

MAPS: USGS Pennington; DEP Washington Crossing State Park map; DEP Delaware & Raritan Canal State Park map

TRAILHEAD GPS COORDINATES:
N 40° 18' 10.5" W 74° 51' 38"

This hike combines an opportunity to learn about a critical battle of the Revolutionary War at Washington Crossing State Park (355 Washington Crossing–Pennington Road, Titusville, NJ 08560-1517; 609-737-0623; www.njparksandforests.org) with a long walk on the towpath of the Delaware & Raritan Canal. On the towpath (the walkway for the mules that pulled the canal boats) you will be exposed to much sun—a blessing or curse depending on the season or the weather. There is plenty to do at this state park. In all, this 3,500-acre park boasts about 15 miles of trails. Other hiking possibilities besides the one described here include several footpaths through a 140-acre natural area with an interpretive center.

The park's Visitor Center Museum (open year-round, 7 days a week, except for certain holidays, from 9 a.m. to 4 p.m.) contains a large collection of Revolutionary War artifacts, maps, and descriptive brochures. It offers a 27-minute video that will give you a feel for the momentous event that led to the establishment of the park, and full-length historical films are shown at specific times. There is no charge for admission to the museum, but a $1 per person fee is charged for viewing the video.

The importance of what happened here in 1776 cannot be overestimated. This was the site of probably the single most important offensive in George Washington's military career. At the very least, it kept him and the country alive during the early days of the Revolutionary War.

Since independence had been declared, the Continental Army, led by Washington, had not scored a point against the British. Washington and his men had tried to stop the British invasion of Long Island (Brooklyn) but were driven back to Manhattan and

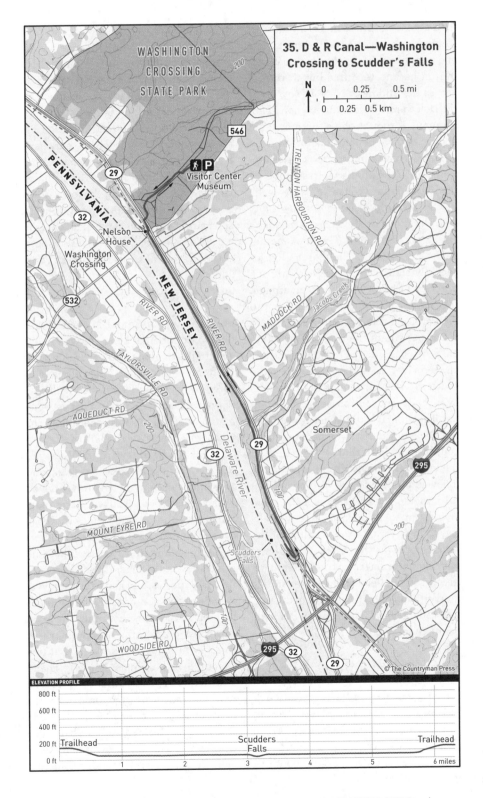

35. D & R Canal—Washington
Crossing to Scudder's Falls

N

| 0 | 0.25 | 0.5 mi |
| 0 | 0.25 | 0.5 km |

WASHINGTON
CROSSING
STATE PARK

546

Visitor Center
Museum

TRENTON HARBOURTON RD

PENNSYLVANIA

29

32

Nelson
House

Washington
Crossing

532

RIVER RD

TAYLORSVILLE RD

RIVER RD

NEW JERSEY

MADDOCK RD

Jacobs Creek

AQUEDUCT RD

200

32

29

Somerset

295

Delaware River

100

MOUNT EYRE RD

200

Scudders
Falls

100

WOODSIDE RD

295   32

29

© The Countryman Press

ELEVATION PROFILE

800 ft						
600 ft						
400 ft						
200 ft	Trailhead		Scudders Falls			Trailhead
0 ft	1	2	3	4	5	6 miles

then across the Hudson to New Jersey. Denied an adequate number of troops and supplies to meet the threat, Washington had no recourse but to retreat across the middle of New Jersey, cross the Delaware, and hunker down in Pennsylvania. Although the situation would appear to have been cause for extreme depression, Washington took a risk and won, and in the process stirred hope for the revolutionary cause.

On the night of December 25, 1776, he ordered three divisions of troops to attack the Hessians (German mercenaries) at Trenton. The plan called for each division to cross the Delaware at a different location and then converge on the enemy. Washington and his 2,400 men crossed the river in ferryboats to reach the site of the present-day state park. After a difficult crossing of the ice-choked river, he and his men marched south to Trenton, caught the Hessians by surprise, and took possession of Trenton. The other two divisions never made the crossing that night because they couldn't navigate their boats through the icy river. Washington immediately followed up the victory with a successful attack on the British at Princeton. Having pushed back the enemy halfway to New York, he took shelter for the remainder of the winter behind the long, curving natural wall of the Watchungs, in central New Jersey. These two battles marked a major turning point in the war, and they kept Washington in place as commander in chief.

GETTING THERE

From I-95, take Exit 1 North (the last exit in New Jersey) to NJ 29 North. About 3 miles from the exit, make a right turn onto County Route 546; you will find the main entrance to the park on your left in 0.7 mile. Between Memorial Day and Labor Day there is an entrance fee on weekends only. Pass the toll gate, follow signs to the Visitor Center Museum, and park in the large lot just to the north of the museum. Parking is free just north of the Nelson House near the river—if there is room. You may wish to park here and walk back to the visitor center to see the museum's collection of artifacts or simply walk south along the towpath as described below. Another option is to spot cars at each end of the hike. There is a parking area for boaters 3 miles south of the park on NJ 29 near Scudder's Falls.

THE HIKE

From the Visitor Center Museum, walk over to Continental Lane, the wood-chip walking path about 100 yards due west (in front) of the center. This path is indicated by a sign and is marked with red-dot-on-white blazes. You'll find it between a long line of trees and other plantings just across the paved road. Turn left onto the trail and head toward the Delaware River. Continental Lane is a pleasant, tree-lined walkway between two paved park service roads. You will note many large tree stumps along the way. These are the remains of tall ash trees that formerly lined the path. These trees became infected with the emerald ash borer, an invasive species, and had to be removed.

When the red-dot-on-white blazes turn off to the right, continue ahead on the wood-chip path, now unmarked. In a few minutes, the path ends at two Colonial-era buildings. Directly ahead is an old stone barn that now houses restrooms and a meeting room (not open to the public). To your left is the Johnson Ferry House, fronted with an herb garden. This house was likely used by General Washington and his staff throughout

NELSON HOUSE

the midnight crossing of the Delaware River on Christmas night in 1776. It is open to the public and is worth a visit.

To continue along the route of the hike, turn left for about 50 feet onto a paved road, then turn right (at a sign for PEDESTRIAN BRIDGE AND OVERLOOK AREA) onto a wide gravel path that heads south. This path will lead you past an overlook by a stone wall (overlooking NJ 29 and the Delaware River), with a large sign commemorating Washington's crossing of the river on Christmas night, and out to a pedestrian bridge over NJ 29. Cross the bridge and turn right, crossing the canal, then turn left and head south on the canal feeder towpath.

The towpath, which formerly served as the railbed of the Belvidere-Delaware Railroad, is flat and is surfaced with very fine, though loose, gravel. It gets much use from joggers and bikers as well as walkers. To the right and quite a drop below is the Delaware River. To the left is the feeder canal and, beyond that, NJ 29. It is unfortunate that the highway is so close, but that is an unavoidable reality. This section of towpath is exposed to sunlight and, during hot summer days, it may be advisable to hike in the late afternoon, when the shade from the taller trees on the west bank covers the entire path.

As you walk along the towpath, you'll see vegetation very different from that of the highland mountains or the Pinelands. The plants are more typical of highways, urban vacant lots, and other places that receive much sunlight. Don't be put off by this; some of the most valuable medicinal herbs are found in such environments.

For example, you'll see thistle, with its prickly leaves and round flower heads, which is used for fevers (it produces sweating). The common mullein—the tall, spikelike plant commonly seen along the roadside—is also found here; a tea made from its leaves and flowers is used for lung complaints and asthma. As for flowers, you'll find purple gentians, black-eyed Susans, goldenrod, and wild carrot (better known as Queen Anne's lace). Poison ivy is in abundance here as well, though it doesn't encroach upon the path. Pokeweed, edible as a young shoot but poisonous when fully matured, is found here also. You'll find the staghorn sumac with its red berry clusters that, when soaked in cold water, make a lemonade-like drink. At the edge of the dense woods that separate the towpath from the river are flowering dogwoods and even a few catalpa trees, with their large heart-shaped leaves and long, beanlike pods.

Where the canal curves slightly to the east, notice the outcroppings of red Brunswick shale, also known as brownstone, on the opposite bank. This rock is the primary bedrock throughout all of central New Jersey, except for the igneous intrusions that make up the Watchungs, Cushetunk Mountain, Sourland Mountain, and Rocky Hill.

A little farther ahead, Jacob's Creek passes under the canal and empties into the Delaware. There's a nice view of this wild and rocky confluence from the towpath, which stands 50 feet above it. Blue herons may be wading in the shallows, where they are safe from intruders. Don't be surprised if you see deer hoofprints on the towpath; they've got dense woods to hide in during the day.

After passing a flood-control structure, which allows the canal to drain into the river if necessary, you'll see a bridge across the canal ahead of you. Bear right here and head downhill on the paved road. Take one of the pathways to your left down to the river, and you'll come out near Scudder's Falls, a Class II set of rapids on the Delaware.

Scudder's Falls is named for the Scudder family, whose 18th-century farmstead and mill were once located in the area. One well-known member of the family was Amos Scudder, one of Washington's scouts at the Battle of Trenton. John Hart, one of the signers of the Declaration of Independence from New Jersey, was married to a Scudder. Unfortunately, nothing is left of the original house.

Notice the huge sections of concrete on the island just across from the falls. A structure located here once utilized the immense power of the water, which drops several feet in a short distance. These falls, more like a channel or chute between shoreline and island, are popular with kayakers. If you are here during high water and on a weekend, you will no doubt be treated to a display of paddling skills. The area, also heavily used by anglers and partygoers, is quite pleasant and very interesting, making it a good spot for lunch. You can sit on some of the big rocks near the river's edge, listen to the roar of the rapids, and gaze out toward Pennsylvania, far off on the other side.

After watching the rapids, return to the towpath (or follow the road along the river to a gas line and then scramble back up to the towpath) and begin the long walk back to Washington Crossing State Park. The benches placed about every quarter mile can provide a welcome rest, should you need one. Before crossing the pedestrian walkway over NJ 29, you may wish to take a look at the Nelson House, just below it, toward the river. The building contains a large collection of period pieces, a flag collection, and, adjacent to the building, a reconstruction of one of the original ferryboats that took Washington and his men across the frozen river on that cold December night.

From the Nelson House, take the pedestrian bridge across the highway and continue on the gravel path toward the Johnson Ferry House and flag museum to Continental Lane. Turn right onto Continental Lane and follow it back to the Visitor Center Museum and parking area—unless, of course, you parked elsewhere.

36

D & R Canal— Bull's Island to Stockton

TOTAL DISTANCE: 7.2 miles

HIKING TIME: 3.5 hours

VERTICAL RISE: Minimal

RATING: Easy to moderate

MAP: USGS Lumberville/Stockton; DEP Delaware & Raritan Canal State Park map

TRAILHEAD GPS COORDINATES: N 40° 24' 37.5" W 75° 02' 07"

For 30 miles (from Frenchtown to Trenton), the Delaware & Raritan Canal and the abandoned Belvidere-Delaware Railroad, on the New Jersey side of the Delaware River, are paralleled on the Pennsylvania side of the river by the Delaware Canal. Six bridges accessible to pedestrians cross the river in this stretch, making possible loop hikes of various lengths. This hike combines a walk along a 3.5-mile section of the path along the Delaware & Raritan Canal, from Bull's Island to Stockton, with a stroll along the towpath of the Delaware Canal on the opposite side of the river in Pennsylvania.

Construction of the Delaware & Raritan Canal began in 1832. The main section of the canal extended from Bordentown on the Delaware River to New Brunswick, on the Raritan River. To assure an adequate supply of water to the canal, a 22-mile feeder canal was built along the east side of the Delaware River from Bull's Island south to Trenton. An artificial island created by the construction of the canal, Bull's Island was named after Richard Bull, one of the original owners. By 1834, the wingdam at Bull's Island that diverted water from the river to the canal was completed, and the entire canal opened later that year.

The Belvidere-Delaware Railroad, which paralleled the Delaware River from Trenton to Belvidere, was completed in 1855. It was acquired by the Pennsylvania Railroad in 1872. Interestingly, about the same time, the Pennsylvania Railroad also acquired the Delaware & Raritan Canal, which remained in operation for another 50 years until it was abandoned in 1932.

The Belvidere-Delaware Railroad operated passenger service until 1960, with service in the 1950s consisting of

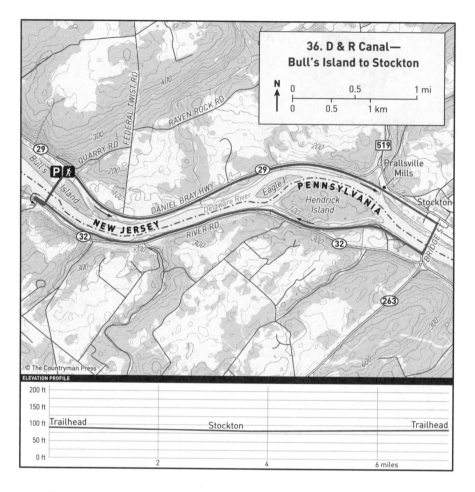

a single weekday round-trip from Phillipsburg to Trenton and back. Freight service lasted until 1978. The tracks were removed soon afterward, and a few years later, the rail line became part of the state park.

This hike follows the abandoned railbed of the Belvidere-Delaware Railroad high above the canal, rather than the historic canal towpath, because the towpath, which separates the canal from the river, is largely overgrown.

The return from Stockton is via the Delaware Canal on the Pennsylvania side of the river, which extends 60 miles from Easton to Bristol. Construction began in 1829, and the canal was

completed in 1832. It was in service as a navigable canal for 100 years, but even after its abandonment in 1932, the canal and its towpath remained intact and are today part of the Delaware Canal State Park.

GETTING THERE

From its junction with US 202, take NJ 29 North for 6 miles to the Bull's Island Recreation Area of the Delaware & Raritan Canal State Park (2185 Daniel Bray Highway, Stockton, NJ 08559; 609-397-2949; www.dandrcanal.com). If you are coming from the north, take I-78 West to Exit 15. Turn left at the first traffic light onto County Route 513 and proceed for 4.2 miles to Pittstown. Turn right to continue on County Route 513 and follow it for another 7.5 miles to Frenchtown. Turn left onto NJ 29 in Frenchtown and continue for 8.9 miles to the Bull's Island Recreation Area. Follow the entrance road over a one-lane bridge and park in a large parking area near the visitor center.

THE HIKE

From the parking area, head back across the one-lane bridge over the Delaware & Raritan Canal. Just before reaching NJ 29, turn right onto the abandoned right-of-way of the Belvidere-Delaware Railroad, now a multiuse trail suitable for walkers, joggers, and bicycle riders (and, in the winter, cross-country skiers). Go around the gate and head south on this wide path, which runs between NJ 29 on the left and the canal and river on the right (although, for much of the way, the canal and the river are separated from the path by a wide swath of woods). The path is popular with bicyclists, so walkers should keep to one side of this wide path to allow bicyclists to pass. For most of the way, the route is shaded by trees.

In a quarter mile, you'll pass milepost 21 on the right. These mileposts were installed at half-mile intervals to mark the distance along the path in the Delaware & Raritan Canal State Park. A short distance beyond milepost 20.5, you'll notice an historic concrete milepost on the right with the number 22. This milepost was placed by the railroad to indicate the distance to Trenton. Just before reaching canal milepost 20, you'll

PRALLSVILLE MILLS COMPLEX

PEDESTRIAN SUSPENSION BRIDGE OVER THE DELAWARE RIVER

cross a high bridge over a stream, with unobstructed views over the canal and river on the right.

Beginning at milepost 19.5, the canal runs closer to the path you are following (although the view of the canal and the river is often obstructed by vegetation). In another half mile (just before milepost 19), an interpretive sign on the right provides historical information on the canal and on a waste gate, used to drain excess water from the canal to the river. There is another unobstructed view over the canal and river here.

A third of a mile farther, the highway moves away from the path, and a stone retaining wall begins on the left. This stone wall was probably constructed in the 1850s, when the railroad was built. The stone used to construct the wall is of the locally quarried Stockton Formation, better known as brownstone. This type of stone has been used in the construction of many historic buildings in New Jersey, including some at Princeton and Rutgers Universities. A short distance ahead, you'll pass canal milepost 18.5, cross a bridge over the Wickecheoke Creek, and reach the Prallsville Mills complex.

Located just north of Stockton, the original mill on the site was constructed by Daniel Howell in 1720. John Prall, after whom the mill is named, bought the property in 1794. He enlarged the original gristmill and sawmill operation by adding a stone building used to mill linseed oil and plaster. In 1874, the original gristmill burned, ignited by a spark from a passing steam engine on the Belvidere-Delaware Railroad, but the mill was rebuilt on the old foundations 3 years later.

After milling came to an end in the 1950s, the entire complex of 10 buildings was acquired by the state and is gradually being restored by the Delaware River Mill Society (P.O. Box 298, Stockton, NJ 08559; 609-397-3586; www .prallsvillemills.org), which leases the site. The buildings are considered to be a significant example of early American industrial architecture. Guided tours of the inside of the historic buildings, where much of the original milling equipment has been preserved, are available on Thursday afternoons from June until September and by appointment. The historic buildings may be rented for special events such as weddings. Public restrooms are available, and there are picnic tables if you'd like to stop for lunch.

After exploring the Prallsville Mills complex, continue south along the path, the former railbed of the Belvidere-Delaware Railroad. Soon, you'll notice a small concrete shanty on the left. This was once used by the crossing watchman who guarded the railroad crossing just to the south (note the white crossbucks on the right side of the path). When you reach the location of the former railroad crossing, turn right and follow the road to the site of a guard lock in the canal, with an historical sign explaining its significance.

When you're ready to continue, retrace your steps to the former railbed and turn right. You'll pass on the right the concrete milepost 21 of the railroad (this milepost is not in its original location). The path you're following now runs some distance from the canal and the river, and you'll go by the backyards of homes along NJ 29 on the left. Soon, you'll cross the dead-end Ferry Street that leads to homes situated between the railbed and the river, and a short distance beyond, you'll reach Bridge Street.

Continue across Bridge Street. On the opposite side of the street, the former Stockton station is now a commercial establishment. Turn right and follow Bridge Street to the bridge across the Delaware River. Officially known as the Centre Bridge-Stockton Bridge, this steel truss bridge was constructed in 1926 on the stone piers of a former covered bridge that had originally been built in 1814, was rebuilt in 1841, and was destroyed by fire in 1923. The present-day bridge, which was extensively rehabilitated in 2006, is owned and maintained by the Delaware River Joint Toll Bridge Commission.

At the west end of the bridge, descend a concrete stairway and turn right onto the towpath of the Delaware Canal. The canal towpath heads north, passing the backyards of large homes. You'll pass under a bridge used to access several homes on the east side of the canal. This section of the towpath is peaceful and quiet.

After walking along the towpath for about three-quarters of a mile, you'll notice that River Road (PA 32) begins to parallel the canal on the left. This road closely parallels the canal and towpath for the next 1.7 miles, and the noise from the vehicles traveling along the road disturbs the tranquility of the setting. The towpath, though, runs directly along the Delaware River for most of this distance, with good views across the river to New

Jersey. This section of the towpath has few trees to provide shade.

Soon, you'll reach the Virginia Forrest Recreation Area, where parking and restrooms are available. About a mile to the north, you'll walk under a low bridge (clearance just under 6 feet) and pass a storage yard for Delaware Quarries.

In another third of a mile, the road moves away from the canal. For the next 0.7 mile, you'll again experience a more pristine environment, with backyards of homes visible above to the left, and the river directly to your right.

Soon, a picturesque pedestrian suspension bridge over the river comes into view. You'll be crossing this bridge to return to the Bull's Bridge Recreation Area in New Jersey, but since there is no direct connection between the towpath and the bridge, you'll need to continue under the bridge and follow the towpath for another 500 feet to Lock 12 of the canal. Here, a path leads left to River Road. Follow the path to River Road, turn left onto the road, and proceed back to the pedestrian bridge.

Turn left again and cross the five-span pedestrian suspension bridge, which offers panoramic views up and down the Delaware River.

The first bridge built in this location was a covered bridge constructed in 1856. This bridge remained in service until 1944, when it was declared unsafe and closed. In 1947, the Delaware River Joint Toll Bridge Commission contracted with John A. Roebling's Sons Co. of Trenton (the same firm that built the Brooklyn Bridge about 65 years earlier) to construct a pedestrian suspension bridge on the original stone piers of the 1856 bridge. The cost was $75,000. In 2013, the bridge was extensively rehabilitated at a cost of $3 million. A plaque commemorating the 2013 rehabilitation of the bridge is affixed to each end of the bridge. Although there is no charge to walk across the bridge, it is maintained by tolls collected at other bridges operated by the commission.

At the eastern end of the bridge, proceed ahead to the parking lot where you left your car.

D & R Canal— Kingston to Rocky Hill

TOTAL DISTANCE: 4 miles

HIKING TIME: 2 hours

VERTICAL RISE: Minimal

RATING: Easy to moderate

MAPS: USGS Monmouth Junction/Rocky Hill/Hightstown; DEP Delaware & Raritan Canal State Park map

TRAILHEAD GPS COORDINATES: N 40° 22' 27" W 74° 37' 08"

When it opened in 1834, the Delaware & Raritan Canal served as a major transportation link between Philadelphia and New York. The canal extended a distance of 44 miles, from the northernmost point of navigation on the Delaware River at Bordentown to the head of navigation on the Raritan River at New Brunswick. To assure an adequate water supply for the canal, a 22-mile-long feeder canal was built to divert water from the Delaware River at Raven Rock to the main canal at Trenton. Both main and feeder canals had towpaths (walkways for the mules that pulled the barges along). When the canal was abandoned as a transportation corridor in 1932, the waterway was retained because it supplied water to nearby communities. In 1974, it became a state park. Today, 34 miles of the towpath along the main canal are used by hikers, joggers, canoeists, and nature lovers. The Delaware & Raritan Canal State Park is a green corridor through the center of the nation's most densely populated state, and though it is never far from suburbia, it offers many miles of walking. For more information, contact the D & R State Park, 145 Mapleton Road, Princeton, NJ 08540; 609-924-5705; www.dandrcanal.com.

GETTING THERE

The linear D & R Canal State Park has many access points. For this hike, you will use a large parking area located near a canal lock on the south side of NJ 27 in Kingston, where the highway passes over the canal and river. (There is additional parking at the Flemer Preserve across the street.)

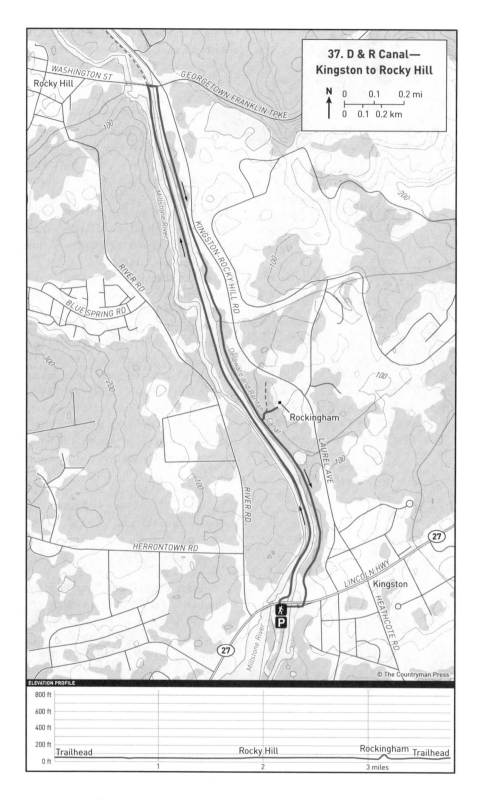

37. D & R Canal—
Kingston to Rocky Hill

N   0   0.1   0.2 mi

0   0.1   0.2 km

WASHINGTON ST

Rocky Hill

GEORGETOWN FRANKLIN TPKE

Millstone River

KINGSTON-ROCKY HILL RD

RIVER RD

BLUE SPRING RD

Delaware and Raritan Canal

Rockingham

LAUREL AVE

RIVER RD

HERRONTOWN RD

27

LINCOLN HWY

Kingston

HEATHCOTE RD

Millstone River

27

© The Countryman Press

ELEVATION PROFILE

800 ft

600 ft

400 ft

200 ft

Trailhead

Rocky Hill

Rockingham Trailhead

0 ft

1   2   3 miles

THE HIKE

Begin the hike by taking a look at the Kingston Lock and the adjacent lock tender's house, both located just south of NJ 27. Locks on the Delaware & Raritan Canal, measuring 220 by 24 feet, allowed boats to move from one section of the canal to another with a different water level. Though seven locks were necessary in the 6-mile stretch of canal from Bordentown to Trenton, only seven more were needed for the remaining 38 miles—a low route that follows the valleys of the Millstone and Raritan rivers. The house behind the lock is one of the old lock tenders' houses found near every lock.

The passage of a boat through a lock was a social event. Exchanges of news would take place between the lock tender and the boatmen. Telegraph connections were in place, and information, such as the arrival of boats, could be sent on to other locations. The lock tender and his family would often trade with the canal boatmen who, like many of today's truckers, owned their own vehicles.

After viewing these interesting remnants of the canal, head under the highway via a corrugated metal tunnel. On the other side, a trail heads to the right and soon reaches the canal towpath. Turn left and head north along the towpath, which runs between the Millstone River (on the left) and the canal (on the right). Although the towpath is wide enough for a vehicle, motorized vehicles are not allowed on the towpath, which is reserved for use by hikers, joggers, bicyclists, horseback riders, and anglers. The densely vegetated strip of land between the river and the canal is part of the river's floodplain.

At one point, a paved road runs relatively close to the towpath, but it soon moves away from the canal, and the sounds of traffic fade away. You will get a feeling of isolation through this stretch. All kinds of wildflowers grow along the towpath here, including yarrow, wild

LOCK ALONG THE CANAL

SPILLWAY ALONG THE DELAWARE & RARITAN CANAL

carrot, pokeweed, and lobelia, as well as clusters of arrowroot, a favorite food of Native Americans. The trees that line the towpath are mostly oak and maple, with some horse chestnut, ash, and sumac mixed in. The great blue heron is also frequently seen along the canal. A word of caution: poison ivy abounds along the towpath. This toxic plant is frequently found along the towpath as a tree-climbing vine. Although the walkway is wide enough to avoid any contact with the plant, when leaving the towpath and approaching either the canal or the river more closely, be sure you know how to identify it.

In about a mile, you'll come to a section of the towpath that is about a foot lower than the level of the towpath on either side. This area is a spillway, which allows excess water in the canal to spill out into the floodplain of the adjacent Millstone River. An interpretive sign explains how this and other, more sophisticated flood-control devices are used to regulate the water level in the canal. Then, about 5 minutes later, you'll notice a square concrete pillar with a tapered top, on the left side of the towpath. This is a canal milepost (actually a replacement for one of the original stone markers). Notice that the number 21 is facing south and that on the other side, facing north, is the number

23. These figures indicate the number of miles from Trenton and New Brunswick, respectively. Adding the two gives the total mileage between these points: 44 miles.

Around this point, you will notice several large buildings on the other side of the canal. These buildings are part of a traprock quarry located just east of the canal. One of the largest and oldest quarries in the area, it supplies traprock, or crushed basalt, to road builders. The rock is quarried from what was once a large igneous intrusion, similar to and the same age as Sourland Mountain, the Watchungs, and the Palisades. If you are hiking during the week, your solitude may be spoiled by the activities of this large operation. Thanks to an exchange of land between the quarry and the state, the property formerly owned by the quarry adjacent to the canal has been transferred to the state, and it is quickly reverting to its natural state. About 45 minutes into the hike, just before you reach the bridge over the canal at Rocky Hill, an inviting rock outcrop extends into the Millstone River, on your left. When you reach the paved road, turn right and cross the canal on a vehicular bridge. On the other side, turn right again and pass the reconstructed stone foundations of the bridge keeper's house. Continue south along the east bank of the canal.

You're now following the right-of-way of the Rocky Hill Branch of the Pennsylvania Railroad, built in 1864 and abandoned in 1983. The line was primarily used to ship rock quarried near Rocky Hill (today, the rock is shipped by truck). The first mile of this rail-trail has a dirt surface and is often somewhat muddy in wet weather.

A little over a mile from Rocky Hill, a bench and a sign along the trail mark the start of a short side trail leading uphill to the historic house known as Rockingham. The oldest part of the house dates back to 1710. In 1783, George Washington lived in the house for over two and a half months. It was during his stay here that Washington composed his "Farewell Orders to the Armies of the United States" on November 2, 1783, which marked the conclusion of the Revolutionary War. During his residence at the house, Washington did much official entertaining—for a few months, this area was the social capital of the new nation. The house has been relocated several times and was moved to its present location in 2001. Guided tours of the house are offered hourly. For more information, go to www.rockingham.net.

For the last part of the hike, a gas pipeline (marked by yellow posts) parallels the trail. After curving sharply to the right, the trail emerges onto a grassy area, with a parking area for the Flemer Preserve on the left. Continue ahead, cross NJ 27 (use extreme care when crossing this busy highway), and turn right to return to your car.

38

D & R Canal—
Weston to
East Millstone

TOTAL DISTANCE: 4.3 miles	
HIKING TIME: 2 hours	
VERTICAL RISE: Minimal	
RATING: Easy	
MAP: USGS Bound Brook; DEP Delaware & Raritan Canal State Park	
TRAILHEAD GPS COORDINATES: N 40° 31′ 43.5″ W 74° 34′ 52.5″	

A century ago, the Delaware & Raritan Canal was the scene of intense commercial activity. Hard coal was the most important item shipped on the canal, accounting for 80 percent of its total tonnage. Many of the canal boats used on the canal were of the hinge-boat variety; they measured about 90 by 10 feet and drew about 5 feet of water. Long strings of these canal boats loaded with coal were pulled by steam tugs, while other canal boats were towed by mules. Towing charges varied according to the service used. At one point, steam tugs were charged a flat rate of $22.22, plus an extra $11.11 per barge, for the trip to New York City. Mules and horses were available from barns at Bordentown, Griggstown, and New Brunswick. The open season on the canal was about 250 days a year, from early April to mid-December. Canal hours were from 6:00 a.m. to 6:00 p.m., and the speed limit for canal boats was 4 miles per hour. When steam tugs began to be used on the canal, the wash began to undermine the banks in places. A stone lining called riprap was installed and can still be seen today in many places.

When the canal closed in 1932, the State of New Jersey took it over and rehabilitated it to serve as a water supply system—a purpose it still serves today. In 1973, the canal and its remaining structures were entered in the National Register of Historic Places, and the following year it became a state park. Today, the Delaware & Raritan Canal State Park is one of central New Jersey's most popular recreational corridors for jogging, hiking, bicycling, fishing, and canoeing.

For more information, contact the D & R State Park, 145 Mapleton Road, Princeton, NJ 08540; 609-924-5705; www.dandrcanal.com.

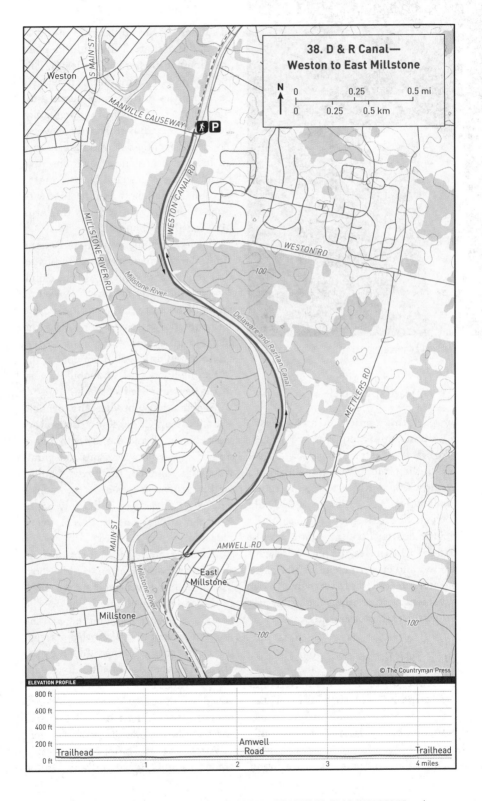

MILEPOST 31 ALONG THE CANAL

GETTING THERE

To reach this section of the Delaware & Raritan Canal State Park from I-287, take Exit 12 (Weston Canal Road). At the end of the ramp, turn left (south) onto Weston Canal Road, following signs to Manville. In 1.7 miles, pass Ten Mile Lock and the lock tender's house on the right and, after that, the community of Zarepath. In 3 miles, the road will swing around and cross the canal. The parking area, created from a remnant of older pavement, is located on the right, just before the road crosses the canal.

THE HIKE

Cross over the bridge and turn left onto the towpath, heading south. On the other side of the canal (the east bank) is the old bridge tender's house, built circa 1831. Originally, a swing bridge spanned the canal here. If you are hiking in summer or early fall, notice the duck-weed, the miniature lily pad-like plant that floats in clusters on the water. This plant tends to accumulate, sometimes covering the entire canal surface for the final 10 to 15 miles of the waterway, before its terminus in New Brunswick. The trees, mostly oak and maple, form an intermittent canopy over the towpath. On the other side of the canal is Weston Canal Road, a country road with light traffic. On your right is the large Millstone River floodplain.

In a few minutes, you'll notice on the right a wooden post, which indicates that you are at milepost 25 of the canal. These mile markers were installed as an Eagle Scout project in 2010, and the mileages do not correspond with the historic mileages of the canal. After another half mile, you'll notice that the Millstone floodplain, undoubtedly very fertile, is being used as a field.

At about the point where the cornfield ends, Weston Canal Road turns away from the canal, and the towpath enters one of its very few sections not paralleled by a road. For the next 1.5 miles, walking through this quiet and somewhat wild area—rare in densely populated central New Jersey—becomes very pleasant.

As the sounds of civilization fade out, the towpath takes on a wilder look. The Millstone River itself swings close to the canal, but 20 feet below it. The sounds of insects, fish jumping, and the hurried scrambling of turtles startled by your intrusion fill the void left by the absence of sounds of traffic. If you are lucky, a great blue heron may wing its way down the canal. The only evidence of civilization is the boat dock for a day camp on the opposite bank of the canal.

After passing milepost 24, you'll come to a stone-faced spillway. On the

ALONG THE DELAWARE & RARITAN CANAL

right, as you reach the spillway, you'll notice a concrete milepost with the numbers 31/13. This original canal artifact tells you that you are 13 miles from New Brunswick and 31 miles from Trenton. About 5 minutes later, you'll reach a footbridge that spans the canal and leads to Colonial Park. Just beyond milepost 23.5, the canal goes over a culvert through which Spooky Brook runs, on its way to the Millstone River. This is an example of one of the many streams channeled underneath the canal in order to keep its water level stable.

All too soon, you'll begin to hear the sounds of traffic, and the quiet and privacy of this section of towpath come to an end. In another half mile, you'll reach Amwell Road in East Millstone, with a parking area and a bridge over the canal. If you're interested, cross over the canal on Amwell Road and take a short walk into East Millstone, a small town that has changed very little over the years. On the left, you'll pass a bridge tender's house and then the historic Franklin Inn, built in 1734. The first road on the right leads to a small grocery store and deli (closed on Sundays). On the way, you'll pass the headquarters of the Millstone First Aid Squad and, behind it, East Millstone Park, a filled-in area that once served as a basin for boats on the canal. Today, it features a basketball court and recreational equipment for children.

After your visit to East Millstone, return to the towpath and retrace your steps to your car.

IV.

COASTAL PLAIN

39

Cheesequake State Park

TOTAL DISTANCE: 3.3 miles

HIKING TIME: 2.5 hours

VERTICAL RISE: Approximately 200 feet

RATING: Easy to moderate

MAPS: USGS South Amboy; DEP Cheesequake State Park map

TRAILHEAD GPS COORDINATES: N 40° 26' 10" W 74° 15' 56"

Located in the transition zone between New Jersey's distinctive northern and southern plant communities, the 1,610-acre Cheesequake State Park (300 Gordon Road, Matawan, NJ 07747; 732-566-2161; www.njparksandforests.org) may be of particular appeal to those interested in botany. There are a variety of habitats throughout the park, including salt- and freshwater marshes, northeastern hardwood forests, pine barrens, and a cedar swamp. Cheesequake is one of the oldest state parks in New Jersey, dating back to 1937, when acquisition of some farms, orchards, and salt marsh began. It formally opened in 1940. Family camping is available April 1 through October 31.

The area was occupied as early as 5,000 years ago by Native Americans who hunted and fished here. The name *Cheesequake* was taken from a word in the language of the Lenni-Lenape tribe, who lived in New Jersey when the Dutch and English colonists first arrived. Some say the word means "upland people." During the 18th and 19th centuries, a fine-quality clay used to make stoneware pottery was mined in the area and shipped to pottery-making sites up and down the Atlantic Coast. Red clay was also mined to make bricks that some say were used extensively in the building of New York City. As late as the early 20th century, a steamboat dock existed on Cheesequake Creek, at the end of Old Dock Road; from there, products and produce were sent to markets.

The park has five marked trails, including one that is multiuse. The two trails followed by this hike (the Yellow Trail and the Green Trail) are hiking-only. The trails traverse a number of wet sections on boardwalks and bridges, and there are also quite a few wooden steps. Most of the blazes are on brown wands,

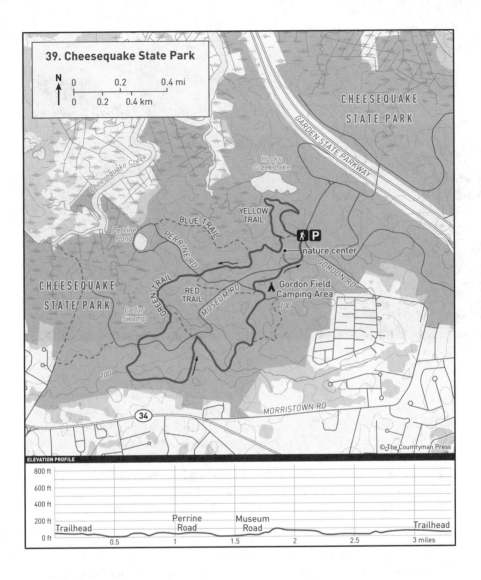

39. Cheesequake State Park

N

| 0 | 0.2 | 0.4 mi |
| 0 | 0.2 | 0.4 km |

CHEESEQUAKE
STATE PARK

GARDEN STATE PARKWAY

Cheesequake Creek

Hooks
Creek Lake

YELLOW
TRAIL

BLUE TRAIL

Perrine
Pond

PERRINE RD

nature center

GORDON RD

GREEN TRAIL

RED
TRAIL

MUSEUM RD

Gordon Field
Camping Area

CHEESEQUAKE
STATE PARK

Cedar
Swamp

100

100

MORRISTOWN RD

34

©The Countryman Press

ELEVATION PROFILE

800 ft							
600 ft							
400 ft							
200 ft		Perrine	Museum				
		Road	Road			Trailhead	
0 ft	Trailhead						
	0.5	1	1.5	2	2.5	3 miles	

and the wands indicate each tenth of a mile along the trails.

GETTING THERE

From the Garden State Parkway, take Exit 120 and turn right (east) at the end of the ramp, following the brown state park signs. Turn right at the first traffic light onto Morristown Road. Turn right again at the next light onto Gordon Road, which will take you to the park entrance in 1 mile. Pass the park office and drive to the parking area on the left, about 0.2 mile ahead. A kiosk with a map of the trails marks the trailhead. A parking fee of $5 daily, $10 weekends is in effect from Memorial Day weekend through Labor Day. There is no charge during the rest of the year.

HOOKS CREEK LAKE

THE HIKE

Begin your hike at the trailhead, marked by an arch just to the right of the kiosk. At the first fork, just beyond the trailhead, turn right onto the Yellow Trail and follow it to a T-intersection, with an arch for the Yellow Trail. Turn left here. The Yellow Trail soon begins to parallel the south shore of Hooks Creek Lake, visible through the trees on the right. This section of the trail is noted for the many lady's slipper orchids that grow alongside the trail.

After descending a flight of wooden steps, the Yellow Trail turns left. You may wish to turn right here and descend a second flight of steps to get a closer view of the scenic lake (with a swimming area on the left), then return to the trail. The Yellow Trail now begins to run along a salt marsh. It then climbs a little to reach a junction with the Red, Green, and Blue Trails. Turn right at the junction, following a sign to the NATURE CENTER. The trails cross a small brook on a wooden bridge, then climb to the park's Nature Center, which contains exhibits illustrating the natural and cultural history of the park. You'll find a turtle display with live turtles in a tank, a model of a Lenni-Lenape village, aquariums, and restrooms. Trail maps and other literature are also available here.

Continue on the Red, Green, and Blue Trails through an understory of sweet pepperbush, perhaps the most common plant along the trail. Sweet pepperbush, mountain laurel and blueberry are the most common understory plants in the park. During the spring, trailing arbutus is in bloom here, as well as along other sections of the trail. In a short distance, you'll come to a viewpoint through the trees over the salt marsh below. Continue downhill on wooden steps and a boardwalk, then climb a long flight of wooden steps. Just beyond the top of the steps, the Blue Trail leaves to the right, but you should bear left, following the green and red blazes.

The Green and Red Trails now pass through a large stand of lowbush and highbush blueberries among some large pines (more typical of the Pinelands of southern New Jersey) mixed with the usual hardwoods. In this dry section are some large clusters of mountain laurel that bloom in June. After paralleling a ravine on the left, the trail descends wooden steps to cross a bridge over a small brook in the ravine. Soon, the trail climbs some more wooden steps, levels off, and crosses a sand road (Perrine Road). Just beyond, the Red Trail leaves to the left, but you should bear right to continue on the Green Trail.

Along this level section are many small sassafras trees, as well as some black cherry, beech, maple, chestnut oak, and white oak. Soon, the trail bears left at a fork and heads rather steeply downhill. At the base of the descent, the trail passes close to the tall sedges, rushes, and grasses of the salt marsh, which forms the western boundary of the park. After a short climb, to the trail descends wooden steps to cross a long boardwalk over a freshwater swamp, heavily overgrown with arrowwood, elderberry, and buttonbush. The end of the boardwalk has been built around several large red maple trees. This quiet area, rich in plant and animal life, is a change from the woods and brush environments traversed so far.

At the end of the swamp, the trail climbs a little and levels off. Soon, it descends wooden steps to cross another boardwalk, this one over a cedar swamp. Here, the environment is even cooler and darker than that of the freshwater swamp you passed a few minutes

ago. The eastern white cedars—which grow out of black clay—dominate. The extreme moisture and the decomposing leaves make the soil very acidic, preserving any cedar logs that become buried. In some similar areas of New Jersey, old cedar logs in good condition have been mined from the dense acidic soil. Great horned owls are known to frequent this swamp. Beyond the swamp, the trail crosses a boardwalk over a wet area, climbs over a ridge and descends to cross another sand road (Museum Road).

After climbing over exposed tree roots and ascending another set of wooden steps, you will reach the highest elevation on the hike. The woods are dry here and composed mostly of chestnut oak, American beech, black birch, and

A LONG SET OF WOODEN STEPS ALONG THE TRAIL

SALT MARSH ALONG THE YELLOW TRAIL

sassafras, with an understory of mountain laurel and sweet pepperbush. From this high area, the trail descends gradually, turns right to cross a ravine on a wooden bridge, then turns left to cross a smaller ravine on another bridge and descend gradually. After coming close to, but not touching, Museum Road, the trail skirts a low-lying area on the left, often flooded during periods of heavy rain. Just beyond a huge fallen oak tree (felled by Hurricane Sandy in 2012), the trail turns left and proceeds across the low-lying area on a long boardwalk. After crossing a bridge over a stream, the trail bears left and continues to skirt the low-lying area. Soon, it curves to the right and crosses a short boardwalk, with a viewing platform that overlooks a grassy, wet area, with many dead trees.

The trail now turns left and crosses another boardwalk. It then climbs over a small hill, turns right to briefly parallel a ravine on the left, and continues along a level footpath. After descending into a ravine and crossing a wooden bridge over a stream, the trail climbs to Perrine Road, opposite a restroom building.

Turn left and follow this paved road for about 900 feet, passing another restroom building at the Gordon Field group camping area. About 150 feet beyond the second restroom building, follow the Green Trail (now joined by the Red Trail) as it turns right at a wooden arch and reenters the woods. The trail skirts to the left of the field, then bears left and descends to Museum Road. Turn right onto the road and follow it, past a turnoff to the Nature Center, back to the parking area where the hike began.

40

Hartshorne Woods Park

TOTAL DISTANCE: 2.7 miles

HIKING TIME: 1.5 hours

VERTICAL RISE: 300 feet

RATING: Easy to moderate

MAPS: USGS Sandy Hook; Monmouth County Park System Hartshorne Woods Park trail guide

TRAILHEAD GPS COORDINATES: N 40° 24' 3.5" W 74° 00' 46"

The 794-acre Hartshorne Woods Park has the most extensive trail network in the Monmouth County park system, with over 14 miles of trails. The area, portions of which rise 245 feet above the Navesink River Bay, is surprisingly hilly for central New Jersey. It features forests of oak, hickory, beech, and maple, interspersed with mountain laurel and holly. For more information, contact the Monmouth County Park System, 805 Newman Springs Road, Lincroft, NJ 07738; 732-872-0336 or 2670; www.monmouthcountyparks.com.

Hartshorne Woods is named for its original owner, Richard Hartshorne, who purchased the tract from Native Americans in the 1670s. The local pronunciation of Hartshorne is "harts horn," or horn of the hart (an old English word for deer).

This hike follows the Laurel Ridge Trail, a loop trail that explores the Buttermilk Valley section of the park. The Laurel Ridge Trail, like nearly all the trails in the park, is a multiuse trail, and it is heavily used by mountain bikes—especially on weekends. Under park rules, bikers are required to yield to hikers, and both bikers and hikers must yield to horses. If you wish to avoid bikes entirely, two very short trails for foot traffic only begin at the main trailhead: the 1.5-mile Candlestick Trail and the 1.1-mile Kings Hollow Trail.

In the late 1980s, Hartshorne Woods, formerly a relatively quiet woods for walkers, became extremely popular with mountain bikers (due in part to the closing of parks in nearby counties to bicycles). Trails in Hartshorne Woods quickly became degraded, forcing the Monmouth County Park Commission to find a solution to this problem.

They launched a major trail rebuilding project and decided to make most of

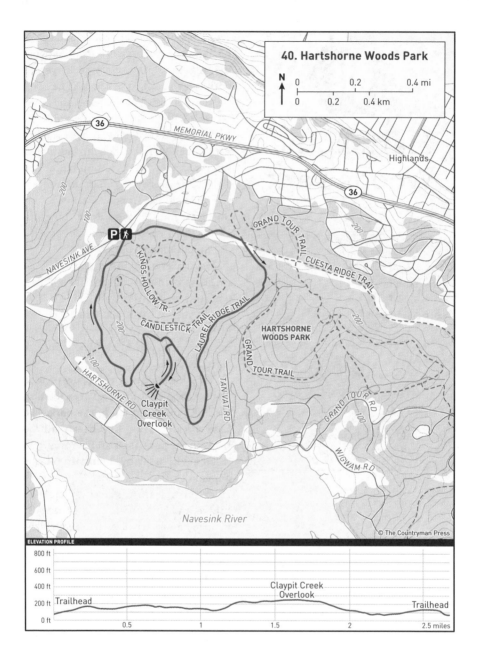

the park's trails multiuse—unlike other county and state agencies, which have chosen to keep bikers and hikers on separate trails where possible.

In 1991, the multiuse trail plan was devised and implemented with the help of some 40 volunteers. New trails were cut and opened to the public, and worn and abused trails were closed and blocked. Junctions were posted with signs, and trails were color-coded and labeled to indicate differing degrees of difficulty.

It should be noted, however, that this

ALONG THE LAUREL RIDGE TRAIL

rating system (modeled after downhill ski standards) is designed with bikes in mind. For hikers, even the "black diamond" trails are no more than moderately difficult.

Hartshorne Woods Park is divided into four sections: Buttermilk Valley, Monmouth Hills, Rocky Point, and Claypit Creek. Trails connect the first three sections, and hikers desiring a longer walk may wish to extend the hike by including a loop on the 3.1-mile Grand Tour Trail. The 2.3-mile Rocky Point Trail, which circles the site of former military fortifications, is another attractive option.

GETTING THERE

Take the Garden State Parkway south to Exit 117. Bear left beyond the toll booths and continue on NJ 36 for 11.5 miles. After passing through Atlantic Highlands, turn right at the exit for Red Bank Scenic Road, then turn right at the stop sign onto Navesink Avenue. Continue for 0.3 mile to the Buttermilk Valley parking area for Hartshorne Woods Park, on the left side of the road. (Do not turn right at the intersection of Memorial Drive and Navesink Avenue in Atlantic Highlands.)

THE HIKE

From the parking area, proceed ahead to a kiosk with a large trail map (free park brochures with maps are usually available here), and turn left onto the Laurel Ridge Trail, marked with a blue circle to indicate it is of moderate difficulty. You'll be following this trail in a clockwise direction for the entire hike. The trail heads gradually uphill on a wide, sandy road. Beyond the crest of the hill, the road descends to a four-way junction, marked by signposts. The Grand Tour Trail begins on the left, and the

Cuesta Ridge Trail proceeds straight ahead, but you should turn right to continue on the Laurel Ridge Trail.

In about 5 minutes, you'll come to another junction. The other end of the Grand Tour Trail is on the left, but you continue ahead on the Laurel Ridge Trail. Follow the path along the side of a slope through thickets of mountain laurel. The trail is named for this plant, abundant throughout the hike. The trail meanders up and down as it swings around the slope, passing a few holly trees, also green throughout the year. After a while, you enter a denser stand of holly and continue through a thickly vegetated section, where greenbrier—a vine-like plant with a green, smooth, and thorny stem—is abundant. You'll also pass a few huge hickory and tulip trees. Smaller sassafras trees are scattered about, and in the understory are jack-in-the-pulpits.

Soon, a view of water appears ahead, particularly when the leaves are off the trees. This is the Navesink River. The trail now curves sharply to the right and begins to climb. You'll notice chunks of conglomerate rock (sand fused with pebbles) along the trail here. This resistant rock has acted as a protective cap over softer sediments, creating highlands among sea-level plains. Another change you may note is in the vegetation itself. There is little mountain laurel or holly along this section of the trail, and oaks are now the predominant tree.

After the trail levels off, you'll reach a junction with a side trail to the Claypit Creek Overlook, the highest point on the hike (elevation 248 feet). Turn left onto this trail and head through dense mountain laurel thickets to the viewpoint over the Navesink River. Unfortunately, the vegetation has largely grown in, and even in leaf-off season, you get only a limited view of the river through the trees. This area makes a good rest stop. Return to the junction when you are ready to continue the hike.

Turn left at the junction and head downhill, first along a stone-bordered switchback and then through mountain laurel thickets. Some of the descent is over soft dirt that in places may be torn up from mountain bike usage. If you are lucky, you may spot a deer or two. Two side trails lead off to the left, but follow the main Laurel Ridge Trail ahead until you reach the kiosk adjacent to the parking area where the hike began.

Allaire State Park

TOTAL DISTANCE: 3.7 miles

HIKING TIME: 2.5 hours

VERTICAL RISE: 120 feet

RATING: Easy

MAPS: USGS Farmingdale, Asbury Park; DEP Allaire State Park map

TRAILHEAD GPS COORDINATES: N 40° 09' 26.5" W 74° 07' 16"

Allaire State Park (4265 Atlantic Avenue, Farmingdale, NJ 07727; 732-938-2371; www.njparksandforests.org) was a gift in 1941 to the people of New Jersey from the widow of Arthur Brisbane, a prominent newspaper man. The original 1,000-plus acres has now expanded to more than 3,200 and includes a narrow-gauge railroad, a car camping area, and a historical village dating from the boom days of the bog iron industry in the 1830s. The park, located in one of the northernmost sections of the Pinelands, straddles the Manasquan River, popular with canoeists. I-195, which bisects the park, pollutes the park with sound, depriving it of the isolation it once had. On the other hand, the interstate highway also makes the park more accessible to the public.

Within Allaire's boundaries are a large number of sand and gravel roads and an abandoned railroad bed used for hiking, biking, and horseback riding. Because the park is essentially quartered by the river and the freeway, a complete tour is not possible, and we have chosen a route that takes you through some wooded areas as well as the park's main attraction, historic Allaire Village.

GETTING THERE

Take the Garden State Parkway to Exit 98. Beyond the toll booths, bear left at the fork, following signs to Route 34 South. After merging onto Route 34, make the first right onto Allenwood Road, and proceed for 0.7 mile to a stop sign at a T-intersection. Turn right onto Atlantic Avenue (County Route 524), and continue for 1 mile to a large gravel parking area on the left, just past the entrance to the Spring Meadow Golf Course. (Alternatively, you can take

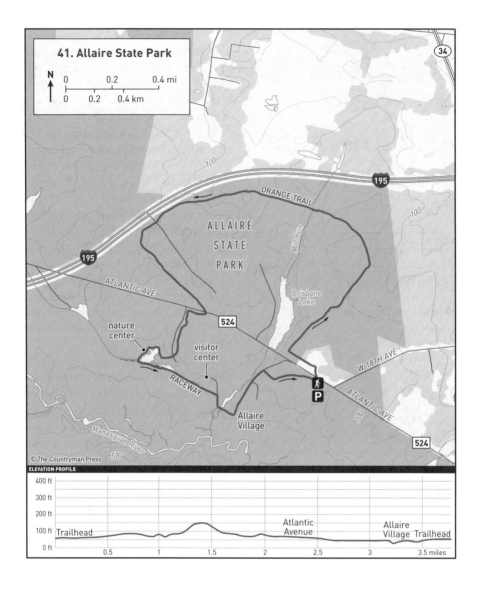

41. Allaire State Park

N

| 0 | 0.2 | 0.4 mi |
| 0 | 0.2 | 0.4 km |

34

195

ORANGE TRAIL

ALLAIRE
STATE
PARK

Mill Run

100

100

ATLANTIC AVE

195

Brisbane
Lake

524

nature
center

visitor
center

RACEWAY

W 18TH AVE

P

ATLANTIC AVE

Allaire
Village

100

Manasquan River

524

© The Countryman Press

100

ELEVATION PROFILE

400 ft						
300 ft						
200 ft						
100 ft	Trailhead				Atlantic Avenue	Allaire Village Trailhead
0 ft	0.5	1	1.5	2	2.5	3	3.5 miles

I-195 to Exit 31B and head east on Atlantic Avenue to the parking area, 0.6 mile beyond (east of) the main entrance to Allaire State Park.) By parking here, you avoid both the fees and the crowds of people who visit the park only to see the historic village. Most of the hike is on sandy trails. Sneakers as well as boots are fine here. A trail map is available at the park office.

THE HIKE

From the parking area, cross the road, turn left, and head west along the grassy shoulder. You'll pass a private residence (#4210) with a split-rail fence and a row of evergreens along the road. In about 750 feet, just beyond the end of the evergreens, you'll see two gates—first a metal gate, then a wooden gate with a State Park Service NO PARKING sign. Go through the opening to the right of the wooden gate and continue along a lane that runs between two properties, with old metal fences on either side. The lane may be somewhat overgrown with grass, but it is the correct route to follow. The park map shows this route as the Orange Trail, but there are no orange markers for the first part of the hike. The lane is shadowed by tall sumac trees and vines, with a few patches of holly along the way. As you move away from the highway and the sound of traffic, the sounds of birds, plentiful in this area, may be heard.

After about 10 minutes, the lane widens into a sand-and-gravel road (typical of the Pinelands), and the walking becomes more pleasant. You'll notice several orange-blazed brown wands on the left, as well as orange paint blazes on trees to the right, indicating that you are following the Orange Trail.

Lowbush blueberry and mountain laurel form the ground cover, and oak and sassafras are the dominant trees (along with stands of holly).

Soon, the trail bears left and begins a gradual ascent. You'll be gaining only about 50 feet in elevation, but this is the most significant climb of the entire hike. As it swings left, the trail begins to parallel I-195 (always busy with cars heading to and from the Jersey Shore), which it follows for about half a mile. At the top of the climb, about 1.3 miles from the start, you'll pass through an abandoned gravel quarry, with a blue water tower visible on the left, through the trees. You'll know when you reach this spot because the oak/sassafras forest is suddenly replaced by a stand of pitch pines.

From the quarry site, the trail begins to descend, now closely paralleling I-195,

POND NEAR THE NATURE CENTER

THE BAKERY AT ALLAIRE VILLAGE

which can be seen through the trees on the right. The noise of the traffic on I-195 spoils the peacefulness of the area, but soon the sand-and-gravel road curves to the left, away from the busy Interstate highway, and the sounds of birds once again become more prominent. The road now begins to parallel the right-of-way of the abandoned Freehold and Jamesburg Agricultural Railroad (visible below on the right). This railroad was built in 1853 to transport produce from Monmouth County farms to city markets, and it was acquired by the Pennsylvania Railroad in 1879. For many years, it served as a main route for passenger traffic from Philadelphia to the Jersey Shore. In 1939, the Royal Train carrying King George VI of England passed over this line. From 1949 until passenger service was discontinued in 1962, the daily passenger train consisted of a gas-electric self-propelled railroad car, popularly known as the "Doodlebug."

Continue along the sand-and-gravel road until you come to Atlantic Avenue, 2.3 miles from the start. (You've followed a semi-circular route to reach this point.) Bear slightly left, cross the road at the crosswalk, and turn right onto a wide paved path with purple blazes. (To your left, you'll see the tracks of the Pine Creek Railroad, a short, narrow-gauge-loop tourist railroad established in Allaire in 1963.) Follow the paved path as it curves left, away from the highway, and enters the woods, paralleling the park entrance road on the right.

After passing a small toll booth, you'll see a sign on the right for nature center parking. Turn right, leaving the paved path, cross the park entrance road, and continue through the parking lot. At the end of the parking lot, bear right and follow a concrete path that crosses a wooden footbridge over a stream and continues through the woods to the Nature Center. If the center is open, you'll want to stop and visit the interesting exhibits. Continue past the Nature Center, following an unmarked path that leads to another footbridge over a stream. Cross the bridge and immediately turn left onto a gravel road known as the Raceway. On the park map, this is shown as the Green Trail, and you'll see some green blazes on trees along the way.

Proceed ahead on the Raceway, passing an attractive pond on the right, and continue along the route of a former canal. Soon, you'll pass a large picnic area on the right. You're now traversing a developed section of the park, and you should expect to see many people here, especially on summer weekends. After passing a large parking lot on the left, you'll enter the historic Allaire Village. Back in the 18th century, this village site was known as Monmouth Furnace and later as the Howell Works, after Benjamin Howell, the first iron maker here. In 1822, the property was acquired by James P. Allaire of New York, who was already established as a brass worker. At the Howell Works, Allaire put together a community of more than 400 people to turn bog iron into pots, kettles, cauldrons, stovepipes, and other common items. The self-contained community included a wide variety of craftspeople to both run the industry and serve the population.

Bog iron, found in the Pinelands, is smelted from iron oxides leached from the sand and deposited in accumulations of decaying swamp vegetation. Interestingly, bog iron is a renewable resource as long as humans do not interfere with the vegetation decay cycle. The operation at Allaire's village prospered in the 1830s, but the discovery of higher-grade iron ore in Pennsylvania, the development of improved smelting technology, and a national depression made the operation less profitable, and it was closed in 1846. Although the village no longer functioned as an active industrial community, the Allaire family continued to live there until James Allaire's son Hal died in 1901.

In 1907, the property was acquired by the journalist Arthur Brisbane, and it remained in his family until, in 1941, it was deeded to the state by his widow. In 1957, a group of concerned citizens, including several descendants of James Allaire, formed Allaire Village, Inc., a nonprofit organization, and restoration of the historic buildings began. Today, most of the historic buildings have been restored, and the village is reminiscent of its heyday in the middle of the 19th century.

The visitor center, a long brick building built in 1820, is on your left and offers a number of interesting displays about the park and the village. A map and guide to the village can be obtained here. After viewing the exhibits, continue straight ahead to the end of the visitor center, make a right, and follow the main road as it heads downhill, turns left to cross a stream, and proceeds through the Historic Village at Allaire. The historic brick buildings you'll pass include a foreman's cottage, a blacksmith shop, a bakery, a general store, and a carpenter shop—all built in the village's heyday, between 1827 and 1836. Many of the buildings are open during summer months from Wednesday to Sunday and feature historical demonstrations. Refreshments are offered for sale in the bakery, and the general store is now a well-stocked gift shop. You'll want to spend some time visiting these historic buildings and exploring the surrounding area.

After taking in the sights of the historic village, continue along the road as it heads north, leaving the village area. A short distance beyond, you'll come to a locked gate. Here, you should turn right onto a paved path (marked with orange and purple blazes) that follows the route of the abandoned Freehold and Jamesburg Agricultural Railroad. Continue to follow the paved path as it bears left, leaving the railbed, and soon reaches the parking area where the hike began.

42

Cattus Island

TOTAL DISTANCE: 3.7 miles	
HIKING TIME: 2.5 hours	
VERTICAL RISE: Minimal	
RATING: Easy	
MAPS: USGS Toms River/Seaside Park; Cattus Island Ocean County Park trail map	
TRAILHEAD GPS COORDINATES: N 39° 58' 55" W 74° 07' 45"	

Cattus Island County Park (1170 Cattus Island Boulevard, Toms River, NJ 08753; 732-270-6960; www.oceancountyparks .org) preserves a small portion of the salt marshes and pine forests on Barnegat Bay. Located in the midst of New Jersey's most popular summer vacation area, which has been extensively developed, Cattus Island offers the hiker a variety of natural environments to explore, including pinelands, open marshes, holly forests, and bay beaches. The excellent views over vast marshes, across inlets, and out over the bay, plus the variety of wildlife found in the park, are further reasons to walk the trails in this 500-acre Ocean County park.

Cattus Island was first settled by the Page family, who moved here in 1763. Timothy Page, born on the island that year, served in the local militia during the American Revolution. Most probably he was a privateer, essentially a pirate licensed by the Continental Congress. During the war, British ships were lured into Barnegat Bay through Cranberry Inlet, only to be attacked and have their cargoes sold for profit. Cranberry Inlet, an opening to the Atlantic near present-day Ortley Beach, existed between 1750 and 1812. It was opened and closed by strong storms.

After the death of Timothy Page, the family house burned down, and the property was sold to Lewis Applegate. He moved there in 1842 and developed the southeastern section of the island, now named for him. He built a sawmill and a port for lumber boats. The island was sold again in 1867 and was slated to be developed as a resort, but the 1873 depression canceled the project.

In 1895, the island was purchased by John V. A. Cattus, an importer and Olympic-class athlete. He used the island and its buildings for weekend

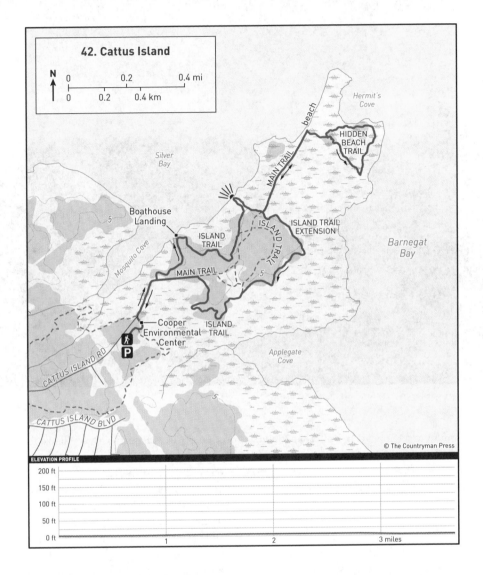

42. Cattus Island

ELEVATION PROFILE

vacations, not as a full-time residence. Cattus loved boating, owned many boats, and built a hunting lodge on the island. Cattus died in 1945, and in 1964, his sons sold the land to developers. New state laws passed in the early 1970s that limited development in wetlands and along the coast discouraged the developers, and they sold the land to Ocean County in 1973. The property was acquired with county tax dollars and state Green Acres funds. In 1976, the park opened to the public, and in the following year trail development began.

GETTING THERE

From Exit 82 on the Garden State Parkway (Toms River/NJ 37), take NJ 37 east 4.4 miles to Fischer Boulevard. Proceed north on Fischer Boulevard for 2 miles, and turn right onto Cattus Island

SALT MARSHES

Boulevard (just after Bellcrest Plaza). The park entrance road is 0.1 mile ahead on the left. Another 0.5 mile will bring you to the large parking area.

THE HIKE

To begin the hike, follow the wide asphalt path to the Cooper Environmental Center, which contains educational displays, including a bird viewing area, a children's activity corner, and collections of live reptiles and fish. After viewing the exhibits, turn right and walk around the porch, descend a ramp, pass a kiosk, and turn right again onto a gravel road (shown on the park map as the "Main Trail"). This road, more like a causeway, crosses the salt marsh that surrounds the slightly higher and drier land ahead. The body of water

on the left is Mosquito Cove. The road leads straight ahead into the woods and eventually out to the tip of the island, which extends well into Barnegat Bay. Our hike utilizes this road and footpaths on either side of it.

Just after leaving the marsh, turn left onto a blue-blazed footpath, called the Island Trail. This path winds through a pine forest, then bears left and swings out to the grassy shore of Mosquito Cove at the old Boathouse Landing, where benches are provided for those who wish to take a break

Leave the landing, and continue following the blue blazes through a forest of oak, pine, and enormous thickets of greenbrier. You'll pass a wildlife observation blind and the fallen trunks of many pine trees toppled by Hurricane Sandy, and you'll traverse a holly forest, green in all seasons. Notice that the red berries do not grow on all the holly trees—only the female trees bear fruit. These bright red berries are found on the trees year-round, and the bird population is well supplied with food.

A short distance beyond, you'll reach a fork where the blue-and-white-blazed Island Trail Extension begins on the left. Bear left and follow the blue-and-white blazes through dense phragmites on a raised wood-chip path and wooden boardwalk. Soon, the trail comes out on the shore of Silver Bay, with broad views across the bay. Several cedar trees shade this pleasant spot, and a bench is provided if you wish to take a break.

Continue on the blue-and-white-blazed trail until you reach the road, then turn left onto the road and follow it across a causeway, bordered by salt marsh on both sides. Towering over the marsh to the left is an osprey nesting site. Other water birds, such as the great egret, may be feeding in this area. In about a quarter of a mile, you'll pass a portable restroom and a group of picnic tables on the right. Just beyond, the road ends at the narrow sandy beach that forms the northern tip of Cattus Island.

After spending some time at the beach (which you can follow to the most northerly point of the island), return to the road. On your left (before reaching the portable restroom) is the trailhead of the orange-blazed Hidden Beach Trail, which loops around Scout Island. Turn left and follow this trail. You'll cross a wet area on a boardwalk and reach a junction, where a sign recognizes the efforts of the local Boy Scout troops to construct and improve the trails on this island.

To follow the loop in the counterclockwise direction, bear right at the junction and head southeast. In a short distance, you'll reach a bench, where a short side trail on the right leads to a secluded beach on Barnegat Bay. The orange-blazed trail now heads north on a grassy path, parallel to the shore of Barnegat Bay, which can be heard (but not seen) on the right. Soon, the trail reaches another secluded beach, with more views across Barnegat Bay. Continue ahead on a wood-chip path through phragmites. After passing more views over the bay and crossing another boardwalk, you'll arrive back at the start of the loop. Turn right to return to the road, then turn left and follow the road across the causeway over the salt marsh.

At the end of the salt marsh, turn left onto the blue-and-white-blazed Island Trail Extension, which follows a raised wood-chip path through a wet area, parallel with a phragmites swamp on the left. After crossing a boardwalk and passing through an open area starting to regenerate with pines, you'll reach an observation blind over a salt marsh, with an osprey nesting platform visible in the distance. The trail now goes through an area dominated by highbush blueberry and ends at a junction with the blue-blazed Island Trail, which comes in from the right. To the right, you'll notice a large clearing, with several benches. This is the site of the Cattus family home.

Continue ahead on the blue-blazed trail, which traverses several stands of holly and highbush blueberries. You'll pass another observation blind, cut through a dense growth of phragmites on a boardwalk, and reach the road that extends to the tip of the island. Turn left onto the road, and follow it back to the paved road. Turn left at the junction and take the wide paved walkway past the Cooper Environmental Center and back to the parking area.

Island Beach State Park

TOTAL DISTANCE: 3.7 miles

HIKING TIME: 2.5 hours

VERTICAL RISE: Minimal

RATING: Easy

MAPS: USGS Barnegat Light; DEP Island Beach State Park map

TRAILHEAD GPS COORDINATES:
N 39° 47' 6.5" W 74° 05' 41.5"

Along the 127-mile boundary between New Jersey and the Atlantic Ocean are a number of long, thin barrier islands. Separated from the mainland by large bays, these islands are part of a chain that runs from New England to the Gulf Coast of Mexico. The constant movement of sand pushed by the ocean waves, called littoral drift, both maintains and changes these relatively fragile land forms. Severe storms often open or close inlets, wash out beaches, and even extend barrier islands, creating new land. With the exception of Island Beach State Park (P.O. Box 37, Seaside Park, NJ 08752; 732-793-0506; www.njparksandforests.org), most of these islands have been developed with row after row of summer beach homes, boardwalks, and restaurants. The 10-mile-long Island Beach is one of the few undeveloped barrier beaches on the coast of the Atlantic Ocean. If it were not for this park, many New Jerseyans would have no idea of what the shoreline in its natural state would look like.

Island Beach State Park occupies the southern end of a long spit joined to the mainland near Point Pleasant. This section of the spit was an island at one time; an inlet connecting the ocean and Barnegat Bay was once located near present-day Ortley Beach. This inlet, known as Cranberry Inlet, was created overnight by a storm in 1750 and was just as quickly destroyed by a storm in 1812. More recently, in 1935, a storm opened up an inlet just south of the present park entrance. Local rum runners wanted it to remain open, but the owners of the tract at the time had it closed.

Originally, Island Beach was owned by Lord Stirling, owner of vast acreages in New Jersey during the 17th century. During this period, the island was called Lord Stirling's Isle. Not much happened

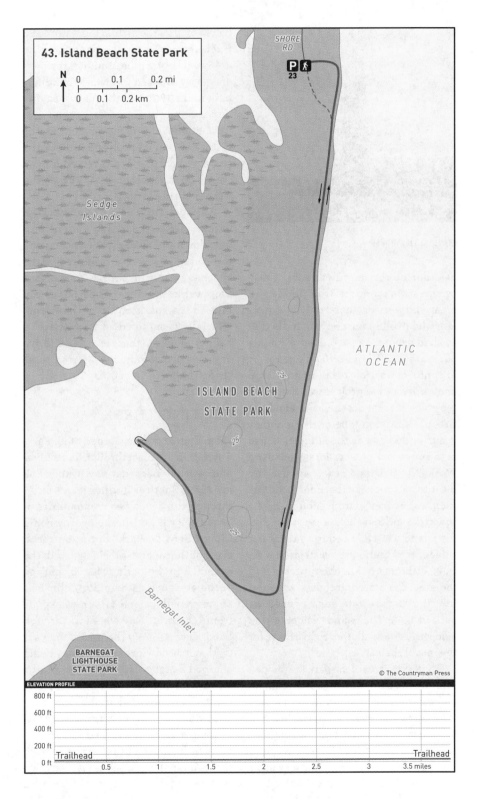

43. Island Beach State Park

N

| 0 | | 0.1 | | 0.2 mi |
| 0 | 0.1 | | 0.2 km | |

SHORE RD

P
23

Sedge Islands

ATLANTIC OCEAN

ISLAND BEACH STATE PARK

25

25

25

25

Barnegat Inlet

BARNEGAT LIGHTHOUSE STATE PARK

© The Countryman Press

ELEVATION PROFILE

800 ft							
600 ft							
400 ft							
200 ft							
Trailhead							Trailhead
0 ft							
	0.5	1	1.5	2	2.5	3	3.5 miles

BARNEGAT LIGHTHOUSE

here during the next 100 years. These beaches were remote from industrial areas and were occupied only by squatters who lived in part on materials that washed ashore. In 1926, Henry Phipps purchased the island with a shore resort in mind. He was able to build three large homes before his project was halted by the stock market crash of 1929 and the Great Depression (one of those homes is currently used as the summer house of the governor of New Jersey). During World War II, Island Beach was used by the army for rocket experiments and, as such, was restricted from public use. The squatters and leaseholders who lived on the island were allowed to remain, but subject to a number of restrictions. In 1953, after much talk about preserving the area, the state purchased the land from the Phipps estate, and it opened the park in 1959. The island residents who held leases were allowed to live there for the rest of their lives.

The 3,003 acres of the park are divided into three sections, the northernmost and southernmost being natural areas, the central section public beaches and concessions. This hike is at the southern tip of the island, beyond the terminus of the 8-mile road that runs along the center of the island. You'll want to stop, either

before or after the hike, at the Nature and Interpretive Center, located at parking area 16 (about 7 miles south of the park entrance). Housed in historic buildings built in the 1800s for the US Life Saving Service and the Coast Guard, the center contains informative exhibits on the history of Island Beach and its flora and fauna. From the center, short self-guided nature trails extend east to the beach and west to Barnegat Bay.

Although there are no roads south of parking area 23, park regulations provide that four-wheel-drive vehicles used for fishing purposes are allowed on the beaches by special permit. You will see these vehicles along the beaches as you hike to the southern tip of the island. Officially designated as "mobile sportfishing vehicles," these four-wheel-drive vehicles are commonly referred to as "beach buggies."

GETTING THERE

From Exit 82 on the Garden State Parkway, take NJ 37 East through Toms River and over the Barnegat Bay Bridge. Follow NJ 35 South as it winds for 2.5 miles through the developed communities of Seaside Park and Berkeley Township (South Seaside Park) until you reach the southern end of NJ 35 and the entrance to the park. A fee is charged at the entrance gate. In 2019, this was $6 on weekdays and $10 on weekends from Memorial Day weekend through Labor Day; $5 daily the rest of the year (with nonresidents of New Jersey being charged a higher fee). Although a large number of parking spaces are spread along the 8-mile road in the park, they often fill up quickly during peak season, and late arrivals are turned away at the gate. In fact, use of the area is so high that computer signs on the Garden State Parkway advise motorists of the park's opening or closing. The best time to explore Island Beach State Park on foot is definitely during the off-season, especially during the week.

To begin the hike, drive the full 8 miles south from the park entrance to parking area 23, the last one on the paved road. This area is very popular and may be filled on sunny days, even during the off-season. If so, park at area 22 or 21 and walk the extra distance along the road.

THE HIKE

From a FOOTPATH sign at the northern end of parking area 23, follow a trail over a sand dune and toward the shoreline, then turn right and head in a southerly direction toward the Barnegat Inlet and Lighthouse. There is no formal trail to follow; you can walk either on the beach buggy tracks or along the water's edge, both far easier to walk on than the soft sand. The compacted sand along the water is probably the most interesting choice because it offers a fascinating variety of ocean debris, constantly being reorganized by the tides and waves. Here there are shells, dead fish, crabs, and driftwood. You will also encounter seagulls and fishermen with beach buggies and campers. You will never be bored, walking along what you may at first think to be a monotonous stretch of beach.

After about 1.75 miles, you will reach the southern tip of Island Beach. This is Barnegat Inlet, where the Atlantic Ocean meets Barnegat Bay. Barnegat Lighthouse, built in 1858, stands across the inlet at the northern tip of Long Beach Island. In Barnegat Inlet, the ocean currents are steadily moving sand southward toward Long Beach Island. The accumulation of sand from this drift is awesome when you consider

that the end of the road, more than a mile back, was once much closer to the end of the island. The Army Corps of Engineers struggles to keep this inlet, which is constantly filling with sand, open to navigation. It was hoped that the inlet would be stabilized by the two jetties, but even these structures don't prevent the sand from filling the inlet. During low tide, either a sandbar or breaking waves are often visible between the two.

Walk west along the jetty toward Barnegat Bay. To your right is a protected bird nesting area and, beyond that, the dunes. The stability of the entire state park depends on these dunes, which are in turn stabilized by dune grass and other plants such as seaside goldenrod and Hudsonia or beach heather. These plants are very tolerant of the salty sea spray, which kills other species. Continue walking westward until you are nearly opposite the lighthouse. Comparing the present topography with that of the geological survey map reveals the incredible changes constantly taking place here. To your right are the Sedge Islands, a large area of salt marsh inhabited by countless birds and visited by many kayakers. Also to the right are the higher back dunes, separating the foredunes and the bay, which support a thick barrier of holly, bayberry, and other shrubs that cannot tolerate salt spray. To the south, the lighthouse and a steady parade of fishing and pleasure boats provide a sharp contrast with the wild, virtually inaccessible Sedge Islands to the northwest.

When you are ready to continue, retrace your steps to the parking area. You'll first notice the beach buggy road that leads back to the parking area, but continue ahead for a short distance until you see the 23 sign that marks the footpath to the parking area, then turn left and return to your car.

Wells Mills County Park

TOTAL DISTANCE: 4.5 miles

HIKING TIME: 3 hours

VERTICAL RISE: 500 feet

RATING: Easy to moderate

MAPS: USGS Brookville; Ocean County Parks & Recreation Wells Mills trail map

TRAILHEAD GPS COORDINATES:
N 39° 47' 45" W 74° 16' 38"

Wells Mills County Park (P.O. Box 905, Wells Mills Road, Waretown, NJ 08758; 609-971-3085; www.oceancountyparks .org) is located at the site of the former town of Wells Mills. Here, sometime in the late 1700s, James Wells established a sawmill. He created the lake, which supplied water power for the mill, by damming Oyster Creek. Others settled in the area, and over the years the ownership of the mill was passed along, with each owner benefiting from the local abundance of Atlantic white, or "swamp," cedar. This wood is not only strong but also extremely rot resistant and was used to build ships. Shingles and house-building lumber were other products of the mill.

During the 1870s, Christopher Estlow and his sons operated two mills in the area, which explains why the name of the hamlet, and now the park, is plural. In addition to the sawmill business, Estlow's grandson Tilden mined clay, which was sent to Trenton to be made into pottery. In 1936, the property was sold to Charles M. Conrad and his brother Grove. A year later, they began constructing the cabin that stands today on the shore of the lake at the boat dock. In 1979, the Conrad family found a buyer for all 200 acres in the New Jersey Conservation Foundation, a private organization that moves quickly to purchase land that might otherwise be developed. Later, it sells the land to public agencies, in this case Ocean County. Additional acquisitions by the county have increased the size of the park to 910 acres.

The staff of the Ocean County Park System has created an excellent trail system.

Several blazed hiking trails traverse the park, the longest being the 8.4-mile Macri Trail. The first section of this trail

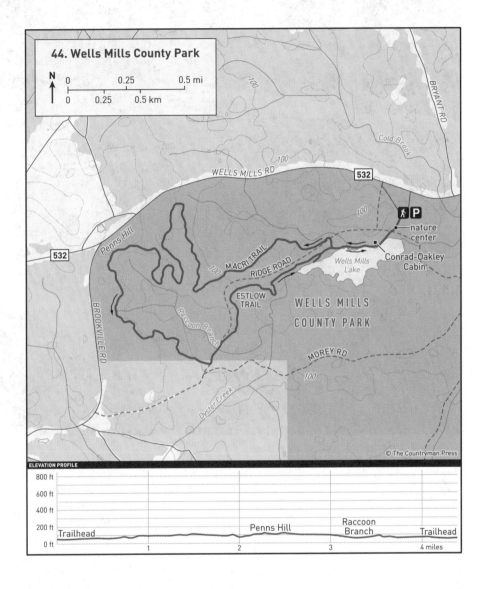

44. Wells Mills County Park

N

| 0 | 0.25 | | 0.5 mi |
| 0 | 0.25 | 0.5 km | |

WELLS MILLS RD

532

BRYANT RD

Cold Brook

100

100

100

nature center

Conrad-Oakley Cabin

PENNS HILL

532

MACRI TRAIL

RIDGE ROAD

Wells Mills Lake

ESTLOW TRAIL

WELLS MILLS COUNTY PARK

BROOKVILLE RD

Raccoon Branch

MOREY RD

100

Oyster Creek

© The Countryman Press

ELEVATION PROFILE

| 800 ft |
| 600 ft |
| 400 ft |
| 200 ft | Trailhead | Penns Hill | Raccoon Branch | Trailhead |
| 0 ft | 1 | 2 | 3 | 4 miles |

will be used in this hike. Except for one designated bicycle trail, which follows a sand road, all of the trails in the park are for hiking only. Among the surprises you will find here are the frequent ups and downs. Most of the New Jersey pinelands are flat. Here, and also just to the north in the Forked River Mountains (privately owned), the flatness is broken by small hills.

GETTING THERE

Wells Mills County Park is on the eastern edge of the Pinelands, not far from the Garden State Parkway. Take the Parkway to Exit 69, turn left at the bottom of the ramp onto County Route 532 West, and proceed for 2.2 miles to the park entrance, on the left. Follow the entrance drive past the maintenance garage to the large parking lot.

PICTURESQUE ONE-LOG BRIDGE ALONG THE MACRI TRAIL

THE HIKE

Walk toward the restrooms and fountain, then follow the paved path to the nature center. Be sure to sign in at the kiosk just past the restrooms, and stop in at the nature center to see the displays illustrating the natural and human history of Wells Mills.

When you are ready to start hiking, descend the steps in front of the nature center and face the lake. You should see a tree with three white paint blazes to your right. This marks the start of the Macri Trail, which first follows the shoreline of Wells Mills Lake and then traverses a remote and hilly section of the park.

Follow the white-blazed trail, which winds through the forest, parallel to the lake. Soon, you'll pass in front of the Conrad-Oakley Cabin, built in 1937. Just beyond, a dock extends into the lake. You can walk out on the dock to get a good view of the lake. Beyond the cabin, the trail goes through a stand of holly and then traverses a deep woods of tall Atlantic white cedar trees, with an understory of highbush blueberry and mountain laurel. You'll cross several streams on wooden bridges, including a picturesque one-log bridge. After bearing right, away from the lake, the trail crosses Ridge Road, a yellow-blazed sand road open to mountain bikes.

From here, the trail winds through a forest of pitch pines and scrub oak, with

After a short but rather steep climb, the trail attains a small ridge. This is Penns Hill, which is about 125 feet above sea level and about 70 feet higher than Wells Mills Lake. Although this relief seems inconsequential when compared with the mountains of northern New Jersey, it is unusual in the Pinelands.

Over the next mile, the trail climbs the 130-foot-high Laurel Hill, descends, and continues along what is called Laurel Ridge. Like Penns Hill, neither of these high points is much more than 50 feet above the surrounding woods, but the many ups and downs you encounter on this hike add up to a total elevation gain of about 500 feet. Along the way you'll walk through a small clearing, descend a few wooden stairways, and cross several wooden bridges and boardwalks over wet areas.

Eventually, you'll cross a wooden barrier and emerge onto Ridge Road. Leave the white-blazed trail and turn left onto this sand road, marked with the green blazes of the Estlow Trail. Soon, you'll enter a cedar swamp. The narrow, perfectly vertical cedars and the dark waters of the brook are a sharp contrast with the pine forest you have traversed for the last few miles. After crossing Raccoon Branch on a wooden bridge, turn right onto a footpath, following the green blazes of the Estlow Trail. For the next mile or so, this trail parallels Ridge Road. As you approach Wells Mills Lake, a short black-dot-on-yellow side trail on the right leads down to an observation blind on the lake.

A short distance beyond, you'll reach a junction with the white-blazed Macri Trail. Turn right and follow the white blazes back through the cedar swamp and past the cabin, and continue to the visitor center, where the hike began.

an understory of mountain and sheep laurel, crossing several fire ditches along the way. The trail snakes its way deeper and deeper into the pineland forest, crossing over wet areas on puncheons. About 20 minutes from the road, the trail reaches the top of a small rise called Raccoon Ridge. This is the 1-mile point. From here the trail alternately rises and descends, a highly unusual pattern for the Pinelands.

About a mile and a half into the hike, you will approach County Route 532 and hear the sounds of traffic. But the trail soon loops away from the road and heads south. As the trail curves to the west, the understory of highbush blueberry and mountain laurel thickens, and in places the vegetation arches over the trail.

45

Bass River State Forest

TOTAL DISTANCE: 4.3 miles

HIKING TIME: 2.5 hours

VERTICAL RISE: Minimal

RATING: Easy

MAPS: USGS New Gretna; DEP, Bass River State Forest map

TRAILHEAD GPS COORDINATES:
N 39° 37' 21" W 74° 26' 25"

Bass River State Forest (762 Stage Road, Tuckerton, NJ 08087; 609-296-1114; www.njparksandforests.org) is New Jersey's first state forest. Land acquisition began with 597 acres in 1905, and today it includes 29,147 acres. The Garden State Parkway passes through the eastern parts of the forest, making it very accessible by automobile. The 50-mile Batona Trail (see also Hikes #46 and #47 in this volume) terminates in the western portion of the forest. The focus of recreational activities in Bass River State Forest is Lake Absegami, which offers swimming and boating and is surrounded by 176 car campsites, six group campsites, and a number of cabins, shelters, and lean-tos. Entrance to this section of the forest is via Stage Road, and there is a fee during the summer season. (The hike below utilizes a free parking area.) Trails in Bass River State Forest are marked with flexible plastic posts containing the trail blaze color.

Bass River State Forest has a memorial to the Civilian Conservation Corps (CCC). The CCC was a New Deal program designed to get many unemployed men, victims of the Depression, working on civic projects. During the 1930s, some 3 million men served in the CCC, and they worked on many park and forest projects that still stand today throughout the United States. Bass River State Forest had its own camp, one of the earliest in the nation. The men who served at this camp, S-55, planted 4,500 acres of timber and were noted for their valor in fighting fires in the Pinelands, including an especially tragic one on May 30, 1936.

The CCC also dammed two streams in the forest and created Lake Absegami. The camp was later used by the military during World War II. Very little remains of this camp today, but you will have the opportunity to hike through its

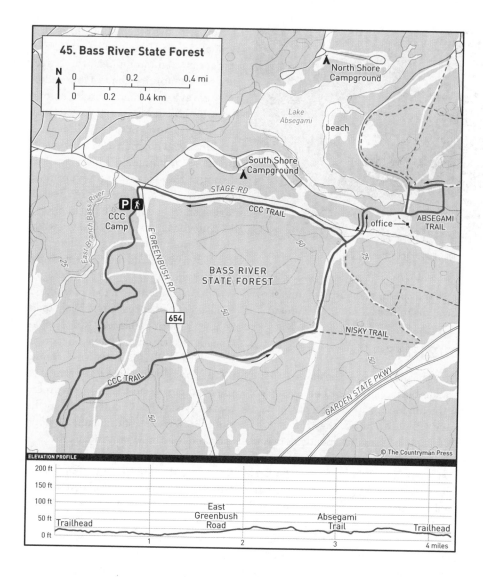

45. Bass River State Forest

N

| 0 | | 0.2 | | 0.4 mi |
| 0 | 0.2 | | 0.4 km | |

North Shore Campground

Lake Absegami

beach

South Shore Campground

STAGE RD

CCC TRAIL

office

ABSEGAMI TRAIL

CCC Camp

E GREENBUSH RD

East Branch Bass River

BASS RIVER STATE FOREST

654

50

50

25

75

NISKY TRAIL

CCC TRAIL

50

GARDEN STATE PKWY

50

© The Countryman Press

ELEVATION PROFILE

200 ft
150 ft
100 ft
50 ft
0 ft

Trailhead

East Greenbush Road

Absegami Trail

Trailhead

1   2   3   4 miles

remnants on the hike described below. A kiosk at the parking area contains photographs of some of the corps back in the 1930s, making the memorial more personal.

This hike follows the orange-blazed CCC Trail, which makes a loop through Pinelands forests south of Stage Road. It also crosses the road to take in the short Abgesami Trail, which includes a magnificent section that crosses a cedar swamp on a raised boardwalk.

GETTING THERE

If you are coming from the north on the Garden State Parkway, take Exit 52 and turn right onto East Greenbush Road (County Route 654), following signs to Bass River State Forest.

Drive 1 mile and park at the CCC Forest Service Memorial on the left. There is parking for about eight to 10 cars. The trailhead is at the northwest end of the small parking area. (If you are coming

STONE FIREPLACE FROM CCC CAMP

You are now proceeding through a typical Jersey Pinelands forest. The coarser-barked pitch pines (three needles per clump) rise above a low understory of several common shrubs, among them highbush blueberry, leatherleaf, and sheep laurel. Soon, you'll cross a sand road and enter an area where oaks are more prominent. The trail winds through the forest and eventually reaches a more open area. Here, the trail curves sharply to the left and begins to head northeast through a forest of white pine. White pines have smoother bark than pitch pines, and they have five needles per clump.

After 45 minutes to 1 hour of walking, you'll cross paved East Greenbush Road. Follow the orange-blazed CCC Trail as it heads east through a pitch pine forest. In a quarter mile, the trail turns left onto a sand road. In another quarter mile, as the road curves to the left, the green-blazed Nisky Trail comes in from the right. Both trails continue ahead along the sand road, now heading north.

Before reaching the paved Stage Road, you'll come to a junction. To the left, the orange-blazed trail will be your return route, but for now you should bear right and continue to follow both orange and green blazes (now joined by blue blazes), which proceed through the woods on a narrower path. Soon, you'll cross the busy Stage Road (use caution when crossing this heavily-trafficked road), with the main entrance to Bass River State Forest just to the right.

After crossing under power lines, you'll come to a T-intersection. Turn right and immediately cross the paved road that leads to the South Shore Campground. The trail bears right and continues parallel to the road, passing the park entrance station and the park office.

A short distance beyond, you'll

from the south, take Exit 50 and follow the signs to Bass River State Forest.)

THE HIKE

From the parking area, head west on the orange-blazed CCC Trail and bear left at the junction just ahead. For the next hundred yards or so, the trail passes alongside the remains, mostly floor and foundations, of the former CCC camp that existed in this location. The first one you pass is labeled Site A, the partial foundation of the kitchen/mess hall for the corps. The trail then swings to the left and passes several other foundations. Site B is unknown, but Site C is distinguished by a wide stairway and is thought to be either a medical building, officers' quarters, or an administration office. Just ahead is Site D, a large slab of concrete with small holes for drainage, which was apparently the bathhouse. Site E was the trash pit, and Site F was where the five wooden barracks of the camp were located. As you walk along the trail, notice that portions of the trail retain the former pavement. At a clearing, the CCC Trail bears right, leaving the camp area.

BOARDWALK ACROSS THE ATLANTIC WHITE CEDAR BOG

come to a junction. Turn right, cross the paved road, and continue ahead on the Absegami Trail, which traverses the beautiful Absegami Natural Area. (The Absegami Trail is officially blazed silver, but the blazes appear to be white.) Proceed east on this easy-to-follow trail through mountain laurel and other common pineland plants and across a white cedar bog. Signs along the way explain the preservative properties of a bog. The anoxic (oxygen-free) conditions in a bog preserve pollen and other botanical remains, as well as ash from fires or even distant volcanic eruptions. A core taken from the bog (3 inches equals about 100 years) contains botanical markers and ash particles dating back as far as 12,000 years, the end of the previous Ice Age.

The bog itself, dark even on a bright day, is crossed on a boardwalk. Here are densely packed Atlantic white cedars rising from a carpet of sphagnum mosses on the moist ground. After leaving the bog, turn left at a junction, and continue to follow the blazes back out to the paved road. Make a left here and, immediately, another left onto the campground road.

Walk back in a southerly direction toward the park office, passing over the Falkinburg Branch drainage that feeds the cedar bog, with a view on the right of the southern end of Lake Absegami. After crossing the drainage, turn right onto the orange-blazed CCC Trail (co-aligned with several other trails) and follow it back across Stage Road (you're now briefly retracing your steps).

When you reach the first junction after crossing Stage Road, cross the sand road and continue ahead on a footpath through the pitch pine and scrub oak forest, following just orange blazes. The trail heads west, closely paralleling Stage Road. After crossing East Greenbush Road, follow the orange-blazed trail as it turns left. Continue for about 500 feet to a T-intersection (marked by a small sign for the CCC Memorial), then turn left to reach the parking lot where the hike began.

46

Brendan T. Byrne (Lebanon) State Forest

TOTAL DISTANCE: 8.1 miles

HIKING TIME: 5 hours

VERTICAL RISE: Minimal

RATING: Moderately strenuous

MAPS: USGS Browns Mills; DEP Lebanon State Forest; DEP Batona Trail maps

TRAILHEAD GPS COORDINATES: N 39° 53' 42" W 74° 34' 32"

With over 37,000 acres, Brendan T. Byrne State Forest (P.O. Box 215, Route 72, New Lisbon, NJ 08064; 609-726-1191; www.njparksandforests.org) is the state's second largest forest. The original name, Lebanon State Forest, came from the Lebanon Glass Works, manufacturers of window glass and bottles, located here during the middle of the 19th century. The availability of sand and wood for charcoal supported the glassmaking industry from 1851 until about 1867, when the wood supply became exhausted. About 150 men worked here, and a small town of 60 homes, a few shops, and a post office was established but later abandoned. In 1908, the state began to acquire land in the area. Brendan T. Byrne State Forest also contains the deserted Whitesbog Village, the birthplace of the cultivated blueberry and at one time the state's largest cranberry farm. The historic village is now being restored, and the not-entirely-abandoned cranberry bogs are appealing to hikers. Cranberries are still harvested in some sections of Brendan T. Byrne State Forest by farmers who lease the land from the state (but the cranberry bogs along the route of this hike have been abandoned). The reservoirs are used to flood the bogs in the early fall for harvesting. Machines are run through the bogs to shake the berries off the vines. The berries, which float, are scooped up and loaded, via conveyor belts, onto trucks that take them to processing plants.

The forest was renamed in 2002 to honor former New Jersey Governor Brendan T. Byrne, who worked to designate the New Jersey Pine Barrens as a National Reserve. During his two terms as Governor of the State of New Jersey (1974 through 1982), Byrne was a leader

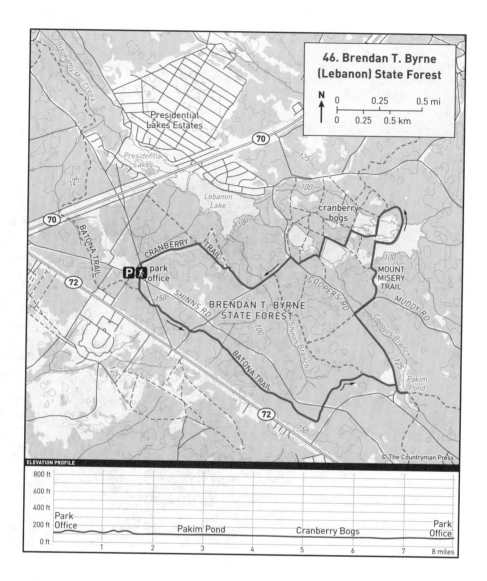

ELEVATION PROFILE

800 ft
600 ft
400 ft
200 ft Park Office   Pakim Pond   Cranberry Bogs   Park Office
0 ft
        1   2   3   4   5   6   7   8 miles

in the difficult and controversial effort to protect the New Jersey Pinelands.

"Pinelands" is the politically correct name, though locals and scientists still respect the historical name "Pine Barrens." With so many interests, public and private, involved in the large Pinelands region, the type of protection eventually settled on involved a combination of local, state, and federal agencies that would manage the Pinelands through land acquisition and land-use controls. This unique arrangement required that the Pinelands be called a National Reserve, the country's first. Without such protective measures, the Pinelands would surely have been developed commercially and for housing by now. The Pinelands National Reserve is said to be the largest assemblage of open space in the northeastern United States and has achieved recognition as a Biosphere Reserve by the United States Man and the Biosphere Program and

RESERVOIR ALONG THE MOUNT MISERY TRAIL

also by the United Nations Educational, Scientific and Cultural Organization (UNESCO).

Utilizing a section of the Batona Trail and the gravel and sand roads that crisscross the Pinelands, the hike described below takes in much of what Brendan T. Byrne State Forest has to offer. A section of the 735-acre Cedar Swamp Natural Area will be traversed twice, and you will visit Pakim Pond, a good spot for lunch. The trail then uses sand roads to explore the shores of reservoirs and cranberry bogs. In this latter section, your navigational skills may be challenged. Though long in mileage, this hike is not especially strenuous because the land is so flat; however, hot weather and biting deer flies could make it seem difficult, and, like most long hikes in the Pinelands, it should probably be hiked in cooler weather. Hikers are advised to

on NJ 72 for 1 mile, turn left at a sign for the park, continue for 0.3 mile, and turn right at the first intersection. The park office is just ahead on the left; park here.

THE HIKE

Facing the park office from the parking lot, turn left and cross a paved road. On the other side of the road, you will see a large sign for the Batona Trail. Follow a blue-blazed trail that heads south toward the Batona Trail. After a short walk, you'll reach the Batona Trail, marked with pink paint blazes (the junction is marked by a sign, PAKIM POND 3 MILES). Bear left here, heading southeast and parallel to, though some distance from, NJ 72 (at times, you will hear the noise of the traffic in the distance). You'll be walking through a mixed pine and oak forest, with an understory of blueberry bushes. The walking is pleasant, and the trail surface, mostly sand, is soft and comfortable.

After a short distance, the trail crosses a wide sand road and reenters the woods, with the trees now forming a canopy overhead. Soon, you'll pass dense stands of mountain laurel. Farther along, the Batona Trail crosses another sand road. The trail now traverses gently undulating terrain, then climbs gradually but steadily to its highest elevation, about 150 feet above sea level. After descending a little, the trail levels off.

About 2 miles into the hike, the trail turns sharply left and crosses paved Shinns Road. In a quarter mile, you'll cross a wet area on puncheons and boardwalks. Soon, you'll come to a junction with a gravel road, the route of the red-blazed Cranberry Trail. Here, a sign indicates that, to the left, it is 2.8 miles to the park office, but you should turn right and follow the pink and red blazes

stay on the trail and out of the brush, because ticks and chiggers have become common in recent years. It is best to wear long, light-colored pants tucked into socks, along with tick repellent.

GETTING THERE

The main entrance to Brendan T. Byrne State Forest is on NJ 72, 1 mile east of the traffic circle where it intersects NJ 70. From the traffic circle, head east through a dense white pine forest planted by the Civilian Conservation Corps (CCC) in the 1930s.

In a short distance, the road swings left and meets a wider sand road, known as Coopers Road. Cross the road and turn right onto a footpath (with pink and red blazes) that briefly parallels the wooden guardrail along the road, then leaves the road and bears left into the Pakim Pond area.

Pakim Pond takes its name from the Native American word for "cranberry." Its water is the reddish brown, acidic water typical of the Pinelands. Known as cedar water, it picks up its color and acidity as it moves very slowly through thick cedar swamps. To the northwest of the pond is a swamp, a former cranberry bog. When the bog was actively cultivated, Pakim Pond was used as a reservoir to store water for the fall flooding of the bog. The Batona Trail (joined by the Mt. Misery Trail) passes between the pond and the swamp. There are restrooms and picnic tables at Pakim Pond, but swimming is not allowed.

A short nature trail, which explores both the pond and the swamp, begins just off the Batona Trail at the southern end of the dam. A guidebook, which explains the points of interest indicated by numbered posts, is available at the park office. Carnivorous plants can be found here, including the pitcher plant and at least two types of sundew. The pitcher plant has funnel-like leaves that are filled with water. Insects are attracted to the leaves because of their odor and color and, should they fall in, are drowned and digested by the plant. The sundew is very small and grows in clumps in very wet but sunny areas. Its leaves, round or stemlike, have numerous sticky hairs that trap insects and then digest them. These plants can be found along the northeastern shore of the pond just off the Batona Trail.

After either exploring or resting at Pakim Pond, leave the way you came in and return to the wide Coopers Road. Do not turn left on the Batona Trail at the junction, though; continue ahead and head west on Coopers Road.

Coopers Road, like most of the sand roads in the Pinelands, is flat and lined with pines. After about 15 minutes (0.7 mile), you'll come to a junction. Turn right here onto another sand road, known as Muddy Road, marked with the white blazes of the Mt. Misery Trail. You will pass through a cedar swamp with towering Atlantic white cedars, densely packed, looking down on you from both sides of the road. You are traversing the Cedar Swamp Natural Area, a dense jungle of Atlantic white cedars surrounded by the pitch pine forest. The cedar wood, which is soft but durable, is used in boatbuilding, for some kinds of furniture, and for shingles and stakes. The management of this tree is an important project in the forest. Below the tall cedars, the vegetation is dense and the lighting is dark. Plant life includes rare orchids, curly grass ferns, pitcher plants, and sundews.

In 0.2 mile, where the road curves to the right, follow the white blazes that lead left onto yet another sand road. To the right, you'll pass a fenced-in area—a former cranberry bog, now being restored as a habitat for the Atlantic white cedar.

Follow the white blazes and the road as it swings around the former bog and heads north (ignore the road going off to the left); then head west again until the road ends at a T-intersection. Bear right here and head north, passing more cranberry bogs. Soon, you'll reach a reservoir, which, like Pakim Pond, was used to flood cranberry fields.

The scenery as you walk along the dam of the reservoir is beautiful, with the backdrop of pines and the green shades of water lilies and other aquatic vegetation. Wildflowers, not found in the shady woods, thrive in this sunny and well-watered environment.

When you come to the corner of the reservoir, bear right, leaving the white markers. Now follow the reservoir's perimeter. The road heads east, then swings to the north, following a causeway between two reservoirs. This section can be quite wet, but you should be able to keep your feet dry by staying to the edge of the road. Eventually, you'll leave the reservoir with its dark cedar water and standing dead trees. The sand road now winds through a quiet and remote pine woods, with a forest carpeting of pine needles.

When you come to a junction with another sand road, keep left. Stay on this sand road (which is the white trail again), heading south for about 750 feet, then make a right turn onto a sand road heading west. (From this junction, the edge of the first reservoir is visible.) You'll pass cedar swamps on both sides of the road. The hike now proceeds through a maze of old cranberry bogs and reservoirs, following unmarked sand roads. Follow the directions carefully, but if you miss a turn, just head south toward the wide Coopers Road. Don't be surprised if some large military aircraft fly by as well—these bogs are not far from Fort Dix and McGuire Air Force Base.

At the next intersection, bear right, but at the following intersection, turn left and head south, out to another reservoir. At this junction, another T-intersection, turn right, heading west along the shore of the reservoir. Next, turn left at the end of the reservoir, and head south along the dam. At the next T-junction, turn right onto a sand road that first swings to the left and then comes to a fork. Take the left fork and follow the road, which swings left and soon arrives at Coopers Road.

Turn right onto Coopers Road, then turn left at the next junction onto a very wide sand road, marked with orange blazes. After a few minutes of walking, the red-blazed Cranberry Trail joins from the left (there is a picnic table near this junction). From here on, you will be following the red blazes back to your car. The trail now bears right and follows a path parallel with but just to the right of the guardrail. Once again, you will cross a cedar swamp. Here the cedars are particularly tall and completely shade the road.

At the end of the guardrail, turn right onto another sand road that heads west. Turn left at the next junction, passing a sign that indicates that the park office is 1 mile away, then bear right. Follow the red markers to the left at the following intersection and continue along a straight sand road, heading southwest. In about half a mile, you'll cross a paved road. Continue ahead for a short distance until you reach the parking area for the park office, where the hike began.

Carranza Memorial to Apple Pie Hill

TOTAL DISTANCE: 8.2 miles (or 5.2 miles with car shuttle)

HIKING TIME: 4 to 5 hours

VERTICAL RISE: 166 feet

RATING: Moderately strenuous

MAPS: USGS Chatsworth, Indian Mills; DEP Batona Trail; DEP Wharton State Forest maps

TRAILHEAD GPS COORDINATES: N 39° 46' 37" W 74° 37' 55"

Walking uphill in the Pinelands is unusual. The entire region is just above sea level, and the very few "hills" are usually only 25 or 30 feet above everything else. There are a few exceptions, however, and this hike leads to the highest elevation in the Pines, a dizzying 205 feet above sea level and about 125 feet above the land around it. This is Apple Pie Hill, on which a fire tower is located. En route, the hike will take you over another hill, 139 feet above sea level, as a warm-up for the big climb. Another feature of the hike is a camping option. One of Wharton State Forest's primitive camping areas is located at the start of the hike and makes a great base camp. Camping permits are issued at the Atsion and Batsto forest service offices.

The Carranza Memorial, where this hike begins, commemorates the tragic crash and death of Mexican pilot Emilio Carranza. Carranza, only 23 at the time of his death, had been a Mexican hero for 5 years, his fame resting on both his aviation and his military accomplishments. On June 11, 1928, he took off from Mexico in a Ryan monoplane, the same as Lindbergh's, and attempted a nonstop flight to Washington. He was grounded by fog in North Carolina but was still received with speeches and parades in both Washington and New York. Carranza was on the return leg of this goodwill flight on July 12, 1928, when he flew into a thunderstorm over this remote section of the Pinelands and crashed. The local American Legion holds an annual observance of this event on the first Saturday after the Fourth of July. Each year on this day, wreaths are placed around the memorial—a stone marker made in Mexico that portrays a diving Aztec eagle.

The destination of the hike, the Apple Pie Hill Fire Tower, offers a panoramic

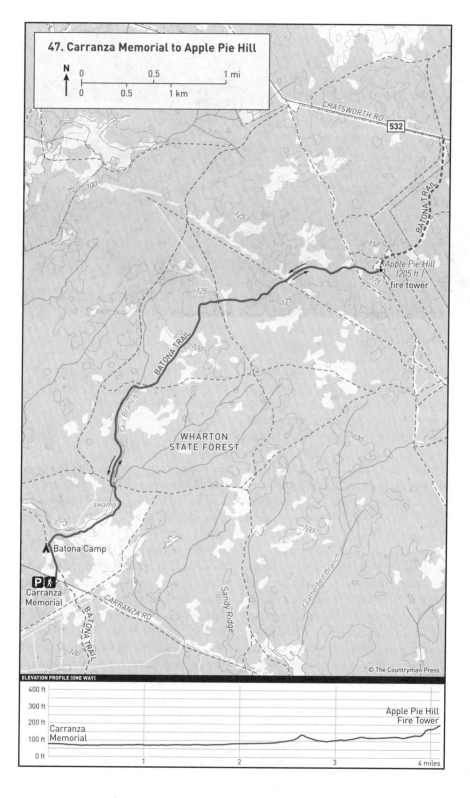

47. Carranza Memorial to Apple Pie Hill

N

| 0 | | 0.5 | | 1 mi |
| 0 | 0.5 | | 1 km | |

CHATSWORTH RD

532

BATONA TRAIL

Apple Pie Hill
(205 ft.)
fire tower

BATONA TRAIL

Skit Branch

WHARTON
STATE FOREST

swamp

Batona Camp

P

Carranza
Memorial

CARRANZA RD

BATONA TRAIL

Sandy Ridge

Featherbed Branch

© The Countryman Press

ELEVATION PROFILE (ONE WAY)

400 ft

300 ft

200 ft

Apple Pie Hill
Fire Tower

Carranza
Memorial

100 ft

0 ft

1   2   3   4 miles

VIEW FROM THE APPLE PIE HILL FIRE TOWER

view over the Pinelands. For many years, the tower (except for the cabin at the very top) was open to the public at all times, and it became a favorite destination for hikers and others. Unfortunately, it also became a scene for parties, and there were many instances of vandalism—including, in 1992, the digging (with an excavator) of a swimming-pool size hole at the base of the tower in search of alleged buried treasure.

Finally, in September 2016, the New Jersey Forest Fire Service (which still uses the tower to search for fires) decided that, in order to preserve the tower for future use, they had to secure the facility. They erected a chain-link fence, topped with barbed wire, around the tower, with a locked gate. At present, the tower is open only when manned by a forest fire observer (generally, during periods of high fire danger). With several days' prior notice, the Forest Fire Service may be able to open the tower to visitors at other times. To find out whether the fire tower is open on a particular day, or to arrange for a special appointment, call 609-726-9010.

GETTING THERE

To reach the parking area at the memorial in Wharton State Forest, turn left (east) off US 206, just south of its junction with NJ 70. The sign here directs you to the town of Tabernacle and the Carranza Memorial. You'll reach the little town of Tabernacle and cross County Route 532 in 2.3 miles. Continue straight ahead through farms and a residential area into Wharton State Forest (Atsion Office, 744 US Route 206, Shamong, NJ 08088; 609-268-0444; njparksand forests.org). Seven miles from Tabernacle, on Carranza Road, you will find the Carranza Memorial, which has ample parking, on the right. If you wish to do the hike as a one-way trip of 5.2 miles, leave a second car on County Route 532 where the Batona Trail crosses it, about

7 miles east of Tabernacle and 3 miles west of Chatsworth. Note: East of the Carranza Memorial, Carranza Road becomes a sand road which, while open to vehicular travel, is in relatively poor condition. It is best to approach the trailhead from the west.

THE HIKE

From the Carranza Memorial, walk east on Carranza Road. Soon, you will see a sign on the left for the Batona Camp. Turn left and follow a sand road towards the camp. A short distance ahead, the road you are following will be joined by the pink-blazed Batona Trail, which comes in from the right. From here to Apple Pie Hill and back, you'll be following these pink blazes. The 50-mile Batona Trail, begun in 1961 by the BAck TO NAture Hiking Club, is a foot trail only. Mountain bikes or motorized vehicles are not permitted. A map of the entire trail is available online at www.njparksandforests.org, as well as at the Atsion and Batsto state forest offices. Signs affixed to trees along the route of the trail give the distance each half-mile from the start of the trail in Bass River State Forest.

A short distance ahead, you'll reach Batona Camp, one of several primitive camping areas located in Wharton State Forest. The site is accessible by car and offers numerous spaces to pitch a tent, with a water pump and several pit toilets available. If you wish to camp here, you'll need a permit, available from the Atsion Ranger Headquarters farther south on US 206 or from the office in Batsto. In 2019, the camping fee was $3 per night per person for New Jersey residents, and $5 per night for nonresidents (there is also a $5 reservation fee). Pets are not permitted in the campsite for overnight camping.

Carefully follow the pink blazes through the camping area, where the trail makes several turns. When you reach the end of the camping area, the Batona Trail bears right past a toilet and enters the woods on a footpath. Immediately, the typical flora of the Pinelands surrounds you. Highbush blueberries, which are found along the trail over much of this hike, make their first appearance. Blackjack oak and, of course, pitch pine surround you. Within a few hundred feet, the trail emerges onto a wide sand road, which it follows for a short distance. Just ahead, the trail bears left, enters the woods on a footpath, and skirts the edge of a cedar swamp. A short side trail on the left leads down to the fascinating swamp. After following along the swamp for some distance, the trail again emerges on the road, then bears left once more and reenters the woods on a footpath.

About half a mile from Batona Camp, the Batona Trail emerges onto the road for a final time to use its bridge. The brook you are crossing is the Skit Branch of the Batsto River. Like all Pinelands water, it is tea-colored from the cedar wood growing in it. The bridge offers a good view of the swampy brook and its plant life. If you look closely at the clumps of grasses growing in and around the water, you'll see hundreds of tiny sundew plants. If you look even closer, you may find a few miniature pitcher plants as well. These plants survive in this nutrient-poor environment by digesting insects that get trapped in their sticky leaves or no-exit entrances.

After crossing the bridge, the trail turns right and reenters the woods on a footpath, this time for good. For the next half mile, Skit Branch and its white

APPLE PIE HILL FIRE TOWER

southern horizon appear between the trees. The trail winds along the hill until the summit and its fire tower appear. This rise is Apple Pie Hill, and at 205 feet, it's the highest summit in the Pinelands.

The view from the fire tower (when open; see above) is of a wilderness of green pines that extends as far as the eye can see in all directions. A white water tower is visible in the distance, and on a clear day, you can see on the horizon the skyscrapers of Atlantic City (to the east) and Philadelphia (to the west), each about 35 miles away. But other than these few intrusions of civilization, the view is one of vastness and wilderness that gives you an idea of the magnitude of the Pinelands.

Fire towers, which are frequently manned, play an important role in controlling the frequent fires (about 400 per year) in the Pinelands. The soil in the Pinelands drains the water so well that the oil- and resin-rich pine needles and dead branches are nearly always dry as tinder. There are no earthworms or bacteria to digest the dead materials on the forest floor, so the tinder accumulates year after year until it burns. The short-leaf pine and the pitch pine, the most common pines here, are two of only three pines in the United States that can sprout from buds lying deep within their trunks or large limbs, thereby assuring their quick recovery following a fire. The persistence of fires in the Pinelands, many of them started by arsonists, has ensured the dominance of these two pines in the forest. Ecologists believe that without regular fires, oaks would probably make up the bulk of a climax forest.

cedar swamp will be on the right. In this section, the trail crosses three wet areas on raised boardwalks.

The Batona Trail now leaves the wet area surrounding Skit Branch and heads into drier and higher territory. About 2 miles from the start of the hike, the first climb begins. The ascent is noticeable by the change from soft white sand underfoot to a harder gravel path. After a "climb" of about 40 feet, you'll reach the table-like summit of this unnamed hill and, before you know it, you'll begin heading downhill. Pay close attention ahead as the trail veers left off the path, crosses a sand road, and then reenters the woods.

After crossing three more sand roads, the Batona Trail begins another climb, this one more serious. Views out to the

If you parked at the Carranza Memorial, you will have to retrace your steps to your car. If you left a car on County Route 532, it is 1.1 miles ahead on the Batona Trail.

Mullica River
Wilderness

TOTAL DISTANCE: 12 miles

HIKING TIME: 6 hours

VERTICAL RISE: Minimal

RATING: Moderate to strenuous

MAPS: USGS Atsion; DEP Wharton State Forest Hiking Trails map

TRAILHEAD GPS COORDINATES:
N 39° 38' 42" W 74° 38' 46"

Beginning at the historic Batsto village in Wharton State Forest (31 Batsto Road, Hammonton, NJ 08037; 609-561-0024; www.njparksandforests.org), this loop hike parallels the Mullica and Batsto Rivers, traversing the heart of the Pinelands. Although it is 12 miles long, the terrain is largely flat, so the hike is not exceptionally strenuous. It can easily be completed in a single day, but the hike also offers a backpacking opportunity, because the Mullica River Wilderness Camp is along the route.

Backpacking in the Pinelands is a unique experience for those more familiar with mountainous areas. The pines are not so dense or tall that they shut out a good view of a starlit sky. In fact, the effect is sometimes more like camping in a desert than in a forest. The pine needle cover on the sandy ground also makes for a comfortable bed. The Mullica River Wilderness Camp has a water pump and pit toilet. You'll have to get a permit from the office in Batsto to camp here, however. In 2019, the camping fee was $3 per night per person for New Jersey residents and $5 per night for nonresidents (there is also a $5 reservation fee).

Batsto was the site of an iron forge that produced kettles, stoves, cannons, pipes, and other iron products during the latter part of the 18th and the early 19th centuries. Like Allaire Village in the northern extremes of the Pinelands, the iron was made from bog iron—accumulations of iron oxides leached from the sand by groundwater and deposited at or near the soil surface. During the Revolutionary War, Batsto was a major source of military iron, and its workers were exempt from military service. At its peak, the village that developed around the furnace had a population of nearly a thousand.

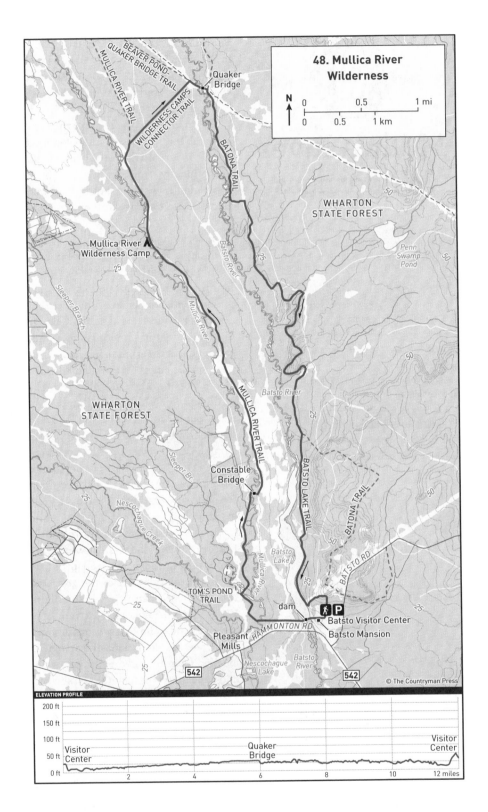

When the iron industry declined, a glassmaking factory was built, and the town produced windowpanes and other flat glass products for a few years. In 1876, after a major fire in the village, Joseph Wharton bought the property as part of his plan to acquire large tracts of land in the Pinelands and sell its water to the city of Philadelphia. The state of New Jersey responded by passing a law prohibiting the export of water, effectively halting this project. Eventually the Wharton holdings were acquired by the state, forming the present-day Wharton State Forest. Information about the interesting history of Batsto and the Pinelands can be found at the visitor center.

The first part of this hike parallels the Mullica River. Hikers will immediately notice its color. "Cedar water" is the usual name for it. The water of the Pinelands is dark, the color of tea, and comes in part from the tannins from decaying vegetation washed out of swamps and in part from the iron-colored sandy mud. Because the water in the Pinelands tends to stay fresher longer, sea captains used to sail up the rivers that drain the Pinelands and take on barrels of what they called "sweet water." The water table in the Pinelands is shallow, but the reserve of water is vast. As an aquifer, there is no equal to the Pinelands in the northeastern United States. Because the water lies so close to the surface, and the sand, which takes in the rain that falls on it, is not a good filter, the Pinelands aquifer is extremely vulnerable to pollution. For this reason, development—which constantly threatens this area—has been kept at bay.

BATSTO MANSION

GETTING THERE

Take the New Jersey Turnpike to Exit 7, proceed south on US 206 for 31 miles, and turn left onto Middle Road. In 1.3 miles, turn left onto South Myrtle Street, and in 0.2 mile, bear left onto Columbia Road. At a T-intersection in 2.7 miles, turn left onto Nesco Road (County Route 542). Continue for 4.5 miles until you see a sign marking the entrance to the Batsto office of Wharton State Forest. Turn left onto Batsto Road and follow signs to the visitor center. Park here.

THE HIKE

The entire hike is within the Batsto Natural Area on sand roads and paths. Although you will be following well-marked trails, pay close attention at junctions, as many paths and sand roads intersect the route. Markers are found on flexible plastic posts, and also as paint blazes on trees. Sections of the sand roads utilized by the trail are very soft.

From the main Batsto parking area, walk to the right of the visitor center and turn right onto a wide gravel walkway (following a sign that reads TO HIKING TRAILS). Proceed past the Batsto mansion, cross the dam at the southern end of Batsto Lake, and continue past the workers' homes. Where the main walkway curves to the left at a fire hydrant, proceed straight ahead until you arrive at a sand road. The trailhead for the co-aligned yellow-blazed Mullica River Trail and orange-blazed Tom's Pond Trail is on the other side of the road.

Continue ahead, following yellow and orange blazes through a pinelands forest of pitch pine and scrub oak. Small signs provide information on plants and trees along the trail. Soon, the trail enters a dark forest of Atlantic white cedar, and

just beyond, it crosses the Mullica River on a wooden bridge. At a junction, the trail turns right onto a sand road, and a short distance ahead, it turns left. At the next junction, follow the yellow-blazed Mullica River Trail as it turns right, leaving the orange-blazed Tom's Pond Trail, and crosses the Sleeper Branch (a tributary of the Mullica River) on a metal bridge. Just past the bridge, there is an interesting swamp on the left. The trail continues through a pitch pine forest on a sand road. For the most part, the road is covered with pine needles that are pleasant to walk on, but several sections have soft white sand.

A little over a mile into the hike, you'll arrive at a bend in the Mullica River noted as a "scenic overlook" on the Wharton State Forest trail map. A bench has been placed here for hikers to pause and take a break.

The Mullica, along with the Batsto, Wading, Great Egg Harbor, and Rancocas, is one of the major rivers draining the vast water reserves lying just below the sands and forests of the Pinelands. Though the river widens considerably farther downstream, the Mullica here in the forest is typical of other rivers in the Pinelands. The river is not wide, but in some places it can be over six feet deep. There are no rapids, but the current is strong. The fact that it remains at a constant water level throughout the year, even during droughts, indicates the extent of the aquifer underlying the Pinelands.

Continue heading north on the yellow trail. In another half mile, you'll arrive at the Constable Bridge across the Mullica River. This bridge is on a sand road open to vehicular traffic, and it is a popular boat-launching point. After crossing the river, continue to follow the yellow markers in a northerly direction, now

on the east side of the river. In another mile, you will reach the entrance to the Mullica River Wilderness Area, a section of the forest where no vehicles (except the rangers') are allowed. A sign here marks the boundary. About a mile from the beginning of the wilderness area is the Mullica River Wilderness Camp, a good place to have lunch—or spend the night.

After resting (or spending the night) at this camp, continue heading north on the yellow-blazed Mullica River Trail. In another mile, you'll reach a junction with the green-blazed Wilderness Camps Connector Trail. Turn right, leaving the Mullica River Trail, and follow the green blazes for a mile to the Quaker Bridge across the Batsto River—another

popular boat-launching site, accessible by vehicle. After crossing the bridge, you'll reach a junction with the pink-blazed Batona Trail.

Turn right and head south on the Batona Trail, which runs along the east side of the Batona River, following sand roads for much of the way. After about 4 miles, you'll reach a junction with the white-blazed Batsto Lake Trail. Turn right and head south on this trail, which continues to parallel the Batsto River. In about a mile, it comes out on the eastern shore of Batsto Lake and runs close to the shore of this scenic lake for half a mile. Near the southern end of the lake, the Batsto Lake Trail turns left and heads east for a short distance, ending at the parking area where the hike began.

Parvin State Park

TOTAL DISTANCE: 3.5 miles

HIKING TIME: 2.5 hours

VERTICAL RISE: Minimal

RATING: Easy

MAPS: USGS Elmer; DEP Parvin State Park map

TRAILHEAD GPS COORDINATES:
N 39° 30' 38" W 75° 07' 53"

In 1796, Leonard Parvin acquired the property that now is known as Parvin State Park (701 Almond Road, Pittsgrove, NJ 08318; 856-358-8616; www.njparksandforests.org). He constructed a dam across the Muddy Run to form Parvin Lake and used the water to power a sawmill. In the early 1900s, the 108-acre lake was the center of the privately owned Parvin Grove Recreation Area.

In 1930, the State of New Jersey acquired the lake and 918 acres of forested land that surrounded it to create Parvin State Park. In October 1933, a Civilian Conservation Corps (CCC) camp was established in the park. The men hacked out trails through the dense forest, using the wood to build bridges across the swamps. They also cleared the main beach and picnic area, created the large parking area across the road, and built the bathhouse/park office using bricks salvaged from 100-year-old buildings in Philadelphia that had been demolished. Between 1939 and 1941, when the CCC camp was closed, the men constructed 18 cabins along the shore of Thundergust Lake, which was created by damming a swamp.

Beginning in 1943, the park housed a summer day camp program for children of Japanese Americans who moved into the area to work at nearby farms and food processing plants. A prisoner-of-war camp for captured German soldiers was established in a section of the park in 1944. The year 1952 saw the last nontraditional use of Parvin. Six years earlier, Soviet dictator Joseph Stalin had the Kalmyck people transported to Siberia because of their alleged anti-Soviet sympathies. Some of the Kalmycks escaped and, after the war, lived in displaced persons camps in Germany. After protracted legal proceedings,

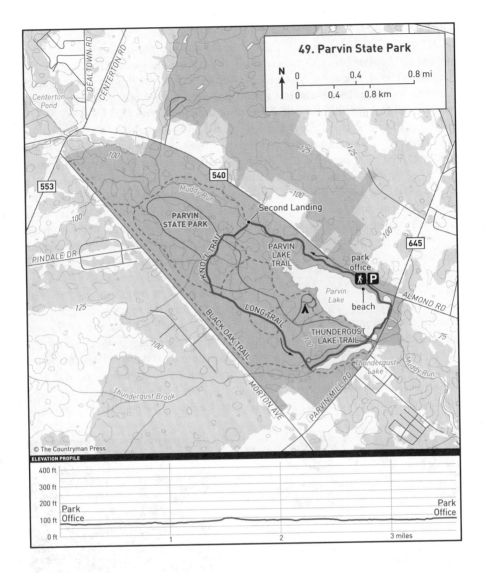

several hundred Kalmycks were admitted to the United States as refugees in 1951–52. They came to Parvin in three groups but stayed only a few months until they were resettled in the Philadelphia area and in Howell Township, New Jersey.

Parvin State Park has a 15-mile network of trails, all of which are multiuse. This hike starts on the Parvin Lake Trail and follows several other trails for the rest of its route.

GETTING THERE

Take the New Jersey Turnpike to Exit 4 and continue onto NJ 73 North. In 1.1 miles, take the exit for I-295 South. Proceed south on I-295 for about 10 miles, then continue on NJ 42. Take the first exit (Exit 13) for NJ 55 South

(Glassboro/Vineland). Proceed south on NJ 55 for 25 miles and take Exit 35B toward Brotmanville. Continue for 2 miles to a complex six-way intersection, where you make a broad left turn onto Parvin Mill Road (following signs for Parvin State Park). Follow Parvin Mill Road for 2 miles and, at a blinking light, turn right onto Almond Road (County Route 540). The park entrance and parking area are on the right in 0.3 mile. After parking your car, cross the road to reach the park office (located in the right side of the large bathhouse building).

THE HIKE

The hike starts just outside the park office. Facing Parvin Lake and the bathhouse, you'll see a sign for the Parvin Lake Trail. Walk to the right (west) along a dirt path, with a green chain-link fence on the left. The trail proceeds between the highway and the lake, passing holly trees and mountain laurel thickets.

After crossing a small brook on a tiny stone bridge, you'll go by several large pitch pines, with their distinctive, thick shingle bark. The trail bears right at a fork and swings closer to the road, then bears left and moves away from the road.

After passing a sign commemorating the work of the Civilian Conservation Corps in the 1930s, the trail approaches Muddy Run, which may be seen on the left. Muddy Run is a typical slow-moving stream of South Jersey. A tributary of the Maurice River, its water eventually empties into Delaware Bay.

Soon, you'll reach a paved road at a pavilion. The park map indicates that this location is known as Second Landing. The paved road forms the main boundary between the developed area and the designated natural area of Parvin State Park—the latter to be retained in a "forever wild" condition.

ALONG THE PARVIN LAKE TRAIL

THE CURVED SPILLWAY OF THE PARVIN LAKE DAM

The League for Conservation Legislation, the New Jersey Chapter of the Sierra Club, and Assemblyman (later Governor) Thomas Kean deserve credit for the passage of the Natural Areas System Act. This landmark legislation, passed in 1976, was modeled after the Forest Preserve article of the New York State Constitution and allows the designation of areas to be left forever in their natural state.

Turn left at the pavilion, continuing to follow the green-blazed Parvin Lake Trail along the paved road. Just ahead, you'll cross the Muddy Run on a wooden footbridge. When you reach the next intersection, turn right onto the orange-blazed Knoll Trail, which proceeds through dense vegetation and crosses a wet area on a boardwalk. After crossing a paved road (the route of the blue-blazed Forest Road Trail), the Knoll Trail continues to follow a wide path through dense vegetation, crossing several wet areas on wooden bridges. Soon, it passes through a more open area, with scrub oak and an understory of blueberry. It then climbs a little and again proceeds through dense vegetation.

After crossing another paved road (still the route of the blue-blazed trail), the Knoll Trail ends at a junction with the red-blazed Long Trail. Bear left and follow the red-blazed trail along a dirt road. You'll soon cross a sand road and pass the trailhead (on the left) of the aptly named Flat Trail, but continue ahead on the red-blazed Long Trail. After a while, the yellow-blazed Lost Trail joins from the right. Proceed ahead, now following both red and yellow blazes, but at the next intersection, where the trails diverge, turn right onto the route of the red-blazed Long Trail.

Soon, you'll traverse an interesting section of trail that is raised from the surrounding forest floor. Continue to follow the red-blazed trail as it crosses the yellow-blazed trail and proceeds through the woods. At the next intersection, where a road goes off to the left, continue ahead on the red-blazed trail. A short distance beyond, you'll reach a junction where the Black Oak Trail begins on the right, and a paved road is visible on the left. Once again, proceed ahead on the red-blazed trail. Just ahead, you'll reach a wooden bridge over Thundergust Brook. Here, the red-blazed Long Trail ends.

Do not cross the bridge. Instead, turn left onto the yellow-blazed Thundergust Lake Trail, which follows the western shore of the brook. The brook soon widens into Thundergust Lake, and the trail runs between the lake on the right and the paved park road on the left. Many short side trails lead down to the lake.

On the left, you'll notice a number of rustic cabins. Each of these 18 cabins sleeps four or six people and contains a refrigerator, stove, toilet, shower, and electric lights. The cabins are available for rental from April to October.

After paralleling Thundergust Lake for about half a mile, the trail approaches Parvin Mill Road. Here, you'll notice a dam with a wrought iron railing on your right and the campground entrance road with a park entrance booth on your left. Turn left toward the booth, then turn left onto the paved park entrance road. Just beyond a gate, leave the road, turn right onto a footpath and proceed toward Parvin Lake, then turn left onto a path that parallels the lake. Bear right at the next intersection and cross a footbridge over an inlet that connects the main lake with a cove on the right. The park office and bathhouse, where your hike began, are visible to the left across the lake.

The trail continues to parallel the lake, soon passing a wooden fishing dock that offers good views of the lake. The sidewalk of the highway bridge is used to cross the outlet stream of the pond, just below the dam. The dam of Parvin Lake is especially interesting, with its unusual curved spillway.

Soon, the trail curves to the left and crosses two wooden bridges, which take you on and off Flag Island. After continuing through a grassy area, the trail reenters the woods and parallels a green chain-link fence on the left until it reaches the bathhouse/park office, where the hike began.

50

Belleplain State Forest— East Creek Trail

TOTAL DISTANCE: 7 miles	

HIKING TIME: 4.5 hours

VERTICAL RISE: Minimal

RATING: Easy to moderate

MAPS: USGS Woodbine, Heislerville; DEP Belleplain State Forest map

TRAILHEAD GPS COORDINATES:
N 39° 13' 27" W 74° 53' 11.5"

Located at the southern tip of the Pinelands, Belleplain State Forest (1 Henkin-Sifkin Road, P.O. Box 450, Woodbine, NJ 08270; 609-861-2404; www.njparksand forests.org) is a popular camping spot containing 168 family camping sites, 14 fully-enclosed lean-tos with propane heaters, five shelters (cabin-like structures with two double-deck bunks and a wood stove), two group campsites (each campsite can accommodate up to 50 people), and a group cabin for up to 30 people. Central to the camping areas in this 23,000-acre forest—90 percent of which is part of the Pinelands National Reserve—is Lake Nummy, a transformed cranberry bog with white sand beaches. It was named in honor of the last Lenni Lenape Native American chief to rule in the Cape May area.

There are about 50 miles of officially designated trails in Belleplain, of which about half are open to "road-legal" motor vehicles. Most of the remaining trails are multiuse, with both hikers and bicyclists allowed (although they are not heavily used by bicyclists). There are several short hiking-only trails near Lake Nummy, but for those seeking a longer hike, the best choice is the 7-mile-long East Creek Trail, a multiuse white-blazed trail that is the route of this hike.

The East Creek Trail, a loop that you will hike clockwise, encircles the area drained by Savages Run between Lake Nummy and East Creek Pond. The trail passes through forests of scrub oak and pitch pine, characteristic of the Pinelands. But, in contrast to the Pinelands, shore vegetation—particularly greenbriers and holly trees—is found throughout the forest, revealing the transitional nature of the region.

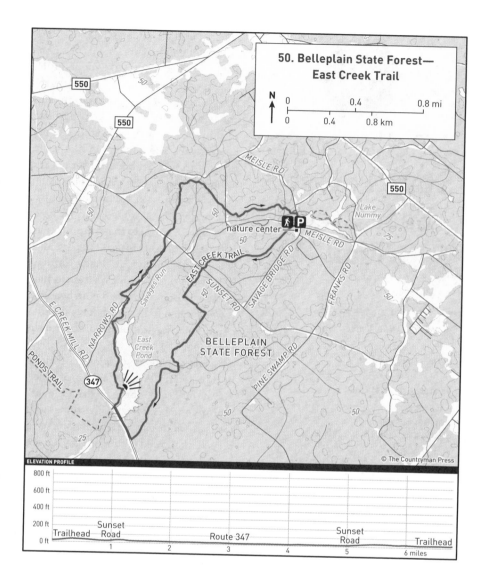

50. Belleplain State Forest—
East Creek Trail

N

| 0 | | 0.4 | | 0.8 mi |
| 0 | 0.4 | | 0.8 km | |

ELEVATION PROFILE

© The Countryman Press

800 ft

600 ft

400 ft

200 ft

0 ft

Trailhead | Sunset Road | Route 347 | Sunset Road | Trailhead

1   2   3   4   5   6 miles

GETTING THERE

Take the Garden State Parkway to Exit 17 (Woodbine/Sea Isle City). Turn left at the bottom of the ramp (following signs for Woodbine), then turn right (north) onto US 9. Continue for 0.6 mile and turn left onto County Route 550 (Woodbine–Ocean View Road). After 6.3 miles, you reach the town of Woodbine, where County Route 550 makes a left turn at the Woodbine Meat Market, then a right turn at a blinking light. This is still County Route 550—stay on it. In another 1.4 miles, you'll see a sign for Belleplain State Forest. Turn left onto Henkin-Sifkin Road and pass the park office on the right (you may wish to stop here to obtain a map). Continue for 0.5 mile to the next intersection and turn right onto Meisle Road. Just ahead, you'll pass the park entry station (a per-vehicle entrance fee is charged from Memorial Day weekend to Labor Day).

Continue ahead for another 0.3 mile, passing Lake Nummy on the right, until you reach the park nature center. If spaces are available (along the side road to the left of the building), park at the nature center. If no parking spaces are available at the nature center, make the next right turn onto Champion Road, cross the dam of the lake, then turn right into the main parking area for Lake Nummy. After parking your car, walk back to the nature center.

THE HIKE

With your back to the lake and facing the nature center, turn right and head west along Meisle Road for about 300 feet. At a sign for the campers-only trash recycling center, turn left, heading towards the recycling center. In 75 feet, a sign on the right marks the start of the East Creek Trail. Follow the white blazes into the woods. The trail—a wide, moss-covered footpath—traverses an open forest of scrub oaks and pitch pine, reminiscent of the Pinelands. About a mile into the hike, the trail crosses a creek on a wooden bridge in the dark shadows of tall cedars. Just beyond, the trail crosses paved Sunset Road.

After traversing an area dominated by mountain laurel, the trail follows the perimeter of an abandoned field, now starting to regenerate with pines and other vegetation. The trail reenters the woods and, in 0.2 mile, turns sharply left and passes through thickets of holly and mountain laurel. In another quarter mile, the trail turns sharply right

EAST CREEK POND

BOARDWALK OVER A CEDAR SWAMP

and crosses several wet areas on long stretches of boardwalk.

Further on, the trail crosses a boardwalk over a branch of a stream at the edge of a stand of cedars. It then crosses another boardwalk over the main stream, with dense cedars on both sides of the trail. As the trail heads south, it proceeds through dense mountain laurel thickets.

You'll know you're approaching Route 347 when you begin to see state park signs and hear the noise of the traffic. A branch trail goes off to the right, but the route of the East Creek Trail continues ahead and soon comes out onto the shoulder of this busy highway.

You've now reached about the halfway point of the hike.

Follow the trail as it turns right and continues along the grassy shoulder of the road for a quarter mile, passing the entrance to a group cabin and crossing the dam of East Creek Pond. If you can ignore the roar of the traffic, the pond appears to be quite calm. Over a hundred years ago, however, this area was the scene of much activity; both a lumber mill and gristmill were located here.

After following the road across the dam of the pond, turn right into a large parking area and, at a sign for the East Creek Trail, reenter the woods. The trail heads north, parallel to the western shore of the pond (which may be visible through the trees), and it soon comes out at the shore of the pond, with a panoramic view over the pond. You're far enough from the road that the traffic can barely be heard, and you can now appreciate the beauty of this wilderness lake. You might see a kayak traversing the waters, but otherwise all is quiet and calm. A bench has been placed here, and you'll want to take a break to rest and take in the vista, which is the highlight of this hike.

When you're ready to continue, proceed north along the trail, which still parallels the shore of the pond. After passing through an area with many cedars, the trail again approaches the water, with a short side trail leading down to the shore of the pond. The trail continues through a typical Pinelands forest of scrub oak and pitch pine and soon bears left, away from the pond.

After crossing a boardwalk over a wet area, the trail curves to the right. A short distance beyond, it turns right onto a sand road. Just ahead, the trail bears left at a fork, but it follows this branch of the road only for a short distance. Watch carefully for a second left turn (marked by a brown wand) where the trail leaves the sand road and continues on a wide footpath through stands of holly and mountain laurel, with an understory of blueberry.

In a quarter mile, the trail bears left and crosses Tom Field Road diagonally to the right. This wide sand road (also known as Narrows Road, and shown on the park map as the route of the pink-blazed Mountain Bike Trail) is open to vehicular traffic (although it is normally little used by motor vehicles). The trail curves to the right and parallels the road, proceeding through mountain laurel thickets, with an understory of blueberry. In several places, the trail approaches the road, which is visible on the right through the trees.

After crossing the paved Sunset Road, the East Creek Trail traverses slightly higher and more open land, where scrub oak, pitch pine, holly, and mountain laurel predominate. In a quarter mile, the trail bears right and recrosses Tom Field Road, and then crosses another sand road. The trail now descends a little to cross a brook on a wooden bridge. It enters an area with many tall cedars, proceeds through a mature white pine forest, and crosses the paved New Bridge Road.

The next trail section parallels Savages Run, the stream that drains Lake Nummy and feeds East Creek Pond. After passing two large stands of cedars on the right, the trail reaches a third stand of cedars, which it traverses on a boardwalk. This is probably the darkest and most interesting cedar stand along the trail. The trail now turns sharply left, then sharply right, and soon comes out on the paved Champion Road. To reach the nature center parking area, turn right and cross the dam of Lake Nummy. To reach the main parking area, turn left.

Resources

Bennett, D. W. *New Jersey Coastwalks*. Sandy Hook Highlands, NJ: American Littoral Society, 1981.

Boysen, Robert. *Kittatinny Trails*. Mahwah, NJ: New York–New Jersey Trail Conference, 2004.

Brooks, Christopher & Catherine. *60 Hikes within 60 Miles: New York City: with Northern New Jersey, Southwestern Connecticut, and Western Long Island*. Birmingham, AL: Menasha Ridge Press, 2004.

Buff, Sheila. *Nature Walks in and around New York City: Discover Great Parks and Preserves Throughout the Tri-State Metropolitan Area*, 1st edition. Boston, MA: Appalachian Mountain Club Books, 1996.

Card, Skip. *Take a Hike: New York City: 80 Hikes within 2 Hours of Manhattan*, 2nd edition. Berkeley, CA: Avalon Travel, 2012.

Case, Daniel. *AMC's Best Day Hikes near New York City: Four-Season Guide to 50 of the Best Trails in New York, Connecticut, and New Jersey*. Boston, MA: Appalachian Mountain Club Books, 2010.

Chazin, Daniel. *Hike of the Week: A Year of Hikes in the New York Metro Area*. Mahwah, NJ: New York–New Jersey Trail Conference, 2013.

Chazin, Daniel. *New Jersey Walk Book: A Companion to the New York Walk Book*, 2nd edition. Mahwah, NJ: New York–New Jersey Trail Conference, 2004.

Dann, Kevin. *Twenty-Five Walks in New Jersey*. Piscataway, NJ: Rutgers University Press, 1982.

DeCoste, Paul E. and Ronald J. Dupont, Jr. *Hiking New Jersey: A Guide to 50 of the Garden State's Greatest Hiking Adventures*. Guilford, CT: Falcon Guides, 2009.

Della Penna, Craig. *24 Great Rail-Trails of New Jersey*. North Amherst, MA: New England Cartographics, 1999.

Harrison, Marina, with Lucy D. Rosenfeld. *A Walker's Guidebook: Serendipitous Outings near New York City: Including a Section for Birders*. Michael Kesend Publishing, Ltd., 1996.

Kjellstrom, Bjorn. *Be Expert with Map and Compass*. Hoboken, NJ: John Wiley & Sons, 1994.

Kobbe, Gustav. *The New Jersey Coast and Pines*. Baltimore, MD: Gateway Press, 1982.

Lenik, Edward J. *Iron Mine Trails*, revised edition. Mahwah, NJ: New York–New Jersey Trail Conference, 1999.

Mack, Arthur C. *The Palisades of the Hudson*. Edgewater, NJ: The Palisade Press, 1909.

McClelland, Robert J. *The Delaware Canal*. Piscataway, NJ: Rutgers University Press, 1967.

McPhee, John. *The Pine Barrens*. New York: Farrar, Straus and Giroux, 1968.

New York–New Jersey Trail Conference. *Appalachian Trail Guide to New York–New Jersey (with 4 maps)*, 18th edition. Harpers Ferry, WV: Appalachian Trail Conservancy, 2019.

Perls, Jeffrey. *Paths along the Hudson: A Guide to Walking and Biking along the River.* Piscataway, NJ: Rutgers University Press, 1999.

Petty, George. *Hiking the Jersey Highlands: Wilderness in Your Back Yard.* Mahwah, NJ: New York–New Jersey Trail Conference, 2007.

Ransom, James M. *Vanishing Ironworks of the Ramapos.* Rutgers University Press. 1966.

Rosenfield, Lucy D. and Marina Harrison. *A Guide to Green New Jersey: Nature Walks in the Garden State.* Piscataway, NJ: Rutgers University Press, 2003.

Scherer, Glenn. *Nature Walks in New Jersey: A Guide to the Best Trails from the Highlands to Cape May,* 2nd edition. Boston, MA: Appalachian Mountain Club Books, 2003.

Waterman, Laura and Guy. *Forest and Crag: A History of Hiking, Trail Blazing, and Adventure in the Northeast Mountains.* Boston, MA: Appalachian Mountain Club Books, 1989.

———. *Backwoods Ethics: Environmental Issues for Hikers and Campers,* 2nd edition. Woodstock, VT: The Countryman Press, 1993.

———. *Wilderness Ethics: Preserving the Spirit of Wilderness,* 2nd edition. Woodstock, VT: The Countryman Press, 1993.

Zatz, Arline. *Best Hikes with Children in New Jersey,* 2nd edition. Mountaineers Books, 2005.

HIKING MAPS

(Published by the New York–New Jersey Trail Conference)

Hudson Palisades Trails five-map set. 2018
Jersey Highlands Trails two-map set. 2015.
Kittatinny Trails four-map set. 2020.
North Jersey Trails two-map set. 2017.

USEFUL ROAD MAPS

AAA New Jersey. Latest edition.
Rand McNally/New York City, Metro Area Counties, Long Island. Latest edition.